Her Hidden Children

Her Hidden Children

The Rise of Wicca and Paganism in America

Chas S. Clifton

ALTAMIRA
P R E S S

A DIVISION OF
ROWMAN & LITTLEFIELD PUBLISHERS, INC.
Lanham • Boulder • New York • Toronto • Oxford

ALTAMIRA PRESS
A division of Rowman & Littlefield Publishers, Inc.
A wholly owned subsidiary of The Rowman & Littlefield Publishing Group, Inc.
4501 Forbes Boulevard, Suite 200
Lanham, MD 20706
www.altamirapress.com

PO Box 317
Oxford
OX2 9RU, UK

British Library Cataloguing in Publication Information Available

Library of Congress Cataloguing-in-Publication Data

Clifton, Chas.
  Her hidden children : the rise of Wicca and paganism in America
/ Chas S. Clifton.
    p. cm. — (The Pagan studies series)
  Includes bibliographical references and index.
  ISBN-13: 978-0-7591-0201-9 (cloth : alk. paper)
  ISBN-10: 0-7591-0201-5 (cloth : alk. paper)
  ISBN-13: 978-0-7591-0202-6 (pbk. : alk. paper)
  ISBN-10: 0-7591-0202-3 (pbk. : alk. paper)
    1. Witchcraft—United States. 2. Paganism—United States.
I. Title. II. Series.
  BF1566.C55 2006
  299'.94—dc22   2005037187

Printed in the United States of America

⊗™ The paper used in this publication meets the minimum requirements of
American National Standard for Information Sciences—Permanence of Paper for
Printed Library Materials, ANSI/NISO Z39.48-1992.

And our Goddess even inclineth to love and mirth and happiness and guardeth and cherisheth Her hidden children in life.

—traditional Wiccan ritual

☾

Contents

☾

Preface

This book tries to tell a story that has never been told: the first decades of the contemporary Pagan movement—particularly Wicca, its largest component—in America. This era, particularly the 1960s to the 1970s, is not only vanishing into the past but is constantly being reinterpreted. Reinterpretation is inevitable; my concern—a concern that originally prompted me to begin this book—would be that key ideas, persons, and events would be excised from the history of this significant new religious movement. "Time, tide, and the Internal Revenue Service affect all public religious organizations, sooner or later," remarked Isaac Bonewits, one American Pagan writer who has made his own contribution in telling this story.[1] Confronted with some of the same material in 1993, another writer, Aidan Kelly, decided that "a comprehensive history of the Craft in America simply cannot yet be written." Instead, he wrote his *Hippie Commie Beatnik Witches* as "creative nonfiction," a personal memoir—with reconstructed conversations and thought processes—of one seminal West Coast group within the overall Pagan revival of the 1960s.[2]

Perhaps the point of "yet" had already passed when he wrote those words. It might have passed in 1979 when Margot Adler completed the first edition of *Drawing Down the Moon*,[3] the last and by far the best of a series of what I elsewhere refer to as the genre of "I go among the witches" books (a genre earlier defined by such writers as Hans Holzer and Susan Roberts who capitalized on publishers' sudden interest in "the occult" and its practitioners). *Drawing Down the Moon* captures the new Pagan movement on a cusp. Adler was able contact most of the movers and shakers with a few cross-country trips, before the growth of Pagan festivals led to an explosion of cross-fertilization and the growth of the Internet made it possible for a "solitary" Pagan to enjoy a simulacrum of community and even an attenuated form of ritual via online mailing lists, chat rooms, and Web sites. But the nature of "the Craft" is changing too, for the larger and more visible it becomes, the more it is shaped by the cultural currents of American religious attitudes in general.

Gathering material in 1976, Adler sent her preliminary research questionnaire to the Pagan magazine *Green Egg*, a home-produced, small-scale "zine" that was the nearest thing to a national Pagan forum at that time. Although she had her own network of potential interview subjects—and she would reinterview several people who were more or less on a circuit for such books—she sought to cast a wider net among a group of people who were widely dispersed and in many cases quite secretive.

Her question number sixty-five asked, "How do you react to the following argument: *'It is going to be impossible to ever write a true history of Paganism and the Craft, because so many people lied about their origins for so many years, lied, because they wrongly thought it necessary to have a lineage, that they now are scared to retract those lies. And these are often the same people who have done the greatest service for Paganism in this country.'* How do you react to that?"

I was one of the *Green Egg* subscribers who read the questionnaire. I responded, but others' responses must have been lengthier and more eloquent than mine. Certainly, *Drawing Down the Moon*, which was updated in the mid-1980s, remains a cornerstone text when assessing contemporary American Paganism. Although written by an insider, *Drawing Down the Moon* avoids fuzziness and sentimentality; the clarity and prescience of Adler's writing have remained.

When I first thought to begin this book, it was because people in the Pagan movement who had strongly influenced me were departing this life—Loy and Louise Stone, Stewart Farrar—and because others whom I knew only through their books—Sybil Leek, Jessie Wicker Bell—were also passing before they could answer any of a number of interesting historical questions. Stories were not being told. Instead, a new narrative seemed to be emerging, at least in certain publishing houses that had newly discovered the Pagan market and Pagan writers; this narrative suggested that something called Wicca had emerged in the 1970s as a sort of spiritual adjunct to the women's movement (Second Wave feminism), that it was mainly founded by women, and that the Los Angeles–raised left-wing daughter of a Jewish psychotherapist—Miriam Simos, better known as Starhawk—was its prophet.

The interplay between Second Wave feminism and contemporary Paganism has been enormous, and it is well documented. But that interplay is the story of the second (or third) generation of twentieth-century American Paganism; it was preceded by both homegrown and imported forms of self-consciously Pagan religion between, at a minimum, the 1930s and the 1960s. This earlier story raises the first question that I have long wished to investigate: what were the mechanisms of this transmission of religious ideas? What about lineages of initiation, which loom so large in Wiccan lore? How are religious ideas passed on, through the mouth-to-ear teaching of initiates (which was the Wiccan myth) or through other means: science-fiction novels, perhaps, or popular journalism? How did a religion that began in England become American? And how does it relate to Paganisms (re)constructed in America? Related to those questions are two others: what other cultural factors might have encouraged Paganism's growth, and how have contemporary Pagans struggled to redefine and reclaim such loaded terms as *witch* and *Pagan*?

Secondly, for the past thirty years at least, American Pagans have been describing theirs as "nature religion" or "earth religion." Given that one of my lifelong concerns has been the relationship between organized religion and the environment, what does "nature religion" mean? I was raised as a "Forest Service brat," and I was always sensitive to the fact that the teachings of the Episcopal Church, in which I was instructed, seemed to end at the edge of town. In other words, aside from occasional prayers for rain, the nonhuman world received little consideration. The same could be said for other Christian denominations, as far as I could tell. Although not articulated in childhood, this incongruity always nagged at me.

My own formal participation in the Pagan movement began in 1972, when I was an undergraduate at Reed College in Portland, Oregon. Not at that time nor in subsequent years have I uncovered any instance of any American Pagan saying, in effect, "Let's position ourselves as the environmental religion." Yet something like that positioning has occurred. Although arguments from absence are risky, I think that the unconscious ease with which American Pagans embraced the term *nature/earth religion* testifies to the strength of Catherine Albanese's argument that nature religion exists in American life, whether as a scholarly construct, as a way of organizing reality (her first description), or as the "spiritual source of secular passion."[4]

I cannot begin to answer Adler's provocative question as to who might have lied about or merely embroidered their spiritual lineage, nor could anyone else, unless there is a sudden, highly unlikely spate of Pagan autobiography in the next few years. Instead, I will offer my own thoughts on how the seeds of a self-consciously reconstructed (for so I believe the evidence suggests) Pagan mystery religion, born in the mid-twentieth century in southern England, crossed the Atlantic and flourished, only to return to Britain and elsewhere born on two new wings, feminism and that wondrous catchall phrase, "nature religion." Since a part of my initial inspiration for writing *Her Hidden Children* came from Rick Fields's pioneering history of Buddhism in America, *How the Swans Came to the Lake*,[5] and since Pagans in general seem to have a heraldic fondness for ravens (as did I at age twelve, when I designed my own raven emblem and inscribed it on my camping gear), I call chapter 1 "How the Ravens Came to the Lake," and hope that Fields will not be insulted.

The roots of the British creation of Pagan Witchcraft are superbly detailed in Ronald Hutton's book *The Triumph of the Moon*.[6] Published in 1999, it offers great insight on the literary and folkloric foundations of the Pagan revival. I also got some other ideas about treating "underground" biography and minority organizations from Stuart Timmons's *The Trouble with Harry Hay: Founder of the Modern Gay Movement*.[7]

As I discuss metaphorically in the introduction, "The Island that Burst from the Sea," the story of contemporary Paganism in America has too many strands to enumerate. Because of my wish to focus on many Pagans' claim to follow "nature religion," I have for the most part set aside those groups that pay more attention to ethnic roots, such as reconstructed Greek, Roman, or Norse religions. Their history remains to be written. Even these, however, may yet welcome the label of *nature religion* or *earth religion* as it becomes more widely accepted in the larger society. Likewise, I have given the origins of feminist Wicca a fairly brief treatment; since the appearance of Starhawk's *The Spiral Dance* in 1979, it has received much attention, perhaps to the point of obscuring its context in a larger Pagan story.

Not only is every new book a conversation with previous books, but no book can be written in splendid isolation. When I first conceived the idea of trying to trace some of the history of American Paganism, Judy Harrow, Gwyneth Cathyl-Harrow, and Kate Slater offered encouragement and shared old books and copies of ephemeral publications. Chapter 4, "The Playboy and the Witch," would have been much poorer without that opportunity.

Every author needs an editor who believes in him, in the project, and that the project might someday be completed despite various catastrophes along the way: that editor was Erik Hanson of AltaMira Press. Two anonymous reviewers provided useful suggestions for revision, as did Wendy Griffin, my coeditor in AltaMira's Pagan Studies series.

Fritz Muntean and Diana Tracy, who in 1997 created what is now *The Pomegranate: The International Journal of Pagan Studies*, helped to nurture an intellectual climate in which a book like this could be written. A small portion of chapter 1 originally appeared as an article about the Wiccan science-fiction writer Margaret St. Clair in *The Pomegranate*, as did the works of other scholars whom I cite. Likewise, I wish to acknowledge the hundred or so members of the Nature Religions Scholars Network (NRSN) and its "natrel" listserv for their constant conversation and stimulation. Much of the material in chapter 4, "The Playboy and the Witch," was originally presented as a paper by the same name to the NRSN meeting in Toronto in 2002. Pagan studies is a small field, with its practitioners often geographically isolated, but we have kept each other from feeling quite so alone.

The New Religious Movements group of the American Academy of Religion, in particular Mike Ashcraft, Catherine Wessinger, Gordon Melton, and Sarah Pike, also entertained some of the ideas in this book and contributed their encouragement, as did Ronald Hutton at the University of Bristol.

Reaching back further in time, I wish also to thank Fred Denny of the University of Colorado's Religious Studies Department, who taught me how to ask the right question (a ten-minute conversation worth a semester in the classroom); Sam Gill for lessons in writing; and Rodney Taylor, for opening the door (both also of the University of Colorado).

More recently, I would like to acknowledge William Sheidley, chairman of the Department of English and Foreign Languages, Colorado State University–Pueblo, for supporting scholarship that, on the face of it, might seem tangential to the department's mission and to my teaching there. Since research is impossible without them, let me also acknowledge the university's librarians, in particular Dan Sullivan, Rhonda Gonzales, Raymond Morris, and Sandy Hudock.

Many people in the larger Pagan community helped with suggestions and by sharing their memories and writing. Among them were Joe Bethancourt, Isaac Bonewits, Raymond Buckland, Julia Carpenter, Cat Chapin-Bishop, Carol Dow, Ann and Dave Finnin, Ed Sitch, Gavin and Yvonne Frost, Grey Cat, David and Kathy Jackson, Harold Moss, Nancy Mostad, Carl and Sandra Weschcke, as well as others whose privacy I must respect. Those now on the Other Side include Evan John Jones, Gwydion Pendderwen, Loy and Louise Stone, Joseph B. Wilson, and Doreen Valiente.

This book is partially dedicated to my father, Otis S. Clifton (1916–2003), who always had interesting books in the house, many of them works on history and comparative religion. The other dedicatee was always there with the encouragement and the champagne suppers to mark milestones in writing: my wife, Mary Currier.

Notes

1. Quoted in Ellen Evert Hopman, *The Origins of the Henge of Keltria 1.1* (2001), www.neopagan.net/OriginsKeltria.html (accessed January 25, 2006).

2. Aidan A. Kelly, *Hippie Commie Beatnik Witches: A History of the Craft in California, 1967–1977* (Canoga Park, Calif.: Art Magical Publications, 1993), 3.

3. Margot Adler, *Drawing Down the Moon* (New York: Viking Press, 1979).

4. Catherine Albanese, *Reconsidering Nature Religion*, ed. Gerald P. McKenny, Rockwell Lecture Series (Harrisburg, Pa.: Trinity International Press, 2002), 48.

5. Fields, Rick, *How the Swans Came to the Lake* (Boston: Shambhala, 1981).

6. Ronald Hutton, *The Triumph of the Moon* (Oxford: Oxford University Press, 1999).

7. Timmons, Stuart, *The Trouble with Harry Hay: Founder of the Modern Gay Movement* (Boston: Alyson Publications, 1990).

❨

The Island That Burst from the Sea

Since the 1960s and 1970s, when it was still largely underground, contemporary American Paganism has grown tremendously. The more it has grown and become visible, the more it is shaped by the cultural currents of American religious attitudes. This book, therefore, seeks to focus on the first critical decades when Paganism, particularly Witchcraft, attracted chiefly people who viewed their religion as an excursus from contemporary life. But, in stepping away from the mainstream, most of them actually stepped into a long-established religious current, that of "nature religion," which quickly, along with "earth religion," became both a euphemistic alternative label and a way of identifying with a source of sacred power.

Here is an extended analogy for the growth of American Paganism since the late 1950s: Imagine a lifeless volcanic island thrust up from the ocean floor into the air above. Soon seeds of a few hardy, colonizing plants arrive somehow, perhaps deposited in bird dung or blown on the wind. Then more plants arrive—nature is on "fast forward" on this little island. There are forbs, grasses, and some shrubs. Other marine life grows in tidal pools. Some lizards and other small animals arrive conveniently on driftwood. Trees sprout here and there. More birds come, and now they are nesting, feeding, and raising their young. A profusion of flowers covers open areas when the seasonal rains arrive. There are rodents in the underbrush, snakes in the trees, and bats clustering in a cave—how did they get there? Sea turtles drag themselves ashore onto the newly created beach to lay their eggs. The whole process has taken perhaps thirty years. Then a boatload of researchers arrives. They be-gin recording, measuring, photographing, and speculating.

Naturally, some want to know which plants colonized the island and in what sequence. But it is too late to tell: the only previously recorded human visitors were a naval landing party from the imaginary nearby nation of Car-itania, which made some basic measurements after the lava had cooled. Oc-casional Caritanian fishermen mentioned seeing this flower or that shrub, us-ing their own names for them and not botanical nomenclature. Using their knowledge from other locales and their knowledge of the botanical genera involved, the botanists in the group construct a possible sequence of events, which they compare to the rougher, less-hospitable portions of the island, which are only now becoming vegetated. They develop a model in which plants seem to have colonized certain accessible areas first and then spread out from there. Likewise, the zoologists and ornithologists try to fit the data that they collect into theoretical models developed elsewhere; and some parts fit neatly while others are confoundingly different.

There is also an archaeologist in the group. Unable to get funding, he has paid his own way. Exploring a man-high lava tube, he finds several rectangular slabs of bark stashed in a recess with what appears to be writing on them.

"That's unlikely," says the entomologist during lunch back at base camp. "Those were markings left by insect larvae tunneling under the bark." The entomologist makes a convincing argument, buttressed by other examples in which susceptible humans have been fooled by insect activity into thinking that they saw signs of a different intelligence at work. The archaeologist is al-most persuaded—almost. Why do some of the "insect markings" form recog-nizable words? Yet others seem to be merely squiggles, he must admit. He knows of nothing to which he can compare the bark slabs; nothing has been published on any similar artifacts—if indeed they are artifacts and not merely the product of natural forces and insect activity. So the question of other hu-man visitors to the island beyond those already known (a shipwreck survivor? prankster-adventurers?) cannot be solved. Certainly, if he writes a popular ar-ticle about the bark slabs, many readers will be caught up in the romance of the unknown visitors. (Before long, a tour boat will probably be named for them.) On the other hand, such a publication would do nothing for his pro-fessional reputation. He can only carry the mystery inside his mind, awaiting further information.

The island analogy illustrates the difficulty in creating a single coherent narrative about the Pagan movement, particularly that part of it more and more denominated by the umbrella label *Wicca*, a label that itself is contested by some contemporary Pagans and actively shunned by others. Can the story of the grasses be told without including the story of the mice that eat the seeds? Then what about the sparrows that also eat the seeds but have nothing to do with the mice? And shouldn't we include the reasonable hypothesis that weather patterns have something to do with the fact that fewer mice inhabit the west side of the island than the east side? And, most importantly, which humans reached the island first, and what did they do there? The Caritanian fishermen are like the popular writers and journalists described in chapter 4, "The Playboy and the Witch"—first on the scene to describe this new religious phenomenon, but with little interest in fitting their observations into a larger scheme. Thus I find that even when I seem to be creating what appears to be a narrative, as in chapter 6, "The Search for Paradise," what I more often have is a chronological series of data points with an arbitrary starting point. The sudden florescence of the analogical island is such that everything seems to be happening at once, without obvious chains of cause and effect.

The missing link, of course, is textual. The story of the Pagan movement is also the story of written texts: of books, articles, letters, and correspondence lessons in Witchcraft. Analyzing the first round of "outsider" publications, such as those described in chapter 4 enables us to see patterns developing and even, particularly in the case of Hans Holzer, how a writer could use the controversies generated in the Pagan community by one book to give him material for a sequel. It is even possible to draw a fairly definite line, at about 1970, to show when a movement that had primarily defined itself as a "magical religion" adopted the additional descriptions of "earth religion" and "nature religion," not coincidentally with the upsurge in environmental consciousness.[1]

Contemporary Pagan Witchcraft owes a great deal to the written word. Beginning in the 1960s, a tide of how-to and journalistic books on Witchcraft began to be published, and today that tide continues to flow, augmented by thousands of homemade Web pages, many of them adhering to conventions of, first, offering Witchcraft's credentials as a religion and, second, providing a reading list. Witchcraft—or "Wicca," to use the name increasingly employed in public discourse—has become a world religion, although a tiny one, beginning in England, spreading to the United States and to other English-speaking nations in the 1960s, jumping to the Netherlands, Germany, and elsewhere in Western Europe in the 1970s, and now reaching such nations as Brazil, which already has a rich tradition of magical religions in Candomblé and Umbanda. Indeed, Wicca has attained the status of "the Other" to reconstructionist Pagan groups in Eastern Europe and elsewhere, something from which they wish to differentiate themselves. All of this growth has been pushed more through the written word than by mouth-to-ear teaching. Frequently, in fact, the travels of Wiccan teachers have a great deal of resemblance to author's tours, and the typical venue is the metaphysical bookstore. It is no coincidence that one of the first public-relations projects of American Pagan Witches was to lobby dictionary publishers to add *Wicca* to their word lists and to define *witch* in a less pejorative way.

Consequently, some of this book is devoted to an analysis of books as well as of the ephemeral Pagan press. I regret that I am unable to study the many works of fiction that contributed inspiration to the nascent movement as well. Two writers will have to suffice: Robert Heinlein (1907–1988), whose *Stranger in a Strange Land* provided a virtual instruction and assembly manual for the Church of All Worlds, and Margaret St. Clair (1911–1995), who gleaned enough from reading Gerald Gardner's *Witchcraft Today* that she could re-create its ethos in fictional form, even before she and her husband became Gardnerian initiates.

Science fiction's impact on Neo-Paganism and Wicca may well have lasted because science-fiction and fantasy characters sometimes offered role models of a sort to a community overloaded with "beginners" and short on "elders." In addition, science/speculative fiction might possibly have been a more potent "growth agent" on American Paganism than in Britain or elsewhere. The interaction between science/speculative fiction and Wicca and other forms of Paganism deserves further exploration. It is a book waiting to be written, or possibly several books. Such literary history lies largely outside this book, but it deserves its own examination.

To draw out the "island" analogy a little bit more, I include myself among the plants, mice, lizards, sparrows, and so on. To some extent, I am describing events in which I myself participated: the coven described in chapter 1 of Adler's *Drawing Down the Moon* was my spiritual home for a time, beginning shortly after her visit.[2] My concern has been that I might confuse my story with the larger story, therefore. To the extent that I might have avoided that error, it was because from the beginning I was a saver of texts—letters, books, and the ephemeral publications of the Pagan movement, and much of what I write here has been reconstructed from those. When I compare my own experience to that of others, such as Aidan Kelly's narrative of the founding of the New Reformed Orthodox Order of the Golden Dawn (NROOGD),[3] I see many of the same patterns forming, which suggests to me, analogically, that many different grasses were sprouting on the island in much the same way during the same period of time. To tell one story, then, is to tell many stories. One walks out into the meadow and samples the flora here, here, and here, trusting that the sampling protocol will produce results similar to what would have happened had the samples been taken there, there, and there.

Finally, a word on terminology. The twentieth-century Pagan revival includes more than Witchcraft, but the self-conscious religion—as opposed to eclectic magical practice—of Witchcraft makes up its largest component. Hence my choice to capitalize *Witchcraft* when referring to what its followers consider to be a religion. Although the term *Neo-Pagan* (or *Neopagan*) was enthusiastically embraced by such influential Pagan writers as Isaac Bonewits and Oberon (Tim, back then) Zell, distinguishing the new Paganism from its ancient predecessors, I have noticed and support a tendency lately to replace it simply with the term *contemporary Paganism*. As Graham Harvey, one of the most engaged scholars of contemporary Paganism, observed in one of our conversations, "After fifty years or more, is it still 'neo-'?" In chapter 3, "The Rhetoric of Wicca," I deal with the issue of nomenclature at greater length.

Notes

1. The upsurge was helped greatly by the passage of major environmental legislation during the presidency of Richard Nixon, who, while focused on international affairs, needed to buttress his environmental record against Senator Edmund Muskie, a possible Democratic challenger. No doubt the Republicans of the time would have been as astounded by the associated resurgence of "nature religion" as those British Parliamentarians who, by repealing an archaic Witchcraft Act in 1951 at the request of the Spiritualists, helped set the stage for the appearance of Wicca in that nation. For more on Nixon, see J. Brooks Flippen's *Nixon and the Environment* (University of New Mexico Press, 2000).

2. Her fieldwork was done in the summer of 1974; I became involved in 1976, together with Mary Currier, to whom I was handfasted the following summer.

3. I cannot help but see some literary kinship between the humorously grandiose name of this Witchcraft group, the slightly earlier (1967) huge success of the Beatles' album *Sergeant Pepper's Lonely Hearts Club Band*, and the elaborate names of certain Bay Area rock bands, some of whose members were socially connected to NROOGD's founders, such as Quicksilver Messenger Service and Big Brother & The Holding Company.

Some Significant Dates in the Growth of American Paganism, 1939–1980

1939   Gleb Botkin incorporates the Church of Aphrodite, believed to be the first American Pagan body. The small group exists until his death in 1967.

1939   (England) Gerald Gardner, leading founder of modern Wicca, claims to have been initiated into a surviving coven of the "Old Religion" in this year.

1948   Robert Graves's *The White Goddess* is published, suggesting that "true poets" always worshiped a muse goddess and offering Graves's interpretation of certain medieval Welsh poems as Pagan allegories. *The White Goddess* becomes a sourcebook for numerous new Pagan groups from the 1950s to the 1970s.

1949   Gerald Gardner's novel *High Magic's Aid* is published, featuring a type of witchcraft bearing little relationship to what Wicca would become.

1951   (England) Cecil Williamson, with financial backing from Gardner, opens a witchcraft museum on the Isle of Man. The British Parliament abolishes the Witchcraft Act of 1735, making it no longer illegal to say that one is a witch.

1954   (England) Gerald Gardner's *Witchcraft Today* is published, supposedly an outsider's view of British Witchcraft, but in reality a clever manifesto by the man who did the most to create it.

1956   (England) Gerald Gardner creates the mock-archaic "Craft Laws," a set of rules for covens.

1959   Tom Delong, then thirteen, meets Victor Anderson, founder of the Feri (or Faerie) tradition of Witchcraft, in the East Bay area of California. Delong becomes better known as Gwydion Pendderwen, the first musician to release albums of Pagan music, beginning in 1976.

1962   College students Tim Zell, Lance Christie, and friends form the Church of All Worlds at Westminster College in Fulton, Missouri, which later becomes an international Pagan organization. The Church of All Worlds newsletter will become the influential Pagan magazine *Green Egg*.

1963   Raymond and Rosemary Buckland, newly arrived from England, begin initiating American students into Gardnerian Witchcraft as the official representatives of the Gardnerian tradition in the United States.

1963   Science-fiction writer Margaret St. Clair publishes *Sign of the Labrys*, probably the first American novel inspired by Gardnerian Wicca, before she makes contact with the Bucklands.

1964   Joseph Wilson, an Air Force enlisted man stationed in Wichita, begins corresponding with British Witches and starts his own newsletter, *The Waxing Moon*.

1964   Students at Carleton College in Northfield, Minnesota, create the Reformed Druids of North America, which goes on to spawn other Druidic groups as Carleton alumni spread its message.

1966   (England) Death of Robert Cochrane, whose correspondence with Joseph Wilson is copied and circulated by nascent American Witchcraft groups.

1967   Gleb Botkin, founder of Church of Aphrodite, dies in Charlottesville, Virginia.

1967   The New Reformed Orthodox Order of the Golden Dawn, an independent American Witchcraft group, is born from a class assignment given by James Broughton at San Francisco State College.

1967   Frederick and Svetlana Adams incorporate Feraferia ("wilderness festival"), a small but influential Pagan group in Pasadena, California, whose membership includes Holman Keith, a former associate of Gleb Botkin.

1968   The Council of Themis is formed as the first umbrella Pagan body in America. Members include Feraferia, Church of All Worlds, Ordo Templi Astartes, and briefly the Psychedelic Venus Church.

1969   The "Pagan Way" is created by several leading American and British Witches as an "outer court" ritual system for people who might later be initiated. Its rituals are later published by Llewellyn Publications. Stephen McNallen forms the Viking Brotherhood (later renamed the Ásatrú Free Assembly), one of the first Norse Pagan groups. Else Christiansen's more politically radical Odinist Fellowship is founded the same year. Hans Holzer's *The Witchcraft Report* is published, the first of several books surveying the new American Paganism by this New York–based author.

1970   First Earth Day is celebrated on April 22, spearheaded by Senator Gaylord Nelson of Wisconsin, who sought to move environmental issues onto the political stage.

1970   Philip Emmons Isaac Bonewits graduates from the University of California with a bachelor of arts in magic. Bonewits turns his undergraduate work into the book *Real Magic* and becomes a leading figure in American Paganism, particularly Druidic organizations.

1971   Zsuzsanna "Z" Budapest founds the Susan B. Anthony Coven No. 1 in southern California and becomes a leading figure in feminist Witchcraft. *Look*, an illustrated American weekly magazine, publishes an article titled "Witches Are Rising" on the perceived occult revival. Susan Roberts' *Witches U.S.A.* is published, linking Witchcraft to nature religion. Llewellyn Publications publishes the hitherto secret Gardnerian *Book of Shadows* from a copy furnished to them by Lady Sheba (Jessie Wicker Bell) of Kentucky.

1972   The Council of Earth Religions, a short-lived successor to the Council of Themis, is formed as an umbrella Pagan body. The first annual Gnostic Aquarian Festival of Astrology, Mind Power, Occult Sciences and Witchcraft, sponsored by Llewellyn Publications, is held in a Minneapolis hotel. The "Gnosticon" continues through the mid-1970s.

1973   Herman Slater, owner of a New York City bookstore, begins publishing a Pagan magazine, *Earth Religion News*. Carl Weschcke, head of Llewellyn Publications, sponsors his own short-lived organization, the Council of American Witches.

1974   *Playboy* magazine covers Llewellyn Publications' Gnostic Aquarian Festival in its July issue.

1975   Covenant of the Goddess is formed in California to provide ministerial credentials and encourage networking among Witchcraft covens. It is still in existence.

1976   *Green Egg* ceases publication in St. Louis.

1979   Two important books on American Paganism are published: *Drawing Down the Moon*, a journalistic survey by Margot Adler of National Public Radio, and *The Spiral Dance*, a how-to guide to Witchcraft by Starhawk.

1979   *People* magazine profiles Witches Jim Alan and Selena Fox of Circle Sanctuary in rural Wisconsin in its November 5 issue.

1979   *Gaia: A New Look at Life on Earth* is published by British biologist James Lovelock, who sees Earth's soils, plants, animals, and atmosphere as working together in dynamic equilibrium to preserve the conditions necessary for life. Many Pagans seize on Lovelock's ideas as confirmation of "nature religion."

1979   The Pan Pagan Festival, the first large, national outdoor Pagan festival, is held at a private campground in Indiana.

1983   Ár nDraíocht Féin ("Our Own Druidry") is formed as a restoration of Indo-European Pagan religion. Its first archdruid is Isaac Bonewits.

1986   Henge of Keltria splits from Ár nDraíocht Féin to form a more specifically Celtic revived Druid organization.

1988   *Green Egg* resumes publication in northern California.

2000   *Green Egg* ceases publication finally.

CHAPTER ONE

How the Ravens Came to the Lake: Wicca's Birth and Atlantic Passage

American Paganism, particularly Pagan Witchcraft—"Wicca" in the broadest sense of the term—has multiple beginnings. Its scheme is more horizontal than vertical, with no central organization and no hierarchy. No one can be truly excluded or "disfellowshipped" from the ranks of Pagan Witches; nor can any one individual speak for a loosely knit community that, as of the first years of the twenty-first century, numbers at a conservative estimate of at least 800,000 persons. Such a horizontal organization makes narrative history difficult. In fact, there is no one narrative about the growth of Pagan Witchcraft in America, but rather multiple narratives springing up at once—the plants and animals of the metaphorical island of the introduction to this book.

Someone telling the history of a broad movement will be tempted to focus on leaders and groups. We usually look at religions in terms of groups, both as groups of followers of this or that teaching, and as subgroups within a "religion," such as Christian denominations. The problem with Wicca in particular is that most Wiccans are not in groups but are "solitaries" who may join with other Wiccans only occasionally, particularly at any of the many summer festivals that have become a fixture on the Pagan scene since the first Pan-Pagan Gathering was held in Indiana in 1980. Solitary Witches count on these festivals to offer the high-energy, communal experience that they do not experience on their own; in fact, many schedule their vacations in order to attend more festivals each year. As one contributor to the Wiccan e-mail list "ColoWiccan" said, "I am a solitary because I just plain haven't met the right group of people. . . . But at the Sabbats, I would like to be able to commune and celebrate with people of like mind and raise some energy for all of our benefit."[1]

During the early 1990s, when I was editing a book series for Llewellyn Publications, the largest American publisher of Pagan books, I was told by a Llewellyn executive that the company's marketers estimated that 70 percent of all self-described Pagans, Wiccan or otherwise, were solitary practitioners. The Wiccan writer Scott Cunningham (1956–1993), one of Llewellyn's best-selling and most prolific authors, is credited (at least within that publishing company) with making solitary practice respectable through his 1988 book *Wicca: A Guide for the Solitary Practitioner*, which had sold more than 400,000 copies by 2000.[2]

More recently, Fritz Jung, webmaster of the Witches' Voice website,[3] has put the percentage of solitary Wiccans at 80 percent of the whole, thanks to the multitude of Internet e-mail lists, chat rooms, and other ways of overcoming distance and isolation. James R. Lewis of the University of Wisconsin–Stevens Point, a researcher on new religious movements, notes that "the explosive growth of Internet neo-Paganism has shifted the median age of movement participants downward, because new neo-Pagans tend to be younger," and he cites two recent studies placing from 15.2 to 25 percent of contemporary Pagans at eighteen to twenty-five years of age at the time of the surveys.[4]

American Pagans, like other Americans, are culturally if not theologically heirs of the Second Great Awakening, a revival that swept the young nation—particularly in recently settled areas—in the early 1820s, in a flurry of camp meetings (outdoor festivals) where itinerant, often self-proclaimed clergy preached a democratic religion that turned the Puritans' predestination on its head. They left a legacy: Camping in the woods and fields, frontier dwellers of the early nineteenth century drank in the fervent sermons of clergy from different denominations who preached new "optimistic understandings" of the individual's role in his or her own redemption.[5] In Wicca's case, we see this legacy both in the highly individualistic practice of the religion and in its seasonal renewals through "camp meetings" that take the shape of campground-based festivals lasting on average four to seven days. What has held Wicca together in the interim—indeed, what brought it across the Atlantic—however, was written texts. People were involved too, of course, but the flow of textual information both preceded and surrounded them. To write a history of American Paganism, both Wicca and other forms, we must therefore focus a great deal on written texts, which moved across the Atlantic and within the United States often more quickly than did individual teachers of "the Craft."

Wicca, a Textual Religion

It is one of the paradoxes of Wicca, which seems intensely somatic,[6] that its propagation and its ongoing life occurred through textual means. Around 1970, the writer Susan Roberts, who interviewed a fairly small group of American Witches, noted, "They are omnivorous readers. I have never been in a witch's home where books and periodicals were not as much a part of the household equipment as pots and pans."[7] At the end of the 1970s, in her list of reasons why respondents to her *Green Egg* questionnaire became Pagans, Margot Adler lists seeking beauty and imagination, personal growth, the freedom of "religion without the middleman," and environmental and feminist concerns, but also bookishness: "In particular, most of the Midwesterners said flatly that the wide dissemination of strange and fascinating books had been the *main* factor in creating a Neo-Pagan resurgence . . . almost *all* [Neo-Pagans regardless of educational level] are avid readers."[8] Adler's research was conducted in the late 1970s, but her conclusion remains appropriate. Today's Pagan websites are replete with reading lists and book reviews. On the ColoWiccan e-mail list, which has more than two hundred members, a Colorado Springs coven leader replied to a question from a new member about the "philosophical areas" of Wicca by writing, "I have what my students affectionately call the 'reading list from hell' that I'd be glad to ship you off-line. It's about 30 pages long in WordPerfect format."[9] Her response was typical. While someone with poor verbal (and typing) skills might make a perfectly fine Pagan Witch, he or she will be excluded from a great deal of community activity.

Combine the fact that a majority of today's Wiccans and Pagans are solitary with the fact that the primary means of transmitting these religious traditions has been textual rather than face to face, and it is easy to see that a great deal of Wiccan life has gone "under the radar," so to speak. Most scholarship has concentrated on groups, or on the intense but temporary experience of large festivals. How would our view of Wicca change if we accepted the solitary Wiccan as the statistical if not the conventional norm, rather than as someone looking for a coven or temporarily between covens?

Wiccans themselves are notably ambivalent about the fact that their religion has been passed along more by written text (including books, letters, correspondence courses, magazines, e-mail, and Web pages), because according to their own values, the way to learn the Craft is face to face, from the archetypal wise and patient high priest and high priestess. (*High* in Wiccan jargon has a sense of being fully initiated, or the leader of a group, but it can also be applied to anyone who serves as a ritual leader, since in theory all initiates are priests and priestesses.) Wiccan groups have certain structural similarities to martial-arts schools: they are usually lineage conscious, they form "traditions" (in the sense that Hsing-i is distinct from Jujitsu in martial arts), and they coalesce around a changing group of teachers and elders. The obvious difference is that while there are many martial-arts books, and one may practice a martial-arts form such as T'ai Chi Ch'uan alone, there exist many formal competitions (not to mention the possibility of an actual brawl) for which practice with other persons is a necessity. The same Witches in whose homes Susan Roberts noted the omnipresent books and periodicals expressed ambivalence about learning from books only: "When they view the current [circa 1970] rash of men and women who, having read a book or two, flamboyantly embrace witchcraft, race out to buy a cape and then publicly proclaim themselves superwitches, they are highly entertained."

Witchcraft Today, the First Key Text

The first key text was published in 1954: Gerald Gardner's book *Witchcraft Today*. In it, Gardner announced that (a) a Pagan Old Religion had survived from the Middle Ages until the present, in the manner suggested by the archaeologist Margaret Murray (who contributed an introduction) and that (b) he himself had made contact with a group of these Witches (referred to as "the New Forest coven" or the "Southern Coven") and been initiated. Murray herself had earlier offered a radical reinterpretation of the late medieval and early modern witch trials in three books of her own, beginning in 1921

Figure 1.1.   Gerald Gardner at the Museum of Magic and Witchcraft, Castletown, Isle of Man, UK, in the early 1960s.

with *The Witch-Cult in Western Europe*.[10] In Murray's narrative, the trials and execution of so-called witches was part of a religious struggle between Catholic (and later Protestant) Christianity and the "Old Religion" of surviving tribal Paganism. Although historians since the 1960s have severely disputed Murray's version of events, she was still considered an authority when Gardner was writing. Gardner carried on her thesis, claiming that followers of the Old Religion worshiped a Mother Goddess and the "Horned God," whom Christians slandered as the Devil. The ritual practice, he wrote, was combined with a knowledge of mind power—the use of massed human wills under heightened circumstances on a particular object or desire. He went her one better by saying that he had found followers of the Old Religion still practicing it in southern England in the 1930s.

Gerald Gardner (1884–1964), a retired civil servant who had spent his career in Britain's Asian colonies before retiring to southern England, claimed to be describing a religion already fully formed, although tiny in number of practitioners. Fifty years of research, however, have failed to uncover exactly who these practitioners were. One American scholar pointed out in the 1980s that there was no source for Gardner's claims except Gardner himself.[11] Subsequent research has uncovered much more information about Gardner's life but no independent verification of the existence of the "New Forest coven" prior to about 1951. It is far more likely that Gardner was the leading figure in the creation of what is now a worldwide movement.[12] Although he placed his initiation in 1939, the picture of Witchcraft in *Witchcraft Today* differs dramatically from the fictionalized medieval magic and Witchcraft in his 1949 novel *High Magic's Aid*,[13] published five years earlier. More likely, what we now know as Wicca was created by Gardner and a small group of associates around 1950–1951.

No American edition of *Witchcraft Today* would be published for several years, but evidence, specifically the writings of science-fiction author Margaret St. Clair (1911–1995), suggests that the British edition would reach the United States several years in advance of the first initiated Gardnerian Witches, Raymond and Rosemary Buckland.

Born in 1934, Ray Buckland had served in the Royal Air Force from 1957 to 1959 and was later employed by BOAC, corporate precursor of today's British Airways. He, too, had read *Witchcraft Today* and entered into correspondence with Gerald Gardner, then living on the Isle of Man. The Bucklands moved because of Ray's employment to Brentwood, Long Island, in 1962, and then returned briefly to the United Kingdom to be trained and initiated by Monique Wilson, one of Gardner's successor priestesses. (Gardner himself was in failing health and would die in 1964 while traveling by ship to Lebanon for a change of climate.) After their initiations, the Bucklands were designated Gardnerian Wicca's official representatives in the United States, although later in the decade, other Americans would receive their initial training and initiation in Britain.

St. Clair was one of those writing to the Bucklands; she and her husband, Eric, would eventually become two of their earliest initiates. But, as an examination of her writing reveals, St. Clair had most likely already read and absorbed not only *Witchcraft Today* but also *High Magic's Aid*, published in 1949, as well as Robert Graves's 1948 "grammar of poetic myth," *The White Goddess*, another seminal text in the Pagan revival. St. Clair's writing demonstrates that Wiccan concepts and imagery arrived in the United States ahead of actual British Wiccans.

The St. Clairs brought to their reading their own interest in classical Pagan religion—Margaret St. Clair was a classics major at the University of California–Berkeley, with additional graduate study in Greek—and ceremonial magic; in effect, like others of the time, they seem to have created their own Pagan Witchcraft before the religion officially arrived. When she did encounter the Bucklands, St. Clair would receive a mild slap on the wrist for "giving away too much." Yet Raymond Buckland mentions her novel *The Sign of the Labrys* with approval in his 1971 book *Witchcraft from the Inside*, noting that "Craft ideas, feelings, beliefs, have been worked into the futuristic story extraordinarily cleverly yet quite unobtrusively."[14] An earlier St. Clair story, "Idris' Pig," published just a year after *The White Goddess*, suggests in some of its themes and images that she had already absorbed Graves's book or was exploring similar sources.

Sign of the Labrys offers a scenario familiar to Cold War readers: a postcatastrophe world where huge underground shelters were constructed and "never actually occupied, and there had been no need for peace to be made for them to be abandoned entirely. People live in them now because they are quiet, even luxurious."[15] Sam Sewell, the narrator, lives in "the tier called E3" under an unnamed city in the former United States. Due to global "yeast plagues," Earth's population has plummeted, government and commerce have dissolved, and the survivors merely drift through their days, finding what they need in the massive stockpiles of emergency supplies, their chief meaningful, organized labor being the collecting and mass burial of victims of the continuing, although abated, plagues.

By page two, Sewell has been contacted by an agent of the FBY (Federal Bureau of Yeast?): "As far as we can be said to have a government nowadays, it is the FBY; I don't know why we dread it so. Perhaps it is the background of 'science,' which, to a man of my generation, is automatically dreadful."[16]

The FBY is hunting a woman named "Despoina, or Spina, or just D. . . . We suspect that she may be a sower [of infectious yeasts]." Despoina, the agent informs him on his next visit, is a witch.[17] Sewell's reaction is predictable: he thinks first of old hags, broomsticks, and so forth, whereas Despoina is described as a "girl . . . slender and small-boned, with a remarkably fair skin [and] very heavy red-gold hair."[18]

If readers have guessed that Despoina is the priestess, that Sewell will become her partner, and that the FBY will play the role of the Inquisition, they have the bare bones of the plot. And if they detect a parallel between Sam Sewell and Jan Bonder and between Despoina and "pliant and graceful" Morven the witch (with "pure ivorine flesh" and "red-gold hair"[19]), they will have plotted a remarkable parallel between *Sign of the Labrys* and Gardner's *High Magic's Aid*.

Sign of the Labrys is sprinkled with signatures of the Gardnerian Craft: people saying "Blessed be" to each other; use of ligatures and drugs to gain "the sight"; recovered memories of the "Burning Times";[20] and an ancient Witches' Sabbat, ritual nudity, ritual garters, and Sewell's initiation by a man in a stag mask with a scourge (a detail that would cause St. Clair some small problems later).[21]

Margaret St. Clair sent Buckland a copy of *Sign of the Labrys* when it was published. "Perhaps a little late in the day, she asked me if I would critique it for Craft details. I thought they were very good at the time except for the fact that she had a man initiating a man."[22]

The error in ritual did not prevent a friendship from developing. "They were absolutely wonderful people, very warm and loving," Buckland recalled. After correspondence and visits, the Bucklands flew from New York to California, and on April 15, 1966, initiated the St. Clairs, who used the Craft names Froniga and Weyland.[23] Eric's Craft name reflected his interest in smith craft and jewelry making; he made the silver witch queen's crown that Rosemary Buckland wears in photographs in *Witchcraft from the Inside*.[24]

The St. Clairs' house "was a great place to visit," Buckland said. "It was high up in the hills [above Berkeley] with a fantastic view—an all-wood house; the walls were plain, bare wood. They had floor-to-ceiling bookshelves and the most incredible collection of the first editions of all the Oz books by Frank Baum. Margaret was very much into herbs and had an herb garden."[25]

Another visitor to that same house was Ed Fitch, a younger American who found the Craft through the St. Clairs. He confirmed that their interest in magic predated their Gardnerian initiation.[26] "When I first walked into their house down at the end of Skyline Drive in Richmond [California] in 1964, the hardwood floor had a triple circle with a pentagram inscribed in it. Me being the innocent, I figured, 'Oh, how very interesting,' And I saw the ceremonial sword on the wall, but I did not connect two and two to make four. The key thing about the circles on the floor is that that's not the way the Gardnerians would have done it. That is pre-Gardnerian, although it's conceivably out of *High Magic's Aid*. What they had there predated their association with the Bucklands."[27]

Like the majority of Wiccans in the 1960s, Fitch, too, made his initial connection through books. He had already read Gardner's *Witchcraft Today*. Later he lived with his parents in Baltimore between enlistments in the Air Force. "When I started getting restless, I would go out to the airport and watch the planes go in and out. I browsed through their really good book section and came across *Sign of the Labrys*. I flipped through it, put it back on the shelf, took a couple steps, stopped, and said, 'Wait a second! Moon phases . . . priestess . . . this fits with what Gardner said and what Robert Graves said.' I read it carefully and said, 'Aha, this is the Craft.' I read it and re-read it. Once I began writing to Margaret in care of the publisher, I began a steady exchange of letters, and they invited me to come out and visit them. Late that year I did exactly that."[28]

When Fitch rejoined the Air Force and was stationed in Massachusetts, "they sent a report on me to the Bucklands and said that I was good material for the Gardnerian Craft. I got a letter from Rosemary, and as soon as I got settled in at the air base, I contacted the Bucklands, went down [to Long Island] to pay them a visit and we were friends instantly. That was how Margaret and Eric got me connected in with the Craft."[29]

Yet another person who connected with Pagan Witchcraft textually first and in person later was Joseph B. Wilson (1942–2004). Like Fitch, he made use of travel provided by the United States Air Force, which sent him to RAF Upper Heyford, Oxfordshire, in 1969. While in England, he met with English Witches whom he had already contacted by mail. Previously, while stationed in Wichita in 1962, Wilson had joined a community theater group that was presenting one of the classic plays of community-theater groups everywhere: *Bell, Book and Candle*, a humorous treatment of fictional modern Witchcraft of the nonreligious, spell-casting-and-psychic-powers sort. (A film version starring Kim Novak and James Stewart was made in 1958.) According to Susan Roberts, Wilson at the time felt that "I was still the only person in the whole world who thought as I did about the Goddess" until he discovered that "another member of the cast was a real witch. . . . I soon found out from him that there were many others who felt the same as I. I was no longer alone. He arranged for my instruction and initiation."[30]

Elsewhere, Wilson speaks of the "Wichita Group," headed by a couple whom he refers to as "Mac and Marlyn," who conducted his initiation in a cave near the Kansas-Oklahoma border. Later he would say that Mac (also known as Sean) never used the term *Witchcraft* but referred only to "some stuff we do in the family." Wilson's experience, however, demonstrates the change that was occurring due to what I will call the "Gardnerian model" of Wiccan Witchcraft-as-religion. What *might* have been some sort of inherited or locally developed form of magical practice was quickly subsumed in the mid-1960s as this English form of Pagan religion acted on other self-described groups of witches as a powerful magnet aligns iron filings within its field.

In 1964, Wilson spotted an advertisement in *Fate* magazine for *The Pentagram*, a small-circulation British Witchcraft newsletter that served as a forum for information and as an arena where various personalities strove for influence. No doubt Gerard Noel, *The Pentagram's* publisher, selected *Fate* for his advertisement because it was at the time the leading nationally distributed magazine dealing with such topics as UFOs, ghosts, extrasensory perception, lost civilizations and fringe archaeology, and other topics often grouped under the heading of "the occult." (*Fate* had been founded in 1948 during the post–World War II "flying saucer" sightings wave; it later was owned for a time by Llewellyn Worldwide Ltd., parent corporation of Llewellyn Publications, a leading publisher of Pagan, astrological, magical, and New Age books.)

Inspired by the copies of *The Pentagram* that he received, Wilson purchased a spirit duplicator[31] and created *The Waxing Moon: A Witchcraft Newsletter*. Sean, he said, did not like the term *Witchcraft*, but Wilson had launched his typographical boat into the current. *The Waxing Moon's* primary purpose was networking, "helping people to find each other because there are *no* covens, *no* groups of people getting together with the exception of the very few closed, secret, and initiatory Gardnerian groups started by Ray and Rosemary Buckland. I write hundreds of letters, almost all in response to people asking for help in finding someone, anyone to teach them. . . . About 85 percent to 90 percent of my subscribers and correspondents are men."[32]

1734 and Tubal Cain

One of these men was Roy Bowers, better known as "Robert Cochrane" (1931–1966), who for the last three years of his life blazed a meteoric path across the British Craft firmament. Doreen Valiente (1922–1999), who had been Gerald Gardner's high priestess and collaborator in the late 1950s, broke with Gardner and then spent a year in Cochrane's coven before his death. She described Cochrane as "perhaps the most powerful and gifted personality to have appeared in modern witchcraft."[33] Evan John Jones

(1936–2003), another member of Cochrane's coven, who collaborated with Valiente years later on a book recapitulating Cochrane's teachings and their subsequent development, was still wrestling with Cochrane's legacy thirty years after the "Magister's" death: "Was Cochrane a real magician of the old tradition, or was he just another magical trickster, a 'tregetour' or mountebank who jumped on the occult bandwagon, as some people who never even met the man now claim that he did?"[34]

Valiente had described Cochrane's version of the Old Religion (the "Old Faith," he often called it, one of the few Craft leaders to use the word *faith* as

Figure 1.2.   Robert Cochrane dressed for caving, circa 1965. His English coven frequently met on hilltops and in caves. Photo courtesy of Evan John Jones.

a descriptor) as more "shamanic" than "formal." Unlike Gerald Gardner's Wicca, rooted partly in the naturist (nudist) movement[35] with its prescribed "skyclad" indoor rituals, Cochrane's coven frequently met on hilltops, in wooded groves, and in caves; in fact, one surviving photo shows him in boots, coveralls, and caver's helmet with light. In the end, while reserving judgment on all of Cochrane's claims to knowledge of a pre-Gardnerian Old Religion, Jones decided that the proof of his leadership was in the "experiential success" of his ritual workings: "We all knew what it felt like to be one of 'Diana's darling crew,' because we had really lived it. 'Traditional witch' or not, Cochrane and his ways lifted us to this pitch. . . . In my opinion, if he was not a hereditary Witch with a handed-down lore, then he must have known someone who was, because so many of his ideas and concepts hark back to a different form of the Craft than modern-day Wicca."[36]

Joe Wilson's correspondence with *Pentagram* editor Gerard Noel was rewarded when Noel placed a small notice about *The Waxing Moon* in what would be *The Pentagram's* final issue, promoting Wilson's American newsletter and indicating that he was looking for correspondents. Cochrane accepted the invitation and wrote to Wilson on December, 20 1965, inquiring whether America had a "ley" system (pathways on which earth energy is believed to flow) and asserting that the Old Faith had come to America with British immigrants: "The symbols used by the state of Texas point towards this being a fact." (Cochrane was probably referring to the "lone star" flag; more conventional historians see it as derived from the Bonnie Blue Flag of the Confederacy.) Cochrane offered some cryptic information about himself as well: "I know the right and left-hand language . . . I come from the country of the Oak, the Ash, and the Thorn," adding as well, "I am against the present form of Gardnerism [sic] and all kindred movements, although . . . I believe they could become something far greater."

Wilson, intrigued, wrote back, and the correspondence continued for the next half year until Cochrane, overwhelmed by some problems in his personal life, committed suicide by an overdose of sleeping pills and alcohol. The west-bound letters provided the symbolic basics of the Old Faith, divided into two parts: the masculine mysteries, symbolized by the control of fire, whose initiates are called the Clan of Tubal Cain (a legendary blacksmith of Middle Eastern origin), and the feminine mysteries, the flow of creation and destruction and life and death. Their combined symbol was the pentagram, whose points, Cochrane said, stood for life, birth, love, maternity, wisdom, and death/resurrection. After one long gloss on the ancient Celtic poem called *The Song of Amergin*, relating its lines to the progress of the ritual of the Cauldron, he concludes, "Wisdom is not dogmatic—and when the pupil becomes wise he must necessarily break from the teacher, and interpret dogma and the promptings of his soul as he sees fit. Therefore I explain to you what I know—but I am not teaching you, you are taking from it what you require—and transmuting these ideas to your own needs."

The young airman and the slightly older English Witch would never meet, since Cochrane's death preceded Wilson's Air Force assignment to England. Once there, he did seek out others of Cochrane's circle. In those years of the late 1960s, Cochrane's letters would be endlessly recopied and circulated, adding their flavor to various new traditions of Witchcraft, often with their origins stripped away. (This was how I first encountered them in a Colorado coven in 1976.) In the United States, this "current" became known as "1734," which is not a date but a group of symbolic numbers. While in England, Wilson developed his own correspondence course and tried to organize what he had learned from Cochrane and elsewhere into a coherent system, succumbing, as he said, "to the pressure of expectations people had about 'the way things should be done.'"[37] Discharged from the Air Force and living in Los Angeles in the early 1970s, he developed an initiation ceremony for the 1734 tradition. His Los Angeles–area initiates included Dave and Ann Finnin, who later made several trips to England, made their own connection with Cochrane's covener Evan John Jones, and started their own legally incorporated body within the Tubal Cain tradition, the Ancient Keltic Church.[38]

Although Cochrane's covens did not use the Masonic-derived three-degree initiation system of Gardnerian Wicca, Wilson's correspondence and subsequent working relationships in England counted as an initiation of sorts. At the time, both Gardner's initiates and Robert Cochrane were claiming, in their own ways, unbroken continuity with ancient pre-Christian religion. Having Gerald Gardner's book in hand, with the imprimatur of Margaret Murray plus their own initiatory lineage, gave American Gardnerians the upper hand in claiming authenticity. During the 1970s, a great deal of energy and ink would be expended on the question of initiation and what constituted a valid initiation, until Ray Buckland broke ranks with Gardnerian tradition and declared that self-initiation could be perfectly valid. But "1734" Witches were able to claim that they, too, were in possession of ancient teachings, even though they had arrived via the postal system. "They were able to say [to the Gardnerians], 'Well, we don't need you to validate us as real Witches,'" as Dave Finnin remembers.[39]

At the time, with Ray and Rosemary Buckland the only official Gardnerian Wiccan leaders in the country (the St. Clairs kept to themselves and did not lead a coven), Wilson, Fitch, and others realized that the one training coven on the East Coast was inadequate to cope with the growing number of American seekers. Between 1963 and 1972, according to one Gardnerian writer, the Bucklands initiated only twenty third-degree high priestesses.[40] Fitch, however, had spent some of his free time during his own Air Force hitch in Thailand writing two books that became underground classics in the Pagan community: *The Grimoire of the Shadows* and *The Outer Court Book of Shadows*, which combined Pagan material from pre-Christian Europe with the basic structure of Gardnerian Wicca. The term "outer court" meant that these rituals and meditations could be used by people seeking to learn if Wicca was right for them without compromising the contents of the *Book of Shadows*, the gradually growing collection of material that was for initiates only. Material from both books was later combined, revised, and commercially published as *The Outer Court Book of Shadows* in 1996.[41]

In addition, Fitch and Wilson also collaborated with Thomas Giles, an American occultist with nineteenth-century roots; several British Witches, including John Score (also known as "M"), who edited *The Wiccan*, a successor to *The Pentagram*; Tony Kelly, author of a widely influential visionary essay called "Pagan Musings"; the writer Susan Roberts (as a consultant); and others to create a new body of Pagan seasonal rituals known as the Pagan Way, also later revised and published in commercial form.[42] Bits of Pagan Way ritual were published in Hans Holzer's *The New Pagans* and Susan Roberts' *Witches U.S.A.* These texts rapidly diffused throughout the new Pagan community, losing connection with their original authors.

Donna Cole Schultz of Chicago encountered the Craft when her husband served as *Fate* magazine's astrology editor in the mid-1960s and brought home Gardner's books. "When we read these, we immediately knew that our search was over." They encountered other self-initiated American Witches before traveling to England to make more contacts. In a 2003 article, Schultz described a typical marathon Sunday-afternoon copying session in her English priestess's home: "We all gathered round the large dining room table and various rituals were laid out for us to copy, either by hand or by my husband's furious strikes on the typewriter. This material was precious as gold to us."[43] Later, as part of the Pagan Way, Schultz helped to create a body of written material that took on a life of its own through such forms of Pagan self-publishing as she describes.

"Twenty years later, material from these books was still surfacing in new traditions and rituals, sometimes being labeled as an 'ancient Celtic tradition from Ireland and Scotland,'" writes Wiccan historian Aidan Kelly. "Pagan Way appealed to two audiences: those just getting started in Witchcraft, and those interested in attending Pagan ceremonies and structuring social and civic activities around them, much as in mainstream churches. The founders and early organizers let the movement take its own course. . . . Some covens of Witches ran Pagan Way groups as training circles for interested persons and potential initiates."[44]

Some of the British creators of the Pagan Way were also involved in 1971 with the founding of an organization called the Pagan Front, later renamed as the slightly less militant-sounding Pagan Federation, which remains in existence today. In America, active Pagan Way groups were maintained during the 1970s by Penny and Michael Novack (students of Thomas Giles) in Philadelphia and by Wiccan leaders Donna Cole Schultz and Herman Enderle in Chicago. Numerous other groups subsequently "hived off" from these and from their successors.

Fitch bemusedly told an interviewer how the Pagan Way texts gained a life of their own:

Every now and then, at a Pagan gathering up in the [California] mountains, I will be enjoying myself with the good company of kindred souls, and perhaps with a tankard of good ale. There will be an announcement that a handfasting will be taking place, and that all are welcome to attend. I will go, of course, since I like such things. Usually, I find a place out in the trees toward the back of the crowd and watch. The bride will be radiant and beautiful, as all brides are, and the groom smiling, strong and handsome, as are all grooms. The ceremony begins, and the liturgy begins sounding familiar. I realize that, although the rite has been modified somewhat, the words are mine. I wrote it, originally! I look at the bride and groom. Their faces show the happiness of a joining that will link them for years, or perhaps for a lifetime. I look at the people around them, smiling or in tears of joy. *I've done something good for someone*, I think to myself. *They'll probably never know that I forged the link that joins them, but I know it. I've given them something really worthwhile, and that's what matters, after all!* I raise my tankard of ale toward them in silent salute and then settle comfortably at the base of an oak tree, way out in back at the edge of the woods, to watch the proceedings.[45]

The Gardnerian "Magnet"

The Bucklands' New York coven lasted from 1963 to 1972, when they stepped back from the leadership position to remain as elders. Shortly after that, however, they divorced. Active leadership had passed to Thomas and Judy Kneitel, known in the Craft as Phoenix and Theos, who began publishing a Gardnerian newsletter, *Gardnerian Aspects*, within the eclectic pages of the Church of All Worlds' *Green Egg* magazine. Like Gardner, Raymond

Buckland started his own tiny Witchcraft and magic museum in his home and began writing books. His 1971 book *Witchcraft from the Inside* paralleled *Witchcraft Today* in making the claim of unbroken continuity: its first page proclaims, "For nearly four hundred years, witchcraft, to all intents and purposes, has been dead"; he goes on to cite Margaret Murray's work approvingly and continues, "Confirmation of [Murray's] scholarly theories was not long in coming for, it seemed, witchcraft had *not* died after all. It had lain hidden, feigning death, awaiting the chance to once more come out and practise openly and unafraid."[46] In a passage expunged from later editions after its author's change of heart, Buckland wrote of the Witchcraft scene circa 1970:

> It says much for the success of Gerald Gardner in obtaining recognition for the Craft as a religion, for its imitators are those who, unable to gain access to a coven, have decided to start their own. These do-it-yourself "witches" would, on the face of it, seem harmless but on closer scrutiny are not so. They are causing considerable confusion to others who, seeking the true, get caught up in the false. . . . These "covens" [in both Britain and the United States] spreading like chicken-pox have no association with "the Craft." Why do people start such "covens"? Why not wait and search? For some it is just that they have no patience. They feel so strongly for the Craft that they *must* participate in some way. By the time they eventually do come in contact with the true Craft it is too late. They are by then so set in their own rites and, unfortunately, have others whom they have led along, that they cannot back down. Some, however, are merely in search of fame and fortune.[47]

Gardner's publicity seeking in the 1950s (which caused a split in his original coven), his own writing, and the writing of his followers contributed to Gardnerian Wicca's becoming the prototype for generic Wicca. What set Gardnerian Wicca apart from some other forms of reconstructed Paganism was its structure—a strictly initiatory mystery religion. As the growth of the Pagan Way demonstrates, far more people were drawn to Witchcraft than the Gardnerian initiatory coven-based structure could accommodate. And that growth intensified the tendency to fragment that remains typical of the Pagan movement in general.

In the United States, with initially only one official initiating high priest and priestess in place, the situation was acute. When Ray and Rosemary Buckland divorced, the Wiccan principle of female religious leadership did hold true, and most of the coveners took Rosemary's side. But despite the American Gardnerians' carefully conserved initiatory records, they have not been immune to the essentially fissile nature of the Pagan movement. After his separation from Rosemary, Ray Buckland initiated a new high priestess, an action that turned many of the earlier initiates against him and led to a great deal of furor over who was a "real" Witch and who was not.

A greater uproar followed Buckland's decision to reverse the position that he had taken in *Witchcraft from the Inside*. In 1974, he produced a new how-to book, *The Tree*, a complete, ready-made tradition of "Seax-Wicca" (Saxon Witchcraft), one of whose tenets was that self-initiation was valid.[48] Other differences included democratic election of coven leaders, the absence of ritual scourging, no degree system, and a choice of meeting in the ritual circle either nude or clothed. Tom Kneitel, the new high priest of American Gardnerian Wicca, exploded:

> The same person who set forth such impressive criteria [for Wicca being a mystery religion] has, himself, recently become the founder of what he terms a new "tradition" of "Wicca," the *non*-secret rituals of which are to be made available to the general public by the founder in handy book form; self-initiation into the *non*-mysteries being open to any and all (no screening whatsoever is involved) who may purchase the book at any drugstore, supermarket, or newsstand, giving the founder an author's royalty and thereby causing the new initiate to pay for the initiation and whatever teachings may be included.[49]

Buckland, however, seems to have caught the spirit of the times, since *The Tree* was merely an forerunner of the dozens of how-to Pagan Witchcraft books published during the decades that followed. (With his subsequent spouses, Buckland also offered mail-order lessons in Seax-Wicca until the early 1990s, when he turned to full-time writing and one of his earlier students took over the correspondence school.)

Indeed, many of the characteristics of Gardnerian Wicca have not been borrowed by other American Witches, including the ritual scourge (admittedly with a soft, nonharmful whip of knotted cords), promoted by Gerald Gardner for "purifying the soul" and "raising power." Nude ritual work is also characteristic of Gardnerian Wicca, justified variously because it is said to eliminate social differences (the same argument made by the secular British nudists with whom Gardner associated in the 1930s), to promote somehow the flow of magical power, and, more esoterically, to lessen the fear of death by having the practitioner confront the variety of human forms. Aidan Kelly, the first "insider" religious scholar to examine Gardnerian Wicca, would cause consternation when he asserted that Gardner was "addicted to being whipped," in the ritual circle or out, and that his ideal high priestess was someone who would appear to dominate him sexually, while he actually controlled the scenario.[50]

But, setting aside that debatable assertion, Kelly actually makes a more convincing argument that "all Neo-Pagan witches [are] Gardnerian witches, because all the current activity results from widespread imitation of Gardnerian practices. The few covens around that might predate Gardner (and that had an utterly different theology from what the Gardnerians propose) have borrowed the Gardnerian system almost whole cloth because of its utility."[51]

The Gardnerian system, Kelly argues, combines the ceremonial magic of the Holy Order of the Golden Dawn (itself based on Renaissance and early modern sources) with the Goddess-centered "thealogy" of Graves's *The White Goddess*. The results are the common elements of Wicca in the broader sense of the word. These include a ritual circle, typically drawn with sword, *athame* (dagger), or finger to demarcate sacred space, further reinforced by invocation to the four traditional elements of air, fire, water, and earth, associated with the four cardinal directions. These ritual elements derive from ceremonial magic, and when Gardnerian Wicca was being codified in the early 1950s, "none of the circle rituals in use . . . were based on a 'Pagan' theology; they were all adapted from the Cabalistic procedures of the *Greater Key of Solomon*."[52]

Kelly credits Doreen Valiente, Gardner's high priestess from roughly 1954 to 1957, with meshing these elements with the God-and-Goddess theology, expressed through the "Great Rite." This term refers to sexual intercourse, either actual or symbolic, between the high priest and priestess. When symbolic, it is usually expressed by dipping an *athame*, the ritual dagger, into the chalice, but it can also be expressed by other symbolic actions, such as the driving of a staff into the earth or the placing of a rope's end through a loop at the other end, forming a noose. (The last is generally not a Gardnerian practice, however.) "Contrary to what many people believe, we never took part in sexual intercourse in the presence of other people in the circle," Valiente wrote in describing that period. "The Great Rite . . . was publicly performed at the Sabbats; but by us it was only 'in token.' . . .We were encouraged to find a partner of the opposite sex within the cult and to be faithful to that partner, working privately with them to perform our own magics."[53]

This Great Rite, usually in its symbolic form, has become another staple of Wiccan practice, whether Gardnerian, eclectic, or denominated by some other name. It is probably derived from Aleister Crowley's Gnostic Mass, Crowley and Gardner having been friendly in the late 1940s, when the former felt Gardner might carry on his magical order, the Ordo Templi Orientis, or OTO.[54] It is likely that Crowley's thoughts on sexual energy in magical ritual influenced Gardner to refocus his Wicca on this central symbolic sexual rite rather than on the evocation of spirits that we see in *High Magic's*

Aid. In Wiccan practice, if a man and woman are leading the ritual, the man holds the chalice and the woman the *athame*; this apparent gender reversal reflects the teaching of Dion Fortune, an influential early twentieth-century English ceremonial magician, who taught that on the "inner planes," traditional gender polarity was reversed, with the woman becoming active and the man passive or receptive—hence, for example, the pattern of the male artist and his female muse. Although Gardner's original texts often spoke of "men and girls," same-sex partners also perform the Great Rite, described in terms of polarity rather than sexuality. In larger group rituals, such as at Pagan festivals, where the basic ritual form is expanded and performed in a more theatrical style, the Great Rite often is presented as an erotic dance of chase, capture, and simulated intercourse.

Stewart Farrar, an English Witch and author, writes that the Great Rite "expresses three fundamental principles of the Craft. First, that the basis of all magical or creative working is polarity, the interaction of complementary aspects. Second, 'as above, so below'; we are of the nature of the Gods, and a fully realized man or woman is a channel for that divinity. . . . And third, that all the levels from physical to spiritual are equally holy."[55]

However the Great Rite is performed, its performance is connected in ritual to the practice known as "drawing down" or "carrying," a form of trance possession. Instructions for trance possession were one of the key elements omitted from the Pagan Way rituals when the latter were prepared for either students of Wicca or for those persons who wanted to worship the Old Gods without going through the full series of three initiations that Gardner borrowed from Freemasonry. Also omitted from the Pagan Way rituals were several key bits of terminology, such as a ritual "charge" delivered to initiates, the informal term *the Craft*, the use of the pentagram as an important symbol, the ritual affirmation "So mote it be," and more. Drawing down or "carrying" the divine brings the central Wiccan mystery directly to the circle. "Authoritarian religious hierarchies claim to mediate between the Gods and the Community, and by controlling access claim for themselves greater power," write two North American Wiccan priestesses. "We don't. Instead we teach all our Elders to Carry."[56]

The term "carrying" parallels the Voudoun practice of describing the trance medium as being ridden by one of the *orishas* (deities); hence the title of Zora Neale Hurston's 1938 book on Haitian religion, *Tell My Horse*. The phrase *drawing down*, or simply *drawing*, usually is short for "Drawing down the Moon [Goddess]," but a similar "drawing down the Sun [God]" is performed by some Wiccan high priests, although less frequently.[57] Here Wiccan practice again somewhat parallels religions of the African diaspora, notably

Candomblé and Umbanda in Brazil, where possession by the deities and spirits is more common for women. Paul Christopher Johnson, author of a recent study of Candomblé, *Spirits, Gossip, and Gods*, notes that "the gendered language of an orixá's 'mounting' of an *iaô* [initiate], his wife, is unmistakable, even if the 'horse' is male and the orixás is female." Johnson's informants told him that "in the old days," men never danced and were never possessed: by the 1930s, "it was still so exceedingly rare that if it did occur it provoked scorn and the actual posting of signs against it in the more traditional houses."[58] In many cases, men who danced and were possessed were either homosexual or, it was suggested, such an experience would turn a heterosexual man into a passive homosexual. In Umbanda, which draws more on European occultism and spiritism as well as on Candomblé's West African roots, spirit possession by men is more common, but Umbanda rituals are frequently more sedate, with the mediums seated. Likewise, "carrying" by Wiccan priestesses is far more common than a similar possession by men.

Throughout Wicca's first decades, the professed ideal of female religious leadership confronted the fact that it was men who were writing the books and providing group leadership, often seeking (and in some cases later discarding) spouses who would step into the role of high priestess. Gardnerian Wicca adheres most strongly to this ideal (exceeded only by those "Dianic" Witchcraft covens that are all female by design), yet this tradition was founded by a man, Gerald Gardner, whose wife, Donna, was uninterested in Pagan religion. Consequently, he initiated a sequence of high priestesses, the first of whom may have been his long-term lover as well. In his study of Candomblé, Johnson observes that men serve chiefly as ritual drummers, priests, and patrons of the "house" who underwrite its financial needs, and suggests that the role of women in channeling *axé* (divine force) and in organizing prestigious rituals does not necessarily undermine Brazilian machismo and the marking of the public sphere as "male."[59] America has a different culture, of course, with a different tradition of female leadership of nonmainstream religion (for example, the Shakers or Christian Scientists). And certainly the figure of the "witch" traditionally is gendered as female. Nevertheless, the tension between the ideal and the reality of Wiccan leadership deserves further exploration.

In Gardnerian Wicca and in those related traditions that practice it, a sacred-possession trance may be induced through a variety of practices, including music and drumming, but also through verbal and tactile cues. One set of clues is found in the Gardnerian *Book of Shadows*, originally a "manuscript tradition" of hand-copied scripts for rituals and spells. The "Charge of the Goddess," a portion written by Doreen Valiente in the 1950s, begins,

"Listen to the words of the Great Mother, who was of old called amongst men, Artemis, Astarte, Dione, Melusine, Aphrodite, Cerridwen, Diana, Arionhod, Bride, and by many other names." The *Book of Shadows* was supposed to be for initiates only, but copies were leaked in both the United Kingdom and the United States during the 1960s. American Wiccan priestess Jesse Wicker Bell (1920–2002), known as Lady Sheba, working with Llewellyn Publications, issued portions of it under her own name in 1971, claiming that while it had been handed down "by word of mouth during the time of persecution," she now had the "blessing of the Gracious Goddess" to make it available to all humanity.[60] In the "Charge of the Goddess," the officiating priestess speaks in the voice of the Wiccan Goddess, but it is quite possible that if the drawing down is successful, the priestess will speak extemporaneously. Stewart Farrar recorded the observation of his wife, Janet, high priestess in the related Alexandrian tradition of Witchcraft:

> The Goddess *does* come through, in the tone and emphasis of the delivery of the Charge—often to the surprise of the priestess delivering it. Janet admits frankly that she 'never knows how it will come out.' Sometimes the wording itself is completely altered, with a spontaneous flow which she listens to with a detached part of her mind. It is as though the Goddess knows better than the priestess just what emphasis, or encouragement, or even warning or reprimand, is called for at that particular Circle, and controls the charge accordingly.[61]

Another East Coast Wiccan priestess went further, dismissing the printed Charge as a "placeholder" from which the entranced priestess almost always textually departs. In their book *The Centre of Our Craft: Drawing the Moon*, Gwyneth Cathyl-Harrow and Judy Harrow describe the state-altered "tone and emphasis of the delivery" as "enhancement" trance, a sense of larger personal presence: "The Priestess in enhancement may speak *about* the Goddess, or even recite or read some text while acting in role as the Goddess." Beyond that comes "inspiration trance," and beyond that, "integration trance," the stage Farrar describes as listening "with a detached part of her mind." True possession trance, as the authors present it, involves a temporary personality change and often the inability to recall what happened: "A Priestess must be willing to yield personal consciousness absolutely, to completely surrender her own will to the will of the Goddess."[62]

The cues for entering possession trance are widely varied—chants, songs, movement, incense, and artwork are a few—but most Wiccan practice insisted on the necessity of having two people, the carrier and the anchor, or the invoker and invokee. In some circles, these roles are rotated to avoid what is humorously called "high priestess syndrome," the idea that trance possession carries over into one's mundane life and sets the recipient above other people. As the writers cited above sardonically note, "There is anthropological record of possessing spirits demanding rich gifts for their Carriers."[63] Wiccans, however, are as likely to mistrust religious authority as they are (in some traditions) to apply terms such as "Lord" and "Lady" to their religious leaders. Certainly one core Wiccan value is mistrust of dogma, often to the point of constantly reinventing the wheel for fear that old Craft teachings are fossilized or irrelevant, even while the same Witch claims ancient roots for his or her teachings. But Wicca does consistently value somatic experience; and as Morris Berman wrote in *Coming to Our Senses: Body and Spirit in the Hidden History of the West*, somatic experience often is linked to the idea of heresy: "The attempt to restore body cognition to the center of human consciousness is a central feature of most heretical movements in the history of the Christian West. . . . Gnosis is not about belief, but about tangible proof of the existence of 'larger forces.'"[64] By encouraging trance possession, those Witches that do so walk a delicate line between avoiding routinization and dogmatism on one hand and encouraging further fissioning in what is already a highly fissile movement on the other.

Finally, during the 1980s, the phenomenon of Pagan festivals, begun on a small scale in the 1970s (often in hotels, with science-fiction conventions as their models), grew to a large extent, to the point that there are on the average more than one per week, although most are concentrated in the warmer months. Most are "outdoor camping affairs that are held at private campgrounds or state parks and involve anywhere from fifty to a thousand people," reports Sarah Pike in *Earthly Bodies, Magical Selves*, a detailed study of Pagan festivals. "In the 1990s approximately sixty festivals took place annually across the United States between May and September."[65]

These festivals—my own state of Colorado hosts two and sometimes three each summer—provide temporary community for the many solitary practitioners, but they have also provided ritualists with opportunities to create and experiment with larger-scale rites than are possible in the traditional coven of a dozen or fewer persons, the form in which the Craft came to the United States. One recent phenomenon has been an increasing practice of trance possession by multiple "carriers," a new development (although with its parallels in such religions as Spiritualism, Umbanda, and others) in Wicca. Typically, several pairs of "anchors" and "carriers," to use the terminology of *The Centre of Our Craft*, will work in their own unique ways within a ritual circle until trance is achieved. Then each entranced priestess or priest will sit apart in a bower or tent. Someone else will be nearby as a watchdog against disruption, while other designated individuals will guide querents to the priestess or priest for private conversations, blessings, or healings. When all have been heard, the "anchor" will help his or her partner back to everyday reality. This practice may represent a significant change from the small-group-based mystery religion of Wicca into something larger and more public, albeit within the "temporary autonomous zone" of a Pagan festival.

Because they seemed to carry a seal of approval based in misty history, all the elements of the specifically Gardnerian Wiccan practice influenced all other forms of American Wicca, as described further in chapter 5. Witches of other traditions had either to adopt these elements, such as female ritual leadership, or articulate reasons why they did not. (One group that obviously had to face this challenge would be all-male groups.) Ritual scourging, far more than ritual nudity, was rejected by other Wiccan traditions, probably because practitioners were unable to see beyond its connotation of sexual bondage-and-discipline role-playing. Nudity, on the other hand, could be rationalized or grouped with ritual elements—including ritual baths, candlelight, incense, and special music—that unlike scourging had no disquieting connotations for most American Pagans. Gardnerian Wicca's emphasis on trance possession by the deities has not been taken up to such a great extent by other forms of Wicca. All Pagan Witchcraft has one root in Western ceremonial magic, which includes a form of trance possession sometimes called "assumption of the god form," but against that we must place a general American cultural wariness or fear of any sort of trance possession. (Since the 1980s, however, there has been some cross-fertilization between immigrant Brazilian Spiritism in the form of Umbanda and American Pagan groups.)

What America contributed to the new world religion Pagan Witchcraft, or Wicca, however, was its emphasis on nature. The very terms "nature religion" and "earth religion" were popularized on this side of the Atlantic, and they soon overtook the earlier description of Wicca as a "fertility religion." In Britain, Gardner and his successors were able to identify with the oldest strata of British history. Theirs was the true indigenous religion, they could claim. When World War II's memories were still fresh, Gardner claimed that followers of the Old Religion had worked magic against both the threatened Spanish invasion of 1588, the threatened French invasion of 1804, and the threatened German invasion of 1940, thus certifying their patriotic credentials.[66] In the United States, however, no such claim was possible. The label of indigenous could be applied only to the peoples living here before European settlement. The new American Pagans, however, found that they could easily adapt both existing American attitudes about the sacrality of nature and the new environmental awareness of the 1960s and 1970s, thus making themselves not so much indigenous as "nature based," as the following chapter will describe.

Notes

1. Lippy (jmchol@rmi.net), "Raising Energy, Part Deux," ColoWiccan mailing list, July 13, 2003.

2. Shelley Rabinovitch and James Lewis, eds., *The Encyclopedia of Modern Witchcraft and Neo-Paganism* (New York: Kensington, 2002), s.v. "Cunningham, Scott."

3. The Witches' Voice website is www.witchvox.com (accessed January 25, 2006).

4. Rabinovitch and Lewis, eds., *The Encyclopedia of Modern Witchcraft and Neo-Paganism*, 305.

5. Catherine Albanese, *America: Religion and Religions* (Belmont, Calif.: Wadsworth Publishing, 1981), 266.

6. The ultimately somatic concept would be the teaching—honored generally in the breach—that the final initiation occur through sexual intercourse between priest or priestess and candidate.

7. Susan Roberts, *Witches U.S.A.* (New York: Dell, 1971), 23.

8. Margot Adler, *Drawing Down the Moon* (New York: Viking Press, 1979), 22–23, emphasis in the original.

9. Rowan Moonstone, "Hi," ColoPagan mailing list (2003).

10. Margaret Murray, *The Witch-Cult in Western Europe* (Oxford: Oxford University Press, 1921).

11. Aidan A. Kelly, *Crafting the Art of Magic: A History of Modern Witchcraft 1939–1964* (St. Paul, Minn.: Llewellyn, 1991).

12. Gardner claimed to have been initiated into an existing coven in 1939, on the eve of World War II. In *Witchcraft Today*, he writes that he had finally found what he was looking for in "Wica," as he spelled it. Yet throughout the 1940s, he hobnobbed with at least three other esoteric religious or magical groups, gathering various initiations and ordinations. In 1951, he became a partner in a for-profit museum of witchcraft and folklore and furnished material for many of its exhibits. It is only then that his writing about the religion of Wic[c]a begins to resemble what we now know under that name. I believe it more likely that the creation of the museum accelerated the formal creation of the new Pagan religion.

13. Gerald Gardner, *High Magic's Aid* (New York: Samuel Weiser, 1975).

14. Raymond Buckland, *Witchcraft from the Inside* (St. Paul, Minn.: Llewellyn, 1971), 84.

15. Margaret St. Clair, *Sign of the Labrys* (New York: Bantam Books, 1963), 2.

16. Ibid., 13.

17. Ibid., 13.

18. Ibid., 8.

19. Gardner, *High Magic's Aid*, 204.

20. A term used by many contemporary Witches to refer to the witch trials of the Renaissance and early modern eras.

21. St. Clair, *Sign of the Labrys*, 53–54.

22. Gardnerian initiations were supposed to be of men by women and vice versa. Hearing of this mistake in the text, a contemporary Gardnerian priestess said, "If I were arguing for St. Clair back then, I would have argued that I had turned it around deliberately." But evidently that was not the case. Another friend of the St. Clairs said they were reprimanded by the Bucklands for "telling too much." Times were different then.

23. A legendary pre-Christian Anglo-Saxon blacksmith.

24. Buckland, *Witchcraft from the Inside*.

25. Raymond Buckland, personal interview, June 5, 1997.

26. Ed Fitch (pseudonym), personal interview, June 6, 1997.

27. Ibid.

28. Ibid.

29. Ibid.

30. Roberts, *Witches U.S.A.*, 42.

31. Used for school classroom handouts, church bulletins, and other short-run printing jobs, spirit duplicators used alcohol to activate the ink on a typed or hand-drawn master page that could produce fifty to one hundred copies before wearing out.

32. Joe Wilson, "Highlights of the Pagan-Craft Time Line in the United States," 1734 mailing list, July 10, 2003.

33. Doreen Valiente, *The Rebirth of Witchcraft* (London: Robert Hale, 1989), 136.

34. Evan John Jones, with Chas S. Clifton, *Sacred Mask, Sacred Dance* (St. Paul, Minn.: Llewellyn, 1997), 156.

35. Ronald Hutton, *The Triumph of the Moon* (Oxford: Oxford University Press, 1999), 214. See also Philip Heselton, "Naturism and the New Forest," in *Wiccan Roots* (Freshfields, Berkshire: Capall Bann, 2000).

36. Jones, *Sacred Mask, Sacred Dance*, 165–66.

37. Joseph B. Wilson, *For Those Who Want the Other Side of the Story*, 1734 mailing list (2003).

38. The Ancient Keltic Church's website is www.ancientkelticchurch.org (accessed January 25, 2006).

39. David and Ann Finnin, October 29, 1997.

40. Aidan A. Kelly, *Notes on Gardnerian History, 1963-1990* (Los Angeles: Art Magickal Publications, 1994).

41. Ed Fitch, *The Outer Court Book of Shadows* (St. Paul, Minn.: Llewellyn, 1996).

42. Ed Fitch, *Magical Rites from the Crystal Well* (St. Paul, Minn.: Llewellyn, 1984).

43. Donna Cole Schultz, "My Quest for Witchcraft in the 1960s," *The Cauldron*, August 2003.

44. Kelly, *Notes on Gardnerian History, 1963-1990*.

45. Sylvana SilverWitch, *Ed Fitch: Revealing the Craft* (1995), www.widdershins .org/vol1iss2/2.htm (accessed January 25, 2006).

46. Buckland, *Witchcraft from the Inside*, xii.

47. Ibid., 80.

48. Raymond Buckland, *The Tree* (York Beach, Maine: Samuel Weiser, 1974).

49. Tom Kneitel, "Gardnerian Aspects," *Green Egg*, June 21, 1974, emphasis in original. Gardnerian Wiccan contained a prohibition against charging money for teaching.

50. Kelly, *Crafting the Art of Magic*, 27–29. Kelly would weaken his own argument by suggesting that Gardner was somehow a product of the English boarding-school milieu in which flogging was common. In fact, his education was left mostly to a very tolerant governess.

51. Aidan A. Kelly, "Inventing Witchcraft: The Gardnerian Paper Trail," *Iron Mountain: A Journal of Magical Religion* 1 (1984): 28n1.

52. Ibid., 27. The English ceremonial magician S. Liddell MacGregor Mathers had published an edited edition of this book in 1888, and it was well known among English-speaking occultists.

53. Valiente, *The Rebirth of Witchcraft*, 59–60. This practice required an under-standing spouse: neither Gardner's wife, Donna, nor Valiente's husband, for example, were involved in Wicca.

54. Translated as Order of the Temple of the Orient; it remains active today.

55. Stewart Farrar and Janet Farrar, *The Witches' Way* (London: Robert Hale, 1984), 32–33.

56. Gwyneth Cathyl-Harrow and Judy Harrow, *The Centre of Our Craft: Drawing the Moon*, 4th ed. (Calgary: Dayshift-Six Roads, 1998), 6.

57. The term *channeling* is considered too New Age by most Witches. Gwyneth Cathyl-Harrow and Judy Harrow write, "New Age channelers charge fat fees. We don't."

58. Paul Christopher Johnson, *Secrets, Gossip, and Gods: The Transformation of Brazilian Candomblé* (London: Oxford University Press, 2002), 44–45.

59. Ibid., 48.

60. Lady Sheba, *The Book of Shadows* (St. Paul, Minn.: Llewellyn, 1971), back cover.

61. Farrar, *The Witches' Way*, 68.

62. Cathyl-Harrow and Harrow, *The Centre of Our Craft: Drawing the Moon*, 49–50.

63. Ibid., 54.

64. Morris Berman, *Coming to Our Senses: Body and Spirit in the Hidden History of the West* (New York: Simon & Schuster, 1989), 138.

65. Sarah Pike, *Earthly Bodies, Magical Selves: Contemporary Pagans and the Search for Community* (Berkeley: University of California Press, 2001), xv.

66. Gerald Gardner, *Witchcraft Today* (Secaucus, N.J.: Citadel, 1973), 104.

CHAPTER TWO

Calling It "Nature Religion"

The first Maypole in America stands nearly eighty feet tall, and a pair of antlers from a buck whitetail deer are fastened near its top. It is raised on the shore of Massachusetts Bay, in what is now Quincy, on the first day of May 1627, and garlanded with wildflowers. Around its base stand a dozen or so Englishmen with cups of wine. Also present, whether dancing or watching, are a number of American Indians of both sexes. One of the Englishmen starts a song:

> Make green garlands; bring bottles out
> And fill sweet nectar freely about.
> Uncover thy head and fear no harm,
> For here's good liquor to keep it warm.

And the rest of them eventually pick up the chorus:

> Drink and be merry, merry, merry boys!
> Let all your delight be in the Hymen's joys;
> Io to Hymen, now the day is come
> About the merry Maypole take a Room.[1]

That the visitors include local tribal women is clearly essential, for another verse of the Maypole drinking song invites, "Lasses in beaver coats come away/Ye shall be welcome to us night and day." And while most contemporary readers may associate the word "hymen" with the vaginal tissue that marks a woman's sexual virginity, the word's origins come from ancient Greece, where Hymen was the god of marriage, or as the *Oxford Classical Dictionary* puts it, "Various stories were invented [of this being], all to the effect that he was a very handsome young man who either married happily or had something happen to him on his wedding night."[2] So it's clear what "Hymen's joys" and "Io [hail to] Hymen" mean when the liquor is flowing and the "lasses in beaver coats" have shown up for the party. The writer Henry Beston sees it in his mind's eye: "All join hands, and round and about the pole dance the fantastic company mid the wild uproar of a drunkenly beaten drum, shouts, the thunderous roar of old-fashioned muskets, and faint silvery piping of an English melody."[3]

Obviously this is a different side of old New England than we associate with Plymouth Plantation, founded nearby seven years earlier. No Puritan clergymen are in evidence; the Maypole with its ornament of deer antlers stands tall and proud. (We are seven years after the founding of Plymouth; one year before the founding of the Massachusetts Bay Colony, three years before the founding of Boston—and seventy-five years before the Salem witch trials.) But when they hear of the Maypole at Merry Mount, the Puritans know what it is: a declaration of war. "They also set up a Maypole, drinking and dancing about it many days together, inviting the Indian women, for their consorts, dancing and frisking together," grumbles William Bradford, the governor of Plymouth.[4]

Two centuries later, American author Nathaniel Hawthorne, haunted by his own Puritan ancestry, invents more details: animal masks on the dancers and an English girl named Edith to serve as Lady of the May together with her young Lord, who whispers in her ear, "Is yon wreath of roses a garland to hang about our graves, that you look so sad? O, Edith, this is our golden time! Tarnish it not by any pensive shadow of the mind; for it may be that nothing of futurity will be brighter than the mere remembrance of what is now passing."[5] Morton's story gives Hawthorne the raw material for another of his shadows-and-sunlight Gothic tales of New England, much like his better-known story "Young Goodman Brown." Here Morton is apparently the inspiration for, or the same as, "the flower-decked priest" who urges the celebrants to show the young English lovers "what life is made of, and how airily they should go through it," only to be "wonder struck" at the pensive looks they give him while withered rose petals fall from the Maypole garlands.[6]

In Hawthorne's fictional treatment, the party is interrupted by an incursion of armed Puritans who chop down the Maypole. Their leader says, "I thought not to repent me of cutting down a Maypole, yet now I could find in my heart to plant it again, and give each of these bestial pagans one other dance round their idol. It would have served rarely for a whipping-post!" The Puritans whip the partiers but spare the young couple, only cutting his long hair "in the true pumpkinshell fashion." The two will be allowed to live as sober residents of Plymouth where Edith "may become a mother in our Israel."

The erection of the Maypole at Merry Mount carried numerous meanings, and to examine them we must know something about the man who hosted the party: Thomas Morton. He was born about 1579 and studied law at Clifford's Inn, one of the Inns of Chancery, where English lawyers learned their profession. In his early forties, he married a widow of similar age whom he had defended in a suit brought by her son over some family property. (She apparently died after only six years of marriage to him.) He came to New England in 1624 together with a group of men to establish a fur-trading post. Morton may have been one of the shareholders or merely the manager; given his connections, he probably was an investor. They began operations at a spot already known as Mount Wollaston; Morton renamed it Merry Mount but often wrote the name as "Ma-re Mount," making a pun on *mare*, Latin for "sea," since they were on the coast. In 1628, a year after the May Day revels described above, Morton was arrested by soldiers from the Plymouth settlement, led by Miles Standish, whom Morton ridiculed as "Captain Shrimp" when he wrote his own history of these events a few years later.

Seen from nearly four centuries later, Morton's Maypole blurs into a double image. In one, it is an English Maypole with several symbolic meanings: revelry; defiance of Puritan extremism; and loyalty to the king, to the Church of England, and to some concept of "merry England" and "the good old days." In the other, it is a New England Maypole, perhaps the only one until the nineteenth-century revival of Maypole dancing. If we imagine an alternative history of Massachusetts, one in which the Puritans were not the dominant party, the Maypole would make an excellent symbol for the state's seal, with an Englishman in high-crowned hat and baggy breeches on one side and one of the "lasses in beaver coats" on the other, offering "a symbolic Indian approval of the American take-over," as one historian described the Florida state seal with its Seminole woman and steamship and Oklahoma's state seal with its native and settler shaking hands before the figure of Justice.[7] But in fact the founders of Massachusetts statehood settled on a standing Native American man with bow and arrows, and it was left to twentieth-century Pagans to reinterpret Morton's Maypole as something more than a Cavalier's defiance of the Puritans.

The changed spirit of the twentieth century saw other reimaginings of Merry Mount as well. While Morton still mingles the character of a Cavalier with that of the Satanic angel Beelzebub in *Merry Mount*, a 1932 dramatic poem by Richard L. Stokes, he becomes a shabbier figure in Robert Lowell's 1965 play set in Pilgrim times, *Endecott and the Red Cross*.[8]

To the popular poet Stephen Vincent Benét, Morton is a fun-loving, irreligious, small-*p* pagan appearing in Benét's 1933 poem "Miles Standish":

> Tom Morton was a merry man and liked a merry frolic
> He said, "These long-nosed Pilgrims give an honest heart the colic!"
> He built a place called Merry Mount to serve his merry ends
> And danced around a Maypole with a lot of rowdy friends.[9]

But in contemporary Pagan hands, the Anglican and Royalist Thomas Morton becomes "Attorney, Historian, Poet, Pagan Hero," according to a 1990 article in *Green Egg*, at the time the largest and oldest American Pagan magazine. Noting the attention always given to the Salem witch trials, the author, Devyn, host of a Pagan radio show and coeditor of *The Merrymount Messenger*, journal of the Massachusetts-based Thomas Morton Alliance, admits that with the "possible exceptions of Tituba and, though unlikely, Giles Corey, it is certain that none of the 'convicted' Witches of Puritan Salem (now Danvers) were Witches at all." But, he continues, "there was a direct link to European Paganism that found his way to these shores 75 years prior to the Salem occurrences and very nearly altered the course of events to follow in the fragile and unstable era of colonization."[10]

Here Devyn overstates Morton's political impact, for Merry Mount was first and foremost a business venture, a fur-trading post. While Morton enjoyed needling the Puritans, his all-male group had no intention of permanent habitation and did not constitute a colony, let alone a "Pagan settlement." While much of the article is a straightforward summary of Morton's legal battles with the Puritans, his deportations to England, and his returns, Devyn's prime interest is in reclaiming Morton as a Pagan founding father. On Beltane 1988, he writes, the knoll of Merry Mount itself, now in a residential area near the intersection of Somerset Avenue and Ridgeway Drive in Quincy, was "reclaimed by members of the Thomas Morton Alliance, a Pagan political network co-founded by Chthonic tradition High Priestess Linda Rutherford."

He continues,

> Although Morton was certainly a part of the English white male upper class, a hunter and a trapper, and may have been one of the original persons to introduce "firewater" to the Natives, the Pagans of the TMA have taken his deter-

mination, openly defiant Paganism, and love of the wild to heart in their ef-
forts to live and act with a Warrior perspective. . . . He was, and is, a true Pagan hero, a Warrior who fought bravely for what he believed in with the means
that he knew best.[11]

Thus Morton has been transfigured. Instead of defying Puritan authority
in the name of Merry England, in the *Green Egg* version he has become a
prophet of the Pagan revival and an eco-warrior—a sort of "white Indian."
This new appropriation of the history of "mine host of Merry Mount" speaks
to a new set of concerns: how the "nature religion" of contemporary Paganism can begin to inch toward a sort of neoindigenous status.

The *Green Egg* version of Morton's life makes him an exemplary Pagan
while smoothing over the controversies of his day, for example, the issue of
giving firearms to the Indians, which doubtlessly alarmed the Pilgrims as
much as did his Anglican religious views. But the appropriation of Morton as
a prototypical American Pagan is more than just an attempt to claim historical priority. Through Morton's life—or their version of it—some American
Pagans move their religion into a long-standing alternative to the so-called
Judeo-Christian or Abrahamic tradition, what has come to be called "nature
religion." The word *nature*, however, brings with it multiple definitions, and
Pagans can shift rapidly between them while still describing their religion(s)
with that convenient label.

In order to understand what "nature religion" means in contemporary Paganism, I will divide it into three categories—"Cosmic Nature," "Gaian Nature," and "Embodied" or "Erotic Nature"—as I attempt to demonstrate how
each has ancient roots and how each furnishes contemporary Pagans with a
fulfilling and empowering self-definition.

When the new Pagan religion of Wicca arrived in the United States from
England in the 1960s, it presented itself as the Old Religion, the ancestral
Paganism of the British Isles, and as a mystery cult of both fertility and magic.
Americans, in turn, would add the label of "nature religion" or "earth-based
religion," which fit well with the rising environmentalism of the mid-
twentieth century and also with the new Paganism's roots in the Romantic
literary movement as well as in Neoplatonic astrology and magic. The notion
of nature religion and also Second Wave feminism would be injected into
British Wicca in the 1980s, subsequently along with a dose of Michael
Harner–style neoshamanism.[12]

Wicca's leading figure, Gerald B. Gardner, was well acquainted with "naturism," in other words, with nude sunbathing tinged with occultism, but, if anything, he thought of Wicca more as a continuation of old fertility-based religion.

[Gardner] felt that he met people [through naturism] whom he did not know existed in England: interesting people, prepared to talk, argue and discuss. Many had a faint occult interest: fortune telling, palmistry, astrology, vague spiritualism. He felt healthier, too, and liked the lack of class-consciousness which naturism brought.[13]

The English historian Ronald Hutton has traced the growth of a more literary "nature religion" through the Romantics. Shelley's invocation of "Sacred goddess, Mother Earth/Thou from whose immortal bosom/Gods, and men, and beasts, have birth,/Leaf and blade, and bud and blossom," exemplifies the trend, but this nature religion remains essentially literary, even while preparing later generations to claim and practice it as revived Paganism. Not so literary, Gardner himself had little to say about nature in his own book *Witchcraft Today*, being more interested in claims that Wicca was a surviving pre-Christian fertility religion and that its power was largely the "Massed Power of Mind." He quotes one of the English Witches of his time as saying, "*Our* gods are not all-powerful, they *need* our aid. They desire good to us, fertility for man, beast, and crops, but they need our help to bring it about; and by our dances and other means they get that help."[14]

In America, meanwhile, nature had spoken with a holy voice for at least two hundred years. Nature, however defined, had endorsed the new American republic. It (or she) had been evoked to purify the immigrant from the corruption of old Europe. The Hudson River school of painters depicted nature as a continuing revelation of the divine. In America, nature could be invoked as a source of sacred value that was impossible in Europe, where Wicca—and subsequent forms of reconstructed Paganism ranging from Iceland to Russia—was invariably cast in historical and/or ethnic terms. For instance, in his writings and interviews, Gardner repeatedly insisted that the Old Religion was "remnants of a Stone Age religion," which carried the suggestion that Wicca was somehow truer and more appropriate for the British Isles than imported, "Eastern" Christianity.[15] The British Witches of the 1950s and 1960s told and retold the tale of the Lammas Ritual of early August 1940, in which allegedly a small but motivated group worked magic to thwart Hitler's invasion plans.[16] The story became a firm part of Wiccan lore, reinforcing British Wiccans' notion of themselves as true patriots repelling all foreign invaders—including Christianity.

American Wicca could not claim to be Americans' ancestral religion, for the United States' history was completely different, not to mention shorter. Instead of Wicca-as-surviving-Paganism, its American practitioners found waiting for them the unarticulated but lively notion of "nature religion" (or "earth religion"), which rapidly became synonymous with revived Pagan religion. In 1970, Susan Roberts, author of *Witches U.S.A.*, would write casually about her Witch friend's encounter with a traffic jam caused by New York City's first Earth Day celebration in "Now, no one loves the earth and the purity of air more than a witch"—and feel no need to explain her statement.[17]

The spirit of Earth Day 1970 did not just happen; its roots could include the gradual stirring of environmental consciousness that accelerated in the 1960s, but that stirring itself had deeper roots in an American consciousness of a special relationship with the land, even if that relationship often was abusive. Still, if there was a year when Wicca (in the broad sense) became "nature religion," as opposed to the "mystery religion" or "metaphoric fertility religion" labels that it had brought from England, that year was 1970. For example, Marika Kriss's *Witchcraft: Past and Present*, published in 1970, is a merrily superficial survey of "witchcraft" that includes quick mentions of Mexican *curanderismo*, touches on Carlos Castaneda's alleged tutoring by the shaman Don Juan, digresses into the evil eye and other topics, bounces from Russia to Hawaii, and briefly touches on 1960s English Wicca. Yet for all that, the author in her introduction simply asserts, "The witches were ecologists." (Her use of the past tense is not surprising, for it comes in the context of witches of the vague past as people with certain talents for manipulating nature.) Discussing how these prehistoric witches used "every natural hallucinogen the earth offers to unlock the secrets of nature," Kriss suggests that these witches "understood that man must live in balance with nature and the vitality they perceived underlying nature."[18] Given that slippery thing, the Zeitgeist, I suspect that Kriss was merely invoking this term *ecologist* in its new expanded definition. What had signified a scientist studying "bionomics," the relationship between organisms and their environment, and the energy flows within that environment, now became a person seeking moral or spiritual harmony with the planetary environment.

This alignment of any sort of witchcraft with "ecology" was, by contrast, missing from the expatriate British Witchcraft authors writing in America, such as Gavin Frost,[19] Paul Huson,[20] Raymond Buckland,[21] or Sybil Leek. Nor was the change to viewing Witchcraft as nature religion instantaneous and universal. For example, the only tree in Sarah Lyddon Morrison's *The Modern Witch's Spellbook*, published in 1971, is the Tree of Knowledge in the biblical book of Genesis.[22]

The Three "Natures"

Identification with a national or ethnic past counted for less in the New World than it had in the old. Some Pagan traditions have continued it—Voudoun, of course, and also Ásatrú and other Norse or "Heathen" groups, where the issue of bloodlines invariably turns into an ongoing and bitter internal feud between those who would cast the religion in racialist terms, requiring Northern European ancestry, and those who would not.[23] Instead, by at least the early 1970s, American Pagans chose to identify their religion not as rooted in ethnic heritage but as "nature religion" or its variant, "earth religion." For instance, by the mid-1970s, Herman Slater, a notable figure in New York City's Pagan scene, by virtue of his ownership of a Manhattan occult bookstore and a small publishing venture, was publishing a tabloid called *Earth Religion News*, something of a competitor to Llewellyn Publications' *Gnostica*.

In the appellation of "nature religion" or "earth religion," American Wicca began to define itself less as a magical practice, or the Craft (a term lifted from the Masons), and more as a self-conscious religion. Wiccans and other contemporary Pagans, however, have made no special attempt to define just what "nature" is, and for the most part in their writings, they merge those definitions in common social use: either "all that is," or "all that is not made by humans," or that which is wild ("natural") rather than tame. Gary Snyder, the Beat poet turned philosopher, attempts to sort out these meanings of *nature* in his essay "The Etiquette of Freedom":

> The word [nature] gets two slightly different meanings. One is "the outdoors"—the physical world, including all living things. Nature by this definition is a norm of the world that is apart from the features or products of civilization and human will. The machine, the artifact, the devised, or the extraordinary (like a two-headed calf) is spoken of as "unnatural." The other meaning, which is broader, is "the material world or its collective objects and phenomena," including the products of human action and intention. . . . By these lights there is nothing unnatural about New York City, or toxic wastes, or atomic energy.[24]

Many Pagans kick this same terminological football back and forth; and since most Pagans, like most Americans, are urbanites or suburbanites, it is common to hear attendance at an outdoor, camping-style festival described as "getting back into nature"—nature conceived of as Edenic, curative, and truer somehow than urban life. Sarah Pike connects the phenomenon of outdoor Pagan festivals (which began around 1979 and continue to proliferate) with a going-out from the city to a spiritual frontier: "Neopagans tap into the frontier myth that is at the heart of American religious diversity because it held the promise of endless imaginative space within which to create a new religious life and community."[25] They feel, as one contributor to the soc .religion.paganism newsgroup writes, that by attending a festival in a nonurban setting, they can more easily experience "direct empathetic or emotional contact between the worshipper and the physical world." They struggle with the perceived disconnection between their urban lives and "natural" realities: "But now we all live in cities and planting a seed is for most [merely] a metaphor, and the coven harvest festival is scheduled three months in advance around everyone's work schedule," mourned a Wiccan with the screen name "Dove" on the ColoWiccan e-mail list.[26] Or as Bast, the protagonist of a series of mystery novels by the Wiccan writer Rosemary Edghill, declares while driving north from Manhattan to a festival, "I still felt the same deviant thrill that leaving the metroplex for the land where green things grow always gives me."[27]

To understand the success with which Wicca and other Paganisms appropriate the term "nature religion," I think that it is most helpful to speak of three rather than two "natures." Instead of rehashing the question whether New York City is part of nature or not, we may roughly separate the Pagan use of "nature religion" into three categories, three natures. These I will characterize as Cosmic Nature, Gaian Nature, and Embodied Nature. Most Pagan uses of *nature religion* can be sorted into one or another of these categories, and their use helps to clarify what may seem on the surface to be contradictory statements. "Gaia" comes from the Greek word for planet Earth; here it means our planet and all its inhabitants collectively.

All three categories can serve as sources of sacred value. To Catherine Albanese, "*nature religion* is . . . a symbolic center and the cluster of beliefs, behaviors, and values that encircles it."[28] Albanese's important study, *Nature Religion in America*, focuses on the Deism of the eighteenth century and the Romantic and curative nature of the nineteenth century, but when speaking of nature among contemporary Pagans, we must look back at least to the fifteenth and sixteenth centuries and the idea of "natural magic."

Cosmic Nature

The 1972 Gnostic Aquarian Festival of Psychological, Qabalistic, and Spiritual Science, held at the Hyatt Lodge, 10th and Hawthorne, Minneapolis, was the second annual such event. It was organized by Carl Weschcke, president of Llewellyn Publications, a publisher of books on astrology, esoteric philosophy, parapsychology, and, increasingly, contemporary Paganism. In 1971, the festival had produced headlines from newspapers as far removed as London's *Daily Express* and the English-language *Paris Herald*, while the *Pittsburg Press*, in its caption to a photo of three Pagan Witches, noted that Minneapolis "is beginning to emerge as headquarters for followers of the occult."[29] The program of the 1972 festival included speakers and demonstrations on yoga, ceremonial magic, parapsychology, astrology (the largest category), graphology (handwriting analysis), Qabalah, reincarnation, several varieties of Pagan Witchcraft, and "mind science." One Spiritualist minister spoke on "Man and Nature." That minister, Lois Mostiller, declared in her promotional blurb that "Man, as a spiritual being, rises and falls, ebbs and flows as the seasons change—at the fall and spring equinoxes and winter and summer solstices." What Mostiller's comments exemplify and what many of the speakers' topics also derive from is the concept of "natural magic," which can be traced easily back to the Renaissance. I often prefer to speak of Cosmic Nature—that is to say, not the Gaian Nature of animals, trees, and flowers, but a more abstract nature whose laws generations of astrologers, magicians, philosophers, and the founders of occult schools and orders perceived as demonstrated in the movement of heavenly bodies. This philosophy of interconnected levels of being is associated with followers of the Greek philosopher Plato, particularly the later, or Neoplatonic, philosophers, who attempted either to compete with the rising influence of Christianity or to synthesize it with Pagan Greek philosophy.

The Italian historian Eugenio Garin, in *Astrology in the Renaissance*, notes the strong connection during the Italian Renaissance between astrology, viewed then as a scientific study of the natural world, and ritual magic, which attempted to understand and to exploit Cosmic Nature for the benefit of the operator. Scholars in Marsilio Ficino's fifteenth-century Medici-financed academy were translating Greek, Arabic, and allegedly Egyptian manuscripts on Platonic philosophy and natural magic. Seeking a grand synthesis of Platonic and Christian thought, Ficino (1433–1499) revived the notion of the *anima mundi*, the World Soul, which functioned as the medium of natural magic, uniting all levels of the physical world, "an animated and consentient universe, connecting and working together."[30]

> Assuming that one seeks a favor of a solar nature, for instance, [the magician is advised to conduct] a rite before an altar fashioned in the image of the sun, clothed in a sun-like color such as gold and scented with oils of solar character. The practitioner would then invoke the sun through music, singing an Orphic hymn to the sun, while burning an incense derived from plants known to correspond with the sun.[31]

Discussing Pagan Witchcraft's deep connection with Renaissance high magic, Ronald Hutton notes that this type of practice, informed by the hermetic texts newly available to occultists, differed markedly from magic's "medieval phase, which really began as an aspect of the twelfth-century Renaissance." Medieval magicians collected spells in *grimoires* (magical recipe books): "The detail of actions was all-important, with little concern shown for the quality of the practitioner. [Medieval magic] was a typical product of a period obsessed with God, geometry, and the angelic and demonic kingdoms, and characterized by an increasing formality and elaboration of religious ritual."[32] In Hutton's view, the subsequent early-modern emphasis on the magician's character was the mark of humanism; likewise, some humanists rebelled against what they saw as an overly deterministic depiction of Cosmic Nature by the astrologers. As Garin ruefully admits, "The most complicated knot of questions emerges where the theoretical moment of understanding fate [the theoretical basis of astrology] seems to clash with the [humanistic] hypothesis that there are techniques for escaping fate."[33]

Setting aside the yogic practitioners, the Gnostic Aquarian Festival's lineup presents strong evidence of the persistence of this older nature religion and its adherence to the doctrine of "as above, so below" and its system of correspondences. The sixteenth-century magician Henry Cornelius Agrippa, who introduced his *Philosophy of Natural Magic* with the premise that "every inferior is governed by its superior, and receiveth the influence of the virtues thereof," so that God passes down divine virtue to the animals, minerals, plants, and stones, has successors in such recent popular Wiccan writers as Doreen Valiente (1922–1999) and Scott Cunningham (1956–1993).

The doctrines of Cosmic Nature persist in contemporary Paganism on both sides of the Atlantic. Valiente, an English Witch who was a key figure of the Wiccan movement from the late 1950s through the 1990s, wrote during the early 1970s a book titled *Natural Magic*, in which she treats of dream interpretation, weather magic, and various forms of divination. Explaining that magic is not "something essentially unnatural . . . overthrowing nature's laws," she makes the argument familiar to Ficino and Agrippa: "To [occult philosophers] magic works because of nature's laws, not in spite of them. It is something built into the universe . . . All is part of nature."[34]

Writing on herbalism, Cunningham positions himself as a conservator of folk wisdom, the "old magics of herbs and plants" known to the "old Witches." Yet what he describes in his 1987 book *Magical Herbalism* is not the herbalism of someone who labors with spade and trowel but the bookish Renaissance system of correspondences: Cosmic Nature revealed through the

Figure 2.1.   Doreen Valiente dressed for a Halloween party. In her left hand is a Witch's stang, a forked walking stick that doubles as a ritual staff. Photo courtesy of Phoenix Publishing.

assertion that horehound, for example, is a plant of Mercury, associated with the element of Earth and the Egyptian god Horus, and used in protective sachets and incenses.[35]

Although the Pagan Witches attending the early 1970s Gnostic Aquarian festivals were a minority among the presenters, at least initially, their influence

expanded during that period. In 1974, a council convened from festival attendees produced a statement, the "Principles of Wiccan Belief." The principles
mark an early example of the use of the term Wicca not to define the initiatory mystery religion brought from England a decade earlier but more broadly
as a new "American tradition . . . not bound by traditions from other times and
other cultures." The first of the council's fourteen stated principles reads, "We
practice rites to attune ourselves with the natural rhythm of life forces marked
by the full of the Moon and seasonal quarters and cross-quarters."[36]

In practice, these principles illustrate the intersection of Cosmic Nature
and Gaian Nature in contemporary Paganism. What should also be understood, however, is that during the early 1970s, almost all American Witches
espoused some version of the truth of Margaret Murray's hypothesized Old
Religion. The Witches positioned themselves as heirs of—and often as directly connected to—ancient Pagan coreligionists. Yet a great deal of the
content of Witchcraft practice was taken from the Renaissance, hermetic
traditions of natural magic—often called high magic to distinguish it from
the spell casting of illiterate peasants, the same illiterate peasants who according to Murray were carrying on their secret Pagan practices. Thus the
new Witches had it both ways; they could claim to be following indigenous
Paganism and yet function comfortably—through such disciplines as astrology, ritual magic, and Tarot—in the world of Cosmic Nature.

The new Pagan Witchcraft that blossomed in the 1970s, however, was not
without its critics from within. Primarily they were those who saw "witchcraft" as closely allied to ceremonial magic and to *doing things*, rather than to
worshiping and celebrating as ends to themselves. This older vision of the
Craft is laid out in Paul Huson's *Mastering Witchcraft*.[37] Nine years later, after
Drawing Down the Moon and *The Spiral Dance* were published, both in 1979,
Huson's use of the word *mastering* would seem suspiciously patriarchal; and of
course *warlock*, which he briefly employed to mean a male witch, was completely rejected as a self-descriptor by Pagan Witches. Huson's invocations of
spirits and spells for love and other purposes represent the formula-driven
magic of the later Middle Ages, combined with a large helping of "natural
magic" based on the inherent virtues of apples in love spells, for instance. In
the 1980s, while do-it-yourself Witchcraft books blossomed, Huson's approach would seem either antique, too "dark," or too "advanced" for the typical Wiccan newcomer. The loyal opposition—those practitioners more
drawn to the knowledge of Cosmic Nature than to Gaian or Embodied Nature (my two categories to follow)—were left to grumble that "Witchcraft
was never meant to be this religious movement," or that today "there has
been less emphasis on magick and authentic paganism as the neo-pagan

crowd has become the mouthpiece for feminism and ecological environmen-tal [*sic*] issues."[38]

Gaian Nature

Participants in the British Pagan revival, whether in literary or hands-on modes, could lay claim to a classical heritage—all the imagery of Pan, nymphs, dryads, and the like—as well as the notion, borrowed from geology, that societies had their strata too, and that by burrowing down among the "eternal" country folk, one could discover preliterate and pre-Christian lev-els. By contrast, in America, such idealized peasants did not exist. Patriotic devotees of American nature had already contrasted "towers in which feudal oppression has fortified itself," in the words of Washington Irving (1783–1859), with "deep forests which the eye of God has alone pervaded."[39] It was a rhetorical commonplace of the early nineteenth century that the natural wonders of the New World trumped the manmade achievements of the Old, besides being more virtuously simple, more revolutionary, and also more godly. During this period, some Americans did turn to the image of the Druid as the embodiment of sublime, Romantic nature. The poet Philip Fre-neau, in a work titled "The Philosopher of the Forest," published in 1781, an-nounces how the tall trees of the Hudson Valley make him feel "Half Druid" and impel him to adore them.[40] Around 1815, a short-lived society in the Hudson Valley town of Newburgh, New York, that celebrated the ideals of the French Revolution was known as the Society of Druids. A former cler-gyman lectured the members—merchants and prosperous farmers—on the ideas of Voltaire, Thomas Paine, and Rousseau, and secret midnight cere-monies were said to have been performed.[41] These Hudson Valley fraternal Druids were admitting through their language the need to turn to Pagan models of religion (or to such models as they imagined) in order to feel at home spiritually on the North American continent.

In her *Nature Religion in America*, Catherine Albanese builds upon cate-gories established by the philosopher Roderick Nash to describe several eras in the American view of nature.[42] In the first seventeenth-century East Coast settlements, nature seems to function chiefly as a devilish wilderness that, in the Puritans' eyes, had to be reclaimed and "saved." Second, in her category of "republican nature," which Nash had called Deist nature, she observes how Americans around 1800 moved beyond seeing God in nature to what had been described as "natural (or nonsupernatural) religion." By the federal period, America's very size and bounty were re-visioned as divine blessings on the new republic: "America was physically grand and awesome, and so was its political project." Yet as any student of nineteenth-century American history knows, that initial hierophany easily was transformed into the doctrine of Manifest Destiny, the political doctrine that Americans were clearly divinely mandated to govern all peoples from the Isthmus of Panama to the Arctic Circle—or as much of that territory as could be brought into the republic.[43] Lastly, Albanese credits the New England Transcendentalists, primarily Ralph Waldo Emerson, with stripping "metaphysical" nature religion—what I have called Cosmic Nature religion—of its "casting of magic spells [and] the pursuit of astrology." What emerged was a more elite version, a scientific nature religion that included Spiritualists, for instance, whose mediums were sometimes referred to as "instruments," as though they transmitted as impersonally as a barometer.

Into this new nature religion poured Swedenborgianism, Mesmerism, Theosophy, and all the earlier currents that in the twentieth century were dubbed the New Age movement. My own Colorado home was built by a Swedenborgian (New Church) minister, Allen Cook,[44] and his letters and sermons themselves bear the mark of one stream of nature religion, for he writes of studying "Historical Geology, Biology, Paleontology (the facts of evolution)." In a sermon delivered to tourists visiting the Colorado mountain resort of Green Mountain Falls, he declares, "Mountains, we know, signify exalted states of affection. . . . It is not possible to adequately convey in words the strength, the mightiness, and the beauty of the *symbols* all around us" (emphasis added), concluding with a quotation from Swedenborg: "All nature is full of confirmation of the Divine."[45]

What Cook expresses certainly represents yet another stream of continuing American nature religion; indeed, his sermon blends to a degree "natural religion" with Swedenborg's theory of correspondences, which he certainly endorsed. But the new Pagan nature religion would turn out to be something else: not natural as opposed to supernatural, not exactly a set of correspondences between the unseen and the seen, and not merely a blessing on the American republic, although these at time might creep in. The new American Pagans, in the view of the most articulate early theorist of nature religion, Tim Zell, editor of *Green Egg*, were willing to give to planet Earth the status of a goddess. Hence my term for the second type of Pagan nature religion is Gaian Nature.

The early 1970s define a period of growing environmental consciousness, exemplified by not just Earth Day festivals but the growth and multiplication of environmental organizations, education, and regulation. Some Americans expressed their relationship with nature, mixed with ideas of health and moral purity, by pursuing or at least dreaming of "living on the land," while others filled their homes with potted plants. The 1974 Council of American Witches also took pains to establish Wicca's credentials as an environmentally sensitive religion. Its second principle reads, "We recognize that our intelligence gives us a unique responsibility toward our environment. We seek to live in harmony with Nature, in ecological balance offering fulfillment to life and consciousness within an evolutionary concept."

Wicca's seizure of the position of the most "environmental" religion was well timed. Environmentalism was trendy: President Richard Nixon had remarked to a Sierra Club leader at a bill signing in 1970 that "All politics is a fad. Your fad is going right now. Get what you can, and here is what I can get you."[46] Meanwhile, many Christians were ambivalent toward the environmental movement, in some cases because they chose to see it as a competing religion—a *pagan* religion. Among the most outspoken right-wing Christian critics of environmentalism was Berit Kjos, author of *The Spell of Mother Earth*, who commented in 1993,

> This summer, while the East roasted and rains deluged the Midwest, tourists flocked to national parks like Yellowstone, Grand Tetons, Mt. Rushmore, and the Rocky Mountains [sic]. In park visitor centers, they could find native American shields and dreamcatchers, Zuni fetishes, kachinas and pagan posters that merge shadowy wolves with unearthly images of shamans. Ignoring the true Creator of America's magnificent vistas, multitudes bought and treasured these immensely popular occult charms and idols.[47]

Kjos's denunciation, coming twenty-three years after the first Earth Day, demonstrates that to one sort of Christian, environmentalism still threatens to become either a false religion or else a distraction from ministering to human suffering—assuming, of course, that humanity is seen as outside of nature. A Roman Catholic bishop once expostulated to Paul Gorman, executive director of the National Religious Partnership for the Environment, "How come I never see any people on a Sierra Club calendar?"[48]

Unlike Kjos or the bishop, Wicca and other forms of new American Paganism stepped right through the door that Earth Day had opened for them—or, perhaps more accurately, the door whose opening the first Earth Day merely marked. Through its heritage of high magic, Wicca already drew on Cosmic Nature. Now it had come to a land where *natural* and *nature* were considered by many people to be positive terms. Already, during the 1960s, American Indian activists had gained some moral high ground by presenting themselves as spiritually close to nature, drawing at least in part on the image created by such non-Indians as Grey Owl (in Canada and the United Kingdom) and Ernest Thompson Seton (in Canada and the United States).

While the contemporary Pagan movement generally displayed an internal taboo against appropriating American Indian ceremonies or nomenclature, Pagans were happy to see these native traditions presented as earth religion or nature religion, because such a presentation in turn helped to promote the idea that an earth religion was a viable spiritual tradition, thus adding the legitimacy of their new religious movements.

Gnostica contributor Carl Jones, separating what we might call "operative" witchcraft (spell casting and the like) from nature religion, commented that "the worship, rites, and magic of nature religions around the world have been called by many names." Significantly, he continues, "'Wiccan' does not necessarily imply psychic talent . . . [but is] a part of dynamic psycho-spiritual realization." In other words, when Jones was writing in 1979, it was becoming increasingly respectable to be "Wiccan," without doing most of the things that "witches" were traditionally expected to do, a trend that has grown only stronger. Instead of spell-casting, Wicca was now nature religion:

> [To the Wiccan practitioner,] Nature is suddenly more than the lives of the trees, ferns, and mosses, the bird and untamable wild ones who rustle through the woods; nature seems to breathe a vibrant magical life of her own, and that life is reflected within the heart of the person sensing it. It is this sudden awakening to nature, this unspeakable communion with her mysteries, that is really the essence of Wicca.[49]

Nevertheless, I would stress that Wicca and other forms of new American Paganism stepped right into the opening created, without, so far as I can tell, any premeditation. In more than a quarter century of involvement in the movement, I have not uncovered any instance of any American Pagan's saying, in effect, "Let's position ourselves as the environmental religion." Risking an argument from absence, I think that the unconscious ease with which American Pagans embraced the terms *nature religion* or *earth religion* testifies to the strength of Catherine Albanese's argument that nature religion does exist in the American worldview, whether as a scholarly construct, a way of organizing reality (her first description), or as the "spiritual source of secular passion."[50]

Albanese had not at first treated contemporary Pagan religion under her heading of nature religion. Her 1990 book *Nature Religion in America* briefly quotes Starhawk's writing but places her in the context of a mental healer.[51] Albanese's primary period was the nineteenth century, and the growth of "natural healing" theories and methods remains one of her chief interests. Initially, she did not seem to have been aware of the use of the term *nature religion* as an alternative label to Paganism or Wicca by practitioners from the early 1970s onward.[52] When *Nature Religion in America* does treat Wicca in particular, Albanese perceptively connects the Wiccan view of nature with *excursus* religion, observing that in the Western experience of religion, "It has historically been a standard metaphor for the devotee to be solitary and alone, gazing into a Presence that distances, seemingly, all human presences, worlds, and constructions." Likewise, Wiccan discourse about nature frequently speaks of it as something "out there," away from the cities and suburbs in which most Wiccans live, as do most other Americans. "Confessions of time in nature," Albanese continues, "are most typically about being *out* of the tribe, away from the group, implicitly constructing a world over against the humanly constructed and organized one, playing with the first early whispers of what later may be mounted as criticism against it. Wiccan groups," she continues, "are ad hoc communities; their proneness to fracture is not the stuff of which strong organizations are made."[53]

These statements need some amendment. Wiccans and other Pagans frequently construct Gaian Nature as the place to which they go, as individuals or small groups, to meet with others in the dozens of summer festivals— "temporary autonomous zones" in which the temporary tribe is itself formed and reinforced. The Pagan festival movement began as campouts and outdoor rituals but might also be dated from the summer of 1980, when the first big nationally advertised festival, open to all comers, was held in the Midwest. (Previous national gatherings, like the Twin Cities Gnosticon referred to earlier, were typically held in hotels and were modeled on science-fiction and fantasy conventions, from which they took the suffix -*con*.) As Sarah Pike describes in her study of festivals, festivalgoers "imagine a harmonious relationship between humans and nature. Neopagans also try to draw closer in this way to their adopted cultures, which they say have a more intimate relationship between humans and nature."[54] It is common to hear festival attendees speaking of getting "out into nature," like any group of weekend campers, with the added element that participants frequently feel that their religion is more powerful and real under open skies. These outdoor festivals, while related perhaps to the large outdoor rock-and-roll festivals such as the Woodstock festival of 1969, have another precursor in the religious camp meetings of the Second Great Awakening, a period during the early nineteenth century, particularly in frontier regions, when Americans went "into the wilderness" for a short but intense period of religious instruction and experience. The guiding metaphors for those nineteenth-century Americans would have been the stories of Moses and the wanderings of the Israelites as well as Jesus's forty days of solitude following his baptism by John the Baptist. But in the tradition of American nature religion, the wilderness is itself the source of spiritual instruction rather than being only a place of removal from distractions or of purification.

Tim Zell, whose wedding to his partner Morning Glory would be a centerpiece of one of the Gnosticons, said that his own version of the "Gaea Hypothesis" (his spelling) occurred on September 6, 1970. As far as he was concerned, his publication of his vision of Earth as one single organism, with humanity (and whales and dolphins) as its "noosphere," the planetary brain, gave him precedence over the more mechanistic "Gaia Hypothesis" formulated shortly thereafter by the biochemist James Lovelock. Ultimately, he predicted, humanity would achieve a telepathic oneness, and this planetary consciousness "would be in complete control of virtually everything that goes on in the planet—from earthquakes to rainfall to ice ages to mountain building to hurricanes—and perhaps influence the rest of its local stellar system as well."[55] Then humanity (and cetaceans) would achieve a state that he compares to Teilhard de Chardin's Omega Point, fusing telepathy and scientific knowledge in a religious framework. All life came from one cell; therefore, all of Earth's life-forms taken together were one vast creature: Mother Earth.

Reformulating his insights, Zell published a longer article, "The Gods of Nature; the Nature of Gods," in the Llewellyn magazine Gnostica; the article later became a Church of All Worlds pamphlet. Here he describes Mother Earth as "the highest level of deity yet attained by that process of emergent evolution which began over two billion years ago and need never end," for deity is also "the highest level of aware consciousness accessible to each living being, manifesting itself in the self-actualization of that being." Thus the Church of All Worlds' cosmology tossed out the Neoplatonic heart of Western magic, replacing it with a philosophy of immanence that also made room for Velikovskian "planets in collision" and Eric von Daniken's extraterrestrial "gods from outer space" (Thoth, Prometheus, Aradia, Quetzalcoatl, and other "ancient astronauts" who came to Earth). Zell categorizes other deities of both ancient polytheists and more recent monotheists as "tribal gods," kept alive only by the energy poured into them by their worshipers.[56]

Despite the highly visible position of the Church of All Worlds in the American Pagan movement of the 1970s through its influential magazine Green Egg, most contemporary Pagans are more likely to speak of the spirit of nature and, as heirs of the Romantic movement, to see humanity as suffering from its spiritual divorce from nature. In 1979, Margot Adler would sum up this attitude as "fueled by romantic vision, [literary] fantasy, and visionary activities, empowered by a sense of planetary crisis and the idea that such a nature vision may be drowned in an ecocidal nightmare."[57] Most Wiccans and other contemporary Pagans would accept Gaia as a goddess—a wounded goddess, in some instances—but their primary religious identification with the planet was through its cycles, rather than its biosphere. In the language that constantly speaks of harmony, cycles, and rhythms, we hear the echoes of the natural magic—Cosmic Nature—of the Renaissance, but with Gaian overtones. To give just one example, which is typical, a Washington-state Wiccan writer named Blacksun, no newcomer to the movement, wrote in 1994, "Any who identify themselves with the worship of the Goddess and the God, who celebrate the rhythms of the Earth and call her Mother, and make a sacrament of joy and wonder are just as much Wiccan as those who formally take on the mantle of priesthood by degrees in a tradition that secrets itself behind closed drapes or in dark woods."[58] An insider will see in this statement a repudiation—or at least a devaluing—of the initiatory mystery religion of Gerald Gardner and friends in favor of a heartfelt, self-proclaimed, anarchic nature religion.

Does following a self-proclaimed nature religion make one into an environmental activist? For a long time, this question was little researched beyond the anecdotal stage, which seemed to suggest, in my experience at least, that the answer was "sometimes, but not necessarily." Beginning as far back as the mid-1980s, however, the coming together of large numbers of Wiccans and other Pagans at warm-weather outdoor festivals provided social scientists with an opportunity to conduct interviews, administer questionnaires, and attempt to quantify the Pagan worldview. Since "significant numbers of informants assert definitively that their practice is a Nature Religion and use the terms 'Paganism' and 'Nature Spirituality' interchangeably," sociologist Regina Oboler wondered if the Pagan belief system did promote an environmentalist ethic.[59] Conducting her survey at Pagan gatherings and in online discussion groups and chat rooms, a generation after the first Earth Day—in the first years of the twenty-first century—Oboler came to a mixed conclusion about whether nature religion indeed produced both political activism and proenvironmental behavior, such as recycling and a consciously reduced consumption of material goods. Certainly the rhetoric was there: 98.5 percent of Oboler's respondents agreed with the statement, "Is the sanctity of the natural world a part of your spiritual belief?" And 72 percent of the Pagans, as against 43 percent of all Americans in a recent Gallup poll, said they were favorable to the environmental movement, with an additional 26.5 percent of Pagans and 40 percent of Americans generally in the "somewhat favorable" camp. Throughout her survey, Pagans scored higher than average both in environmental commitment and in activities such as recycling, contributing money to environmental causes, and signing petitions.[60]

Nevertheless, Oboler remained cautious about drawing a direct causal relationship between Pagan religion and environmental activism. For one thing, environmental values generally rise with a person's educational level, and, in her survey and in others, contemporary Pagans tend to have higher-than-average amounts of formal education. (In the 1970s, while noting that the social class of the Pagans whom she met varied widely, Margot Adler added, "Almost *all* are avid readers."[61]) While her statistics supported the hypothesized Pagan environmentalism, "the difference between Pagans and non-Pagans is not as great as one might expect, and it is not clear that it is not attributable primarily to confounding variables such as education. Further, many if not most Pagans report that they were environmentalists prior to being Pagans."[62]

Certainly the rhetoric of Pagan environmentalism has only increased over the years since Earth Day 1970, and Oboler's research indicates that it may well be matched by action, although more work remains to be done on the connection between a profession of nature religion and environmental action.

Finally, there is a theological question: Is it nature being worshiped or the gods of nature? In general, contemporary Pagan theology[63] is more poetic than systematic. Followers of reconstructionist paths, such as revived Egyptian, Roman, or Norse Paganism, are least likely to use the terminology of nature religion and more likely to insist on being called simply polytheists. Reconstructionist Pagans depend on literary sources supplemented by their own intuition, imagination, and experience to re-create the worship of a limited pantheon of gods, seen as distinct nonhuman entities but not omnipotent deities. Most Wiccan concepts of deity, on the other hand, allow for considerable variation. To many Wiccans, gods are not wholly separate from human beings, but neither are they merely personified powers of the individual unconscious mind or of the collective unconscious, the submerged unity of all human unconscious minds postulated by C. G. Jung. The writers Janet and Stewart Farrar straddle that divide nicely in their book *The Witches' Way*:

> The working power and the appeal of the Craft do arise from the emotions, the intuition, the 'vasty deep' of the Collective Unconscious. Its Gods and Goddesses draw their forms from the numinous Archetypes which are the mighty foundation-stones of the human racial psyche. . . . [The Goddess] has two main aspects. She is both the Earth Mother, whose fecundity bears and nourishes [the Witches] during physical incarnation, and the Queen of Night [in some references, the Star Goddess], "she in the dust of whose feet are the hosts of Heaven, and whose body encircles the Universe," whose most vivid symbol is the Moon.[64]

The Great Goddess of Wicca, therefore, can be both an Earth Mother and a goddess of Cosmic Nature. The more feminist forms of Pagan Witchcraft make Her primary, projecting Herself to form Her opposite polarity, the God. "Differentness awakens desire, which pulls against the centrifugal force of projection. The energy field of the cosmos becomes polarized," writes Starhawk, the San Franciscan who emerged in the late 1970s as the leading voice of Wiccan theology.[65] Other more conservative Wiccan traditions cling to an essentially Neoplatonic cosmos, in which an undivided godhead produces male and female aspects. In practice, either approach leads to a certain bricolage, a combining of many different divine images and aspects. Wiccans frequently follow the approach outlined by the early-twentieth-century occultist Dion Fortune, who said, "All the gods are one god, and all the goddesses are one goddess, and there is one initiator." That "initiator" is the person's own High Self, or divine spark within, a concept shared with a wide variety of religious traditions.

Thus far, I have discussed the contemporary Pagan definition of nature religion in two forms: the Cosmic Nature of celestial cycles, magical herbalism, and other forms of natural magic, and a Gaian Nature of the Earth as embodied divinity and of service to that divinity. A third locus of nature religion remains: the human body, and here contemporary Paganism, while having a root in "naturism"—therapeutic nudity and sunbathing—has developed its own "erotic theology."

An Erotic Theology

An album released in 1980 by the Pagan singer Holly Tannen[66] included the song "Heretic Heart," composed by Catherine Madsen and set to a traditional English tune, "Forest Green," sometimes used for "O Little Town of Bethlehem."[67] Madsen's lyrics declare, "My skin, my bones, my heretic heart are my authority," and otherwise encapsulate an entire outlaw culture of resistance to "priest or scripture, man or law."[68] Wiccan writer Margot Adler was so fond of the song that she borrowed its title for her autobiography, published in 1997.[69] The singer makes it clear that she rejects male religious authority and its cosmology, linking that rejection to her control of her body: "My body shall not be subdued, my soul shall not be saved." The singer connects herself to Cosmic Nature ("the Lady Moon"); as the Pagan folklorist Sabina Magliocco comments, the song "sacralizes the body and the cycles of nature, and rejects any form of authority imposed from without or perceived as coming from a locus of power within the hegemony."[70] In the truest sense, the singer is wild and her body is wild.

In his essay "The Etiquette of Freedom," mentioned earlier, Gary Snyder investigates the etymologies of the words *nature*, *wild*, and *wilderness*. *Nature*, he writes, comes from the Latin word for "to be born," with cognates in Greek and Sanskrit, and means at some times "all nonhuman creation" and "all of the material world." *Wild* links to *feral* and to the Latin *silva* ("forest, savage") and to *fierce*. It is usually defined by what it is not: untamed, insubordinate, uninhabited, and uncultivated. But Snyder turns those definitions on their heads. A wild animal is a free agent, a wild plant is self-maintaining, wild behavior is unconditioned and spontaneous. Wild individuals, therefore, follow "local custom, style, and etiquette without concern for the standards of the metropolis or nearest trading post. Unintimidated, self-reliant, independent. 'Proud and free.'"[71]

All the etymology goes to support another piece of Snyder's argument: that wilderness and "the wild" are not just "out there" but "in here" as well, in both our bodies and our psyches:

> Our bodies are wild. The involuntary quick turn of the head at a shout, the vertigo of looking off a precipice, the heart-in-the-throat in a moment of danger, the catch of the breath, the quiet moments relaxing, starting, reflecting—all universal responses of this mammal body. . . . The body does not require the intercession of some conscious intellect to make it breathe, to keep the heart beating. It is to a great extent self-regulating, it is a life of its own. . . . There are more things in mind, in the imagination, than "you" can keep track of— thoughts, memories, images, angers, delights, rise unbidden. . . . The body is, so to speak, in the mind. They are both wild.[72]

Even before the Pagan revivals, Witchcraft was connected with the body and with nudity. Renaissance and early modern witch-hunters considered the physical flight to the Witches' Sabbath to be a point of church doctrine and believed that the body itself, through various marks such as a third nipple, could betray a person's alleged contract with the devil. In larger terms, however, both heresy and excursus religion are connected with the body, and their proponents value firsthand bodily experience more than doctrine and scripture. The cognitive anthropologist Harvey Whitehouse uses the concept of "doctrinal" and "imagistic" modes of religiosity, linking the second with what psychologists call "episodic memory," while the doctrinal or "semantic" mode is more connected with orthodox, large-scale religiosity: sermons, creeds, and scriptures. "Religious identity, in the doctrinal mode, is primarily conferred on the basis of presumed commonalities in the thought and behavior of anonymous others, a state of affairs which is only conceivable with references to semantic knowledge." On the other hand, the imagistic mode is more common in smaller societies and in breakaway groups where, Whitehouse suggests, "religious life is focused around very infrequent, traumatic ritual episodes. . . . Common identity among religious adherents in the imagistic mode is fundamentally particularistic, based on lasting episodic memories of undergoing the traumatic lows and highs of sacred events together with a specific group of individuals."[73]

Where episodic memories are lodged is in the mammalian body. They are born in the slowly warming feel of a smear of oil on the skin, the warmth of a flame, the touch of a sword point. ("It were better to rush upon my weapon and perish than to make the attempt with fear in the heart," says the high priestess to the candidate in one version of the Gardnerian Wiccan initiation ritual.[74]) It is the weight of the animal mask on the head: all these speak to the wild body.

Indeed, control of the body or a different attitude toward the body marks many so-called heresies. Some, it is true, followed the ancient formula of *soma sema*—the body is a tomb—and sought to minimize its importance, such as the medieval Cathar "Perfects" who would eat no food produced by sexual intercourse (for example, meat or eggs) and demonstrated their spiritual agency through deliberate suicide. Small groups of "Adamites" in different eras proclaimed through their nudity that they were no longer in a state of sin but could live as did Adam and Eve in the Garden of Paradise; one such group split off from anti-Catholic Hussite reformers of fifteenth-century Bohemia. More recently, in the mid-twentieth century, the Sons of Freedom, a radical splinter of the pacifist Russian sect of Doukobors, immigrants to Canada, would take off their clothes (in courtrooms, for example, or in the street) to protest what they felt was governmental interference in their lives. "They marched in the nude, 'in the manner of the first Adam and Eve.'"[75] Wiccan nudity, however, sets this contemporary Paganism apart from a great deal of occult tradition, which is more likely to downplay the body in favor of spirit, as in the Hermetic dictum, "Unless you first hate your body, my child, you cannot love yourself." In that sense, Wicca follows the counter-tradition of occult philosophy, sharing an outlook with certain Cabalists and with the twentieth-century magic of Aleister Crowley, whom Gerald Gardner knew.[76]

Wiccan ritual nudity is more common in those traditions directly derived from Gardner's covens or in their close cousins, the Alexandrians, named after Alex Sanders, 1926?–1988, another British Wiccan innovator. Most other Wiccan ritualists wear either full-length robes, some other variety of special ritual clothing, or in some cases their ordinary clothing. Ritual nudity remains an option—one that is frequently exercised in the protected space of festivals—and it usually is justified in several ways. One claim, which Gardner promulgated, is that clothing blocks magical energy. (This belief connects with folklore about female witches unbinding their hair to cast spells, or even with customs of opening doors, etc., when a baby is being born.) Second, as Ronald Hutton points out in his essay "A Modest Look at Ritual Nudity," the practice is promoted as erasing social distinction and creating "a feeling of equality and democracy."[77] (Perhaps that was a more urgent concern for the English Witches of the 1950s.) One reason that I have heard but that Hutton does not list is that ritual nudity, confronting the various shapes and ages of one's fellow coveners leads to an acceptance of physical life and lessens the fear of death. Finally, nudity, when combined with candlelight, incense, and other sensory cues, "conveys a very powerful sense that something abnormal is going on; that the participants in the circle have cast off their everyday selves and limitations and entered into a space in which the extraordinary can be achieved."[78] Here is the place for the creation of episodic memory.

After a cross-cultural survey of ritual nudity, which too frequently is associated with workers of evil magic as well as other liminal and transformational figures, Hutton credits Wiccans with "investing that symbolic function with positive qualities, and its worldwide distribution strengthens a characterisation of Wicca as a counter-cultural religion par excellence."[79] Nudity, however, implies sex. In its sacralization of sexual activity, both literal and metaphorical, Wicca and some other types of modern Paganism enact "nature religion" at the level of the human body, rather than at the level of the cosmos or of the planet. Here, although I have grouped Wicca (broadly defined) and other types of contemporary Paganism together, it is necessary to make some distinctions. Whereas Wicca was heavily eroticized from the beginning, not all types of reconstructed Paganism can be so described. Some, of course, can be: for instance, Feraferia (see chapter 6).

When it came to America in the 1960s, whether transmitted by texts or by individuals, Wicca in particular was described as the pre-Christian Old Religion reborn and rediscovered. (Another of Gardner's justifications for ritual nudity had been that it was one of the "old ways" passed down from the Stone Age.) To the Wiccans of the mid-twentieth century, the Old Religion was automatically a fertility cult. "In the Stone Ages man's chief wants were good crops, good hunting, good fishing, increase in flocks and herds and many children to make the tribe strong," Gerald Gardner had written. "It became the witches' duty to perform rites to obtain these things."[80] The first twentieth-century Wiccans were mainly urbanites not directly concerned with flocks and herds, but they made sexual intercourse between priest and priestess a central feature of their seasonal or lunar rituals, whether carried out literally (actually less common) or metaphorically, through lowering of the ritual knife, the *athame*, into a chalice. The metaphor need not be knife and cup: one of my own episodic memories involves a spring equinox ritual in an old schoolhouse on the eastern Colorado prairie, where at its climax the high priestess pressed a seed into a small flower pot that I held out to her. The psychic jolt that I felt was certainly eroticized spirituality.

The "fertility cult" Wicca of 1950s England carried the intellectual fingerprints of Sir James Frazer (1854–1941), the anthropologist whose magnum opus, *The Golden Bough* (1890), a study of ancient cults, rites, and myths, continued to inspire and provide intellectual underpinnings for British Craft writers such as Stewart Farrar and Evan John Jones into the 1990s. Musicians such as R. J. Stewart kept alive the notion that traditional folk songs contained bits of pre-Christian religion: rituals of sacrificed sacred kings and bits and pieces of a hypothetical pre-Christian Witch cult. "This has led to many people within the [contemporary Pagan] community believing in the existence of an extant body of song in honor of pagan goddesses (or the Goddess) and gods."[81]

Yet within the American context, the work of another "countercultural"—in the broadest sense—thinker might be equally important as Frazer's. Wilhelm Reich (1897–1957), a psychoanalyst and maverick natural scientist, developed his own version of the persistent "vitalist" theory—that a uniform energy pervades the natural world. Certainly a heretic within the medical community, he suffered what his followers still regard as martyrdom at the hands of the "inquisition," played by the American Medical Association and the federal Food and Drug Administration. Reich termed this energy "orgone energy":

> As Reich conceived it, orgone energy is present in the atmosphere, is related to the sun, extends through all space like the 'ether,' is drawn in by all organisms, and is what accounts for the movement—contraction and expansion—of all living things. It flows through organisms, creates a field around them and can be transmitted from organism to organism (among human beings, by the laying on of hands, for instance). . . . In the sexual orgasm a large discharge of orgone takes place, whose biological function is to restore energy equilibrium to the organism. If the orgone flow is unnaturally checked in an organism (e.g., by character armoring), disease will set in.[82]

A refugee from Nazi Germany, Reich built a lab in Forest Hills, New York, where he experimented on concentrating orgone energy for therapeutic purposes. His claim that his orgone-accumulator box could cure cancer would ultimately bring down the wrath of the FDA and lead to the actual burning of his published works. Later, Reich moved to a more isolated spot near Rangely, Maine, where he worked together with his followers, mostly unconventional psychiatrists and doctors. The last ten years of his life were tempestuous. Attacked in magazines such as *Harper's* and the *New Republic* as a dangerous quack and founder of a "love cult," Reich responded bombastically and ultimately lost a federal contempt-of-court trial. He received a two-year sentence and died in prison in 1957. To the medical establishment of his day, the verdict was clear: a once-promising psychiatric career had ended by going over the cliff.

Reich's partial rehabilitation coincided with the first growth spurt of contemporary American Paganism. His book *The Mass Psychology of Fascism* received a favorable review in the *New York Times* in early 1971, and the *Times* and other intellectual publications began to reexamine Reich as something more than a crackpot. Within a couple of years, T. Edward Mann, in his generally sympathetic biography, announced that "in the world of intellectual sophistication, Reich is becoming a name to conjure with."[83]

Reich's vitalistic ideas were not completely new; they can be traced back to the Renaissance physician Paracelsus, among others. In the 1970s, all of his concerns seemed to fit the Zeitgeist: treatments such as Rolfing, deep massage designed to break up chronic muscular hypertension and "armoring," gained popularity, as did a variety of psychotherapies that urged clients to "let it all out," among them, Primal Scream therapy. For eclectic, socially experimental Pagans such as those in the Church of All Worlds, or readers of its journal, *Green Egg*, his was indeed a name to conjure with. All of his concerns were catnip to this new Pagan network: life energy, the human electromagnetic field (the vehicle for magic?), the manipulation of weather and planetary energy, all were fascinating, as were Reich's attacks on authoritarian families and patriarchy. In Reich's work lay "women's liberation . . . the need for a pleasure-centered, instead of pleasure-denying culture . . . [and] the tremendous significance of sexual happiness for emotional and social health." At Reich's core lay his own nature mysticism, not theistic but not incompatible with the new polytheism, an eroticized, "primitive" metaphysics tremendously appealing to those who saw scientific civilization bound up in war and ecological disaster.[84]

Reich's name and those of his intellectual associates, such as the radical British educator A. S. Neill, began to show up in *Green Egg*. Geneva Steinberg's article in 1974, "Wilhelm Reich & Neo-Paganism," praises Reich's work and his alternative technologies for making possible an ecologically friendly, paradisiacal world. "WE COULD HAVE THE COMFORTS OF CIVILIZATION WITHOUT AN INDUSTRIAL ECONOMY!" she trumpets in capital letters. Reich helped to justify Pagan perceptions: "Pagans were not 'anthropomorphizing' when they detected intelligent forces at work in Nature. Probably, we are '*mis*anthropomorphizing' when we *fail* to see them." To her, Reich is not only a misunderstood genius but a prophet, even if the "Neo-Paganism" that he referred to in his writings was the alleged Nazi variety. "It's a shame that Reich couldn't be around to see the real Neo-Paganism come into its own—I think he would have heartily approved."[85]

Another *Green Egg* article the following year, "Omega," by Richard Alan Miller, biochemist and herbalist,[86] traced the history of the invisible energy of nature: "It has been called by many names: animal magnetism, orgone, mana, prana, life force and the like." Reich's thought clearly contributed to Miller's conclusion: "There is no such thing as absolute order," but there are patterns in the randomness, and "magic can be thought of as the science of patterning."[87]

Reich's ideas gave an intellectual justification to where Paganism—Wicca in particular—was headed in the 1970s. More than the 1930s Church of Aphrodite, more than Feraferia, Wicca had turned sex into a sacrament and sexuality into an expression of connection with the earth, ratified not by marriage but by ritual intention. "We were created by the sacred sexual union of our flesh-and-blood mothers and fathers, and born in a great gush of blood and water, children of Earth, all of us," declares an essay by Rhiannon Asher, an editor of the Pagan magazines *Hole in the Stone* and *All Acts of Love and Pleasure*.[88] The latter's title comes from a line in the traditional Gardnerian Wiccan ritual when the high priestess—unless she is inspired to speak more spontaneously as the Wiccan Goddess—may recite a charge in the Goddess's name that includes the phrase, "All acts of love and pleasure are my rituals." As Asher puts it, "The Gods move through us in sacred sexual ecstasy." The idea that human beings may channel divine forces through sexual intercourse is not unique to Wicca, but it is codified in Wicca. "Witches know that the Universe is a living entity, a dance and union of sacred forces," writes Valerie Voigt, formerly editor of the magazine *Pagana*. "When we make love, we can be especially aware of our place in the Creative Force because we are focusing our divine energy. We can actively and consciously connect with God, with Goddess, and experience that creation."[89] The erotic interplay of divine forces is at the core of the religion. And the sex does not need to be heterosexual: gay and bisexual Pagans have outspokenly emphasized the *all* in "all acts."

Many Pagan religions include invocation of and possession by their gods. Wicca, in particular, extends that possession to sexual acts, whether literal or metaphorical, and significantly refers to them as *the* Great Rite. (In public ritual, those acts are almost always metaphorical.) This sacralization of sex does indeed build on a long association in the dominant culture between folk witchcraft and sex, even although the modern practice and the historic myth are far from identical. Consider, for example, the instructions by the witch-goddess Aradia in Charles Leland's 1898 compilation of alleged Tuscan Pa-gan survivals, that at their monthly festivals the witches should play the game of "Moccala di Benevento," or extinguishing the lights and having a sexual orgy—an accusation made against heretics and "foreign cults" as long ago as ancient Roman times.[90] Most Wiccans, like most Americans in gen-eral, are urbanites, but the body is everywhere that we are. To embrace na-ture, religion in the body does not require studying the heavens, nor does it require going "out into nature" as a conscious excursus from the city. It is in the body that Wiccan ritual unites Cosmic Nature—the cycles of divine power seen in astrological symbolism—and even Gaian Nature. "It seems to me that either littering the Earth or brashly using others for your own [sex-ual] pleasure (and calling it religion) is not conducive to ecological or egali-tarian balance," one writer warns.[91]

When Wiccans and other Pagans celebrate the cosmic cycles, they express a deep human religious heritage. In seeing planetary or Gaian Nature—and even the body's own natural healing powers—as divine, they express a view that, while not mainstream, has its own traditions. In sacralizing sexuality and creating a small but growing world religion around that central act, im-age, or metaphor, they brought nature religion into the most intimate of hu-man interactions and fueled it with one of humanity's most basic and in-domitable drives. What had come to America from Britain as a domesticated "fertility cult"—insofar as Wicca in particular was presented in the 1950s and 1960s as surviving, underground, Stone Age Paganism—was recast here as "nature religion." That appellation (or its near synonym *earth religion*) gave the new Pagans a standing in the religious marketplace that dovetailed neatly with the growing environmental consciousness of the late twentieth century, as well as a self-description that could be reexported to Britain as well as elsewhere. By sacralizing sexuality in particular—by taking a "wild" aspect of human life and framing it in religious terms, "approach[ing] one an-other as Deity and sex as worship"[92]—Wiccans in all countries set their own stamp on nature religion, uniting in their bodies the cosmic and the most personal energies of planetary life.

Finally, I would close with this story, taken from Susan Roberts's *Witches U.S.A.*, which I mentioned earlier in brief, because sometimes a particular anecdote illustrates a historical turning point. On April 22, 1970, Roberts was standing on a midtown Manhattan sidewalk trying to hail a taxicab, to-gether with Joe Luckach, one of her principal informants (along with Joseph Wilson and another couple from the Pagan Way group in Philadelphia). As she tells the story,

Neither of us had remembered that this was [the first] Earth Day in New York City and that several main traffic arteries had been closed to automobile traffic in order to observe the event.

Now, no one loves the earth and the purity of air more than a witch. But when it finally dawned on us that the traffic was worse than usual and that this official observance of Earth Day was to blame, Joe began to grumble about how stupid he thought it was to deliberately block already choked streets for any purpose, no matter how laudable.

"Then, how would you observe Earth Day, witch?" I asked.

"Well, I don't know. I haven't thought about it. Through witchcraft, I guess."[93]

But in the 1970s, Earth Day would be observed not as a Wiccan holiday but in a wholesale use of the terms *earth religion* or *nature religion* to redefine Witchcraft. What had previously been either the practice of spell craft and divination or an initiatory mystery religion seeking connection with Pagan deities and believed to be a continuation of pre-Christian European religious practices, now in America discovered what Catherine Albanese has called "a way of organizing reality and relating it to a *religion*."[94] The Pagan use of the term *nature religion* had a different rhetorical purpose than does Albanese's, while her definition includes a great deal more.[95] It was in the wider diffusion of environmental consciousness in American society, symbolized by that first 1970 Earth Day celebration, that *nature religion* begins to join and even replace *the Old Religion* as a description of what Pagan Witchcraft might otherwise be called.

Notes

1. Henry Beston, *The Book of Gallant Vagabonds* (New York: George H. Doran Company, 1925). I have modernized the seventeenth-century spelling here and elsewhere.

2. *Oxford Classical Dictionary*, 2nd ed. (Oxford: Clarendon Press, 1970), s.v. "Hymen."

3. Beston, *The Book of Gallant Vagabonds*, 160.

4. Donald F. Connors, *Thomas Morton* (New York: Twayne, 1969), 99.

5. Nathaniel Hawthorne, *The Complete Short Stories of Nathaniel Hawthorne* (Garden City, N.Y.: Hanover House, 1959), 42. Originally published in *Twice Told Tales*, 1837.

6. Ibid., 43–44.

7. Richard A. Grounds, "Tallahassee, Osceola, and the Hermeneutics of American Place Names," *Journal of the American Academy of Religion* 69 (2001): 309.

8. Connors, *Thomas Morton*, 128–29.

9. Rosemary Benet and Stephen Vincent Benet, *A Book of Americans* (New York: Holt, 1961).

10. Devyn, "Mine Host of Ma-Re Mount," *Green Egg*, Beltane 1990, 16.

11. Ibid.

12. The shamanic revival, prefigured by the works of Carlos Castaneda, gained its first hands-on workbook when anthropologist Michael Harner produced *The Way of the Shaman* (San Francisco: Harper & Row, 1980).

13. Jack Bracelin, *Gerald Gardner: Witch* (London: Octagon, 1960). It is widely believed that the book's putative author, Jack Bracelin, was not its actual author but that it was actually written by the esotericist Idries Shah.

14. Gerald Gardner, *Witchcraft Today* (Secaucus, N.J.: Citadel, 1973), 140. Emphasis in the original.

15. Ibid., 20.

16. The legendary Lammas ritual also furnished the plot of Katherine Kurz's novel *Lammas Night* (New York: Ballantine Books, 1983).

17. Susan Roberts, *Witches U.S.A.* (New York: Dell, 1971), 78.

18. Marika Kriss, *Witchcraft Past and Present, for the Millions* (Los Angeles: Sherbourne Press, 1970), 10–11.

19. Gavin Frost and Yvonne Frost, *The Witch's Bible* (New York: Berkeley, 1972). Although the Frosts described their methods as Wicca, their version in the 1970s differed considerably from the Gardnerian-influenced version, a source of much controversy. Their "Celtic Wicca" honored an "overseeing God who delegates authority throughout the universe" (p. 23) and seemed to combine American Spiritualism, a Theosophical view of progressive reincarnation, New Thought–style "mind development," and Golden Dawn–style magic.

20. Paul Huson, *Mastering Witchcraft: A Practical Guide for Witches, Warlocks, and Covens* (New York: G. P. Putnam's Sons, 1970).

21. Raymond Buckland, *Witchcraft from the Inside* (St. Paul, Minn.: Llewellyn, 1971).

22. Sarah Lyddon Morrison, *The Modern Witch's Spellbook* (New York: Citadel Press, 1971).

23. Jeffrey Kaplan, "The Reconstruction of the Ásatrú and Odinist Traditions," in *Magical Religion and Modern Witchcraft*, ed. James Lewis (Albany, N.Y.: State University of New York Press, 1996).

24. Gary Snyder, *The Practice of the Wild* (San Francisco: North Point Press, 1990), 8.

25. Sarah Pike, *Earthly Bodies, Magical Selves: Contemporary Pagans and the Search for Community* (Berkeley: University of California Press, 2001), 18.

26. Dove, e-mail to ColoWiccan mailing list, October 30, 2002.

27. Rosemary Edghill, *Bell, Book, and Murder: The Bast Novels* (New York: Forge Books, 1998), 291.

28. Catherine L. Albanese, *Nature Religion in America* (Chicago: University of Chicago Press, 1990), 7, emphasis in the original.

29. *Gnostica News*, "First Annual Festival Receives International Attention," August 21, 1972. Today, the Twin Cities area of Minnesota is referred to by some American Pagans as "Paganistan."

30. Eugenio Garin, *Astrology in the Renaissance*, trans. Carolyn Jackson and June Allen (London: Penguin, 1990), 70.

31. Mary Currier, "The Myth of the World Soul: Moving Towards an Ecological Psychology" (Master of Arts thesis, Regis University, 1997), 33.

32. Ronald Hutton, *The Triumph of the Moon* (Oxford: Oxford University Press, 1999), 67.

33. Garin, *Astrology in the Renaissance*, 34.

34. Doreen Valiente, *Natural Magic* (Custer, Wash.: Phoenix Publishing, 1986).

35. Scott Cunningham, *Magical Herbalism* (St. Paul, Minn.: Llewellyn, 1987), 156.

36. Quoted in Chas S Clifton, ed., *Shamanism and Witchcraft*, vol. 3, *Witchcraft Today* (St. Paul, Minn.: Llewellyn, 1994), xii.

37. Huson, *Mastering Witchcraft*.

38. Tarostar, "Witchcraft and Ecology," *The Cauldron*, November 2003.

39. Roderick Nash, *Wilderness and the American Mind*, rev. ed. (New Haven, Conn.: Yale University Press, 1973).

40. Albanese, *Nature Religion in America*, 61.

41. Mark C. Carnes, *Secret Ritual and Manhood in Victorian America* (New Haven, Conn.: Yale University Press, 1989), 40.

42. Nash, *Wilderness and the American Mind*.

43. Catherine Albanese, *Reconsidering Nature Religion*, ed. Gerald P. McKenny, Rockwell Lecture Series (Harrisburg, Pa.: Trinity International Press, 2002), 9.

44. The Rev. Allen T. Cook (1893–1984) was a minister in the General Convention of the New Church in the 1920s and 1930s.

45. Allen T. Cook, "A Letter from Colorado," *Ohio New-Church Bulletin*, September 1928.

46. Melvin Small, review of *Nixon and the Environment*, by J. Brooks Flippen, www.h-net.org/reviews/showrev.cgi?path=32584973114436 (accessed March 6, 2006).

47. Berit Kjos, "America Is Summoning Pagan Gods," *Colorado Christian News*, September 1993.

48. James Gerstenzang, "Religion Lured to Nature," *The Denver Post*, February 9, 1997.

49. Carl Jones, "Rising Goddess: The Nature Religion in the Modern World," *Gnostica*, May–June 1979.

50. Albanese, *Reconsidering Nature Religion*, 48.

51. Albanese, *Nature Religion in America*, 183.

52. She certainly understood the connection after a panel discussion at the 1998 annual meeting of the American Academy of Religion in Orlando, Florida, in which members of the ad hoc Nature Religions Scholars Network participated, some of whom were themselves Pagans.

53. Albanese, *Reconsidering Nature Religion*, 31–32.

54. Pike, *Earthly Bodies, Magical Selves: Contemporary Pagans and the Search for Community*, 45.

55. Otter G'Zell, "Theagenesis: The Birth of the Goddess," *Green Egg*, May 1, 1988.

56. Tim Zell, "The Gods of Nature; the Nature of Gods," *Gnostica*, October 21, 1973.

57. Margot Adler, *Drawing Down the Moon* (New York: Viking Press, 1979).

58. Blacksun, "The Earth Altar," *Panegyria*, November 1, 1994.

59. Regina Oboler, "Nature Religion as a Cultural System? Sources of Environmentalist Action and Rhetoric in a Contemporary Pagan Community," *The Pomegranate: The International Journal of Pagan Studies* 6, no. 1 (2004): 89.

60. Ibid., 93–94.

61. Adler, *Drawing Down the Moon*, 22, emphasis in the original.

62. Oboler, "Nature Religion as a Cultural System?"

63. Many Pagan writers prefer the feminine *theology*, emphasizing the primacy of a Great Goddess.

64. Stewart Farrar and Janet Farrar, *The Witches' Way* (London: Robert Hale, 1984), 111, 113. The Farrars' viewpoint was British, but they spoke as well for a great many American Wiccans.

65. Starhawk, *The Spiral Dance* (San Francisco: Harper & Row, 1979), 26.

66. Holly Tannen, *Between the Worlds* (Gold Leaf Records, 1980).

67. Arranged by the prolific English composer R. Vaughn Williams, "Forest Green" suggests a bouncy fife-and-drum tune such as "Yankee Doodle" or "The British Grenadier." See *The Hymnal of the Protestant Episcopal Church* (New York: The Church Pension Fund, 1940, 1961), hymn no. 21.

68. Sabina Magliocco and Holly Tannen, "The *Real* Old-Time Religion: Towards an Aesthetics of Neo-Pagan Song," *Ethnologies* 20, no. 1 (1998).

69. Margot Adler, *Heretic's Heart: A Journey through Spirit and Revolution* (Boston: Beacon Press, 1997).

70. Magliocco and Tannen, "The *Real* Old-Time Religion."

71. Snyder, *The Practice of the Wild*, 9–10.

72. Ibid., 16.

73. Harvey Whitehouse, *Arguments and Icons: Divergent Modes of Religiosity* (Oxford: Oxford University Press, 2000), 10.

74. Lady Sheba, *The Book of Shadows* (St. Paul, Minn.: Llewellyn, 1971), 35.

75. Ian Morfitt, "Naked City," *Fortean Times*, 1999, www.forteantimes.com/articles/119_naked.shtml (accessed January 25, 2006).

76. B. J. Gibbons, *Spirituality and the Occult: From the Renaissance to the Modern Age* (London: Routledge, 2001), 68–70.

77. Ronald Hutton, "A Modest Look at Ritual Nudity," *The Pomegranate: The Journal of Pagan Studies*, August 2001.

78. Ronald Hutton, *Witches, Druids and King Arthur* (London: Hambledon and London, 2003), 193.

79. Ibid., 209.

80. Gardner, *Witchcraft Today*, 31.

81. Magliocco and Tannen, "The *Real* Old-Time Religion."

82. W. Edward Mann, *Orgone, Reich and Eros: William Reich's Theory of Life Energy* (New York: Simon & Schuster, 1973).

83. Ibid., 22.

84. Ibid., 349–50.

85. Geneva Steinberg, "Wilhelm Reich and Neo-Paganism," *Green Egg*, June 21, 1974, emphasis in the original.

86. Richard Alan Miller, *The Magical and Ritual Use of Herbs* (New York: Destiny Books, 1983).

87. Richard Alan Miller, "Omega," *Green Egg*, December 21, 1976.

88. Rhiannon Asher, "When Sex Is a Sacrament," in *Living between Two Worlds*, ed. Chas S Clifton, *Witchcraft Today* (St. Paul, Minn.: Llewellyn, 1996).

89. Valerie Voigt, "Sex Magic," in *The Modern Craft Movenet*, ed. Chas S. Clifton, *Witchcraft Today* (St. Paul, Minn.: Llewellyn, 1992).

90. Charles Godfrey Leland, *Aradia, or the Gospel of the Witches*, trans. Mario Pazzaglini and Dina Pazzaglini (Blaine, Wash.: Phoenix Publishing, 1998), 362.

91. Diane Teagarden, "Just My Opinion: Pc Pagans," *Pagan Digest*, Ostara–Beltane (spring) 1994.

92. Asher, "When Sex Is a Sacrament," 186.

93. Roberts, *Witches U.S.A.*, 78.

94. Albanese, *Nature Religion in America*, 6.

95. Ironically, Albanese seems to have written *Nature Religion in America* unaware that contemporary Pagans utilized the term nature religion as a self-descriptor until she encountered openly Pagan scholars at American Academy of Religion meetings a few years after its publication.

CHAPTER THREE

The Rhetoric of Wicca

From the 1950s onward, the new Pagan religions, particularly Wicca, turned to various rhetorical strategies to build and defend themselves—and to "outbid" more-established rival religions where they could.[1] Not only did they have to launch new, more favorable definitions of such established pejorative terms as *witch* and *Pagan*, but they had also to introduce the new name *Wicca* as well and to negotiate its meaning in relation to the other two. In so doing, they made other claims as well, such as that Wicca represented the true soul of Britain, or that *Pagan* included not just themselves but could be legitimately stretched to include what had otherwise been labeled animism or tribal religion. This redefinition, in turn, reinforced the claim that many of the new Pagan religions, in particular Wicca, were "earth religions" and hence shared a great deal with native or tribal religions. In some cases, this claim permits today's Pagans to share the mantle of victimhood with Native Americans and other cultures suppressed by capitalistic Western Christianity. The Pagan songwriter Gwydion Pendderwen (1946–1982) wrote in his rousing ballad, "We Won't Wait Any Longer," "You [Earth-destroying Christians] have driven native peoples from the places that they love," rhymed with "razed the sacred groves" of European Paganism—thus the identification between Pagans and "natives" is complete.[2]

Words such as "Wicca" and "Neo-Pagan" were and are contested not only between witches and nonwitches but within the Pagan community as well. Some persons claim that they are "non-Wiccan witches," and others call themselves "Wiccan" but not "witches." Members of initiatory lineages

Figure 3.1.   Pagan songwriter Gwydion Pendderwen in his bardic performing costume, 1981. His 1976 album *Songs for the Old Religion* was the first widely distributed collection of American Pagan music. Photo by Chas S. Clifton

traced back to Gerald Gardner's original coven often wish to keep the word *Wicca* for that initiatory tradition only, even though the term has grown to encompass much more of contemporary Pagan Witchcraft. Likewise, while *Pagan* in its "neo" sense is often employed by both scholars and participants to include all who practice a religion called Witchcraft, it must also be stretched to include practitioners of revived Paganisms based on Greek, Roman, Slavic, Germanic, and other roots. Some practitioners, however, try to escape the label. Followers of revived Germanic and Norse religion, for example, prefer the word *Heathen* or *Northern*, insinuating in their rejection of words with Germanic etymology that *Pagan* carries a connotation of Mediterranean effeminacy.[3]

Based on thirty years of observation, however, I can offer the following generalizations. First, *Wicca* has gained a fair degree of acceptance as the name of a new Pagan religion, and *Pagan* itself is slowly becoming a newly redefined descriptor, thanks in large part to an increasingly vocal group of Pagan scholars in religious studies and the social sciences. But as we can see in countless examples from the history of popular music, when "alternative" becomes "mainstream," a new alternative term is often generated. Now, in the early twenty-first century, some Wiccans have begun to complain that *Wiccan* has been degenerated to a mere fashion statement and no longer really means anything except for a set of preferences in dress, jewelry, and music— a criticism that is often leveled by an older against a younger generation!

Definitions

Employing their new definitions, the pioneers of the Pagan revival began in the 1950s to carry out the task of self-defense. Their method was to redefine words with negative connotations—such as *pagan* in the sense of "irreligious"—in new positive ways. Their second task, having carved out a sliver of space on the religious spectrum, was "outbidding." In Britain, in particular, this outbidding came in the suggestion that Wicca represented a more authentic British faith than Christianity, and that British Pagans, collectively, were following "indigenous religion." In the United States, a nation of immigrants, a different sort of outbidding occurred: nascent Paganism quickly, almost unconsciously, appropriated the discourse of the well-established alternative tradition of nature religion, as described in the previous chapter.

By the 1970s, contemporary Pagans were lobbying publishers of encyclopedias and dictionaries to reform their definitions of such words as *witchcraft* to encompass their religion. True to its text-based nature, the Wiccan revival owed part of its vigor to an encyclopedia, the 1929 edition of the *Encyclopedia*

Britannica. For that edition, the editors chose the English anthropologist Margaret Murray (1863–1963) to write the *Witchcraft* entry. Murray was then advocating a new interpretation of the Renaissance and early-modern witch trials: that they had represented the persecution of an actual pre-Christian religion with a clandestine clergy, a religion that had, under some of the Plantagenet kings of England, received a degree of royal protection and patronage—even outright adherence.

Better known as an Egyptologist, Murray had developed her thinking on the witch trials while waiting out World War I in Glastonbury. In 1921, she published *The Witch-Cult in Western Europe,* which was followed in subsequent decades by two more works taking up the same theme.[4] While subsequent historians refuted her work, showing, for instance, how she seemed to have selectively quoted a limited number of witch-trial records, *Britannica's* prestige and wide use contributed to the diffusion of the "Murrayite hypothesis," the actual existence of an Old Religion in those times. Her ideas were highly influential in academia until the 1970s, and outside academia still today. Some historians continued to doubt Murray's views all along; the skepticism gained momentum in the last quarter of the twentieth century. "Perhaps more potent still in bringing about its demise was the revival of intensive study of archival records of the trials, and the setting of them in their local context," notes Ronald Hutton in *Triumph of the Moon,* adding that a speaker at an academic conference on the witch trials in 1991 "despaired that the public would ever forsake the mythology which had grown out of the work of Murray and her predecessors and followers." Hutton further observes that the Murrayite hypothesis, preceded as it was by the assertion of Matilda Gage in the nineteenth century that "nine million women" had been executed for witchcraft, had already become embedded in feminist thinking as well, which viewed the trials as a "war against women."[5] No wonder it has lasted a long time.

Murray's portrayal of an underground Old Religion defying Christianity merely anticipated the string of claims made by the Pagans who followed her. In order to discuss the changing definitions of such words as *witch* and *Pagan,* it helps to summarize the rhetorical claims and positions underlying them. To begin with, the fundamental claim made by Gerald Gardner (and supported by Murray herself in her introduction to his 1954 book *Witchcraft Today*) was that Pagan Witchcraft was a rival cult to its younger competitor, Christianity, focused on the Great Mother and particularly concerned with mysteries of death and rebirth. But at the same time as he portrayed Witchcraft as a religious cult, Gardner also utilized the other common meaning of *witch*: "men and women who have had a knowledge of cures, philtres, charms and love potions and at times poisons."[6] Nevertheless, his goal was to demonstrate that "Wica," which he often spelt with one c, was not only a religion but the true native English faith.

Later, confronted with increasing evidence that there was no unbroken chain of practitioners of the Old Religion linking the 1950s to the distant past, contemporary Wiccans and other Pagans would shift their goals to being defined as a valid group of somewhat-related religious traditions. In a theological if not a historical sense, after all, they could still claim to be carrying forth the ancient Paganisms, the Old Gods having returned once again—or rather, never having left us altogether.

The first rhetorical goal, therefore, was to convince the world that Witchcraft, rather than being heresy, Satanism, mental delusion, or something else, was in fact the Old Religion. Up through the 1970s, in fact, this claim of antiquity was taken literally by most Pagan Witches, and some still adhere to it. Ed Fitch, an influential figure in early American Wicca, remarked later that, in the mid-1960s, "we were all convinced that the Gardnerian Book of Shadows was cast in granite and that it had been that way with every word unchanged for centuries."[7]

However, reeducating the public to believe that *witchcraft* referred to an English mystery cult rather than to black magic, sorcery, or an "irresistible influence" was a tall order. Consequently, the second goal would be to promote a new term, *Wica/Wicca*, as the name of that mystery religion. In time, the term Wicca would escape that small, initiatory mystery religion and become the catchall name of a fast-growing but poorly defined religious movement.

Finally, a parallel movement would grow in the 1960s and 1970s to reclaim the word *Pagan*, either alone or with the *neo-* prefix. Earlier definitions of *Pagan*, whether capitalized or not, had all been negative: the term signified either a person of no religion, someone following a non-Christian religion, or, more broadly, someone neither Christian, Muslim, nor Jew, "often employed synonymously with 'uncivilized,' 'hedonistic,' or 'primitive.'"[8] Contemporary Pagans would first strive to elevate *Paganism* to equivalent status with other world religions and then, more recently, to extend its definition to include elements of those religions. Since *Pagan* and *Paganism* are broader terms than *Wicca*, I will begin with tracing some of the struggle over their definitions.

Pagans and Paganism

In the introduction to his 1972 book *The New Pagans: An Inside Report on the Mystery Cults of Today*, journalist and parapsychologist Hans Holzer playfully contrasts the then-common meaning of *pagan* with his intended subject: "'See Pagan Rites in Full Technicolor,' screamed the movie marquee at the innocent passerby. Pagan rites indeed!" After explaining that the lurid advertising merely led moviegoers to a series of anthropological documentaries about tribes in Africa and New Guinea, Holzer discusses the etymology of the word *pagan*— from the Latin *pagus*, a province, whose inhabitant was a *paganus*, "a 'country cousin' by Roman standards of sophistication."[9] He then outlines an argument still accepted by many contemporary Pagans: While sophisticated urbanites were drawn to the new faith of Christianity as the Western Roman Empire crumbled, the "suspicious and stubborn" country folk were not. "Priests would scorn these continuing habits of worshiping in the old way and referred to the people clinging to their old gods as pagan people. . . . The pagan gods were all devils, or demons, and those worshiping them evil per se."[10] But today, after the Romantic revival, "The term 'pagan' has taken on additional meanings. . . . Some very special people, highly sophisticated and frequently intellectuals, are the new pagans. A pagan, in today's terms, is simply a person who prefers to worship a multitude of gods or deities representing the various forces in nature." And Holzer acknowledges much of modern Paganism's Neoplatonic background without naming it, adding, "Pagans are also monotheistic in the sense that all gods are part of the One Force representative of the universe."[11]

The idea that at some unspecified point in the past, stubborn country Pagans had tried to fend off proselytizing urban Christians was already commonplace. Undoubtedly it owed something to Murray. Furthermore, it had already been expounded by, among others, Charles R. F. Seymour, a British occultist who bridged the Christianized ceremonial magic of his teacher, Dion Fortune, with the first stirrings of the Pagan revival. In "The Old Gods," an essay written in 1936–1937 and published in the magazine of her magical order, The Fraternity (later Society) of the Inner Light, Seymour had written of "the modern pagan . . . a lover of open air, one who worships God made manifest in nature." He contrasts the "pagan" Jesus with "the city-dwelling Saul [Paul] who founded that which we call Christianity."[12]

A digression: Alert readers may notice that while Seymour and Holzer did not capitalize *Pagan*; I do—and that is part of the rhetorical struggle, expressed through capitalization. Given the English language's conventions of orthography, a capital letter is a mark of attention and respect. Although *pagan* is still used to mean an irreligious, worldly, or materialistic person, I myself prefer to capitalize it when referring to followers of polytheistic religions, whether ancient or modern. (When my book *The Encyclopedia of Heresies and Heretics* was in production, I fought for and won the capitalization battle for *Pagan*, although I lost on the substitution of the more secular *Common Era* and *Before Common Era* in place of the religiously flavored *Anno Domini* and

Before Christ for dates throughout the text.) Thus even orthography serves today's Pagans' struggle for notice and respect.

Not all Pagan writers take that position on capitalizing, however, nor do all historians. For one thing, in the ancient world, there was no one "Paganism," nor were scholars of religion attempting to create such a category. As Robin Lane Fox wrote in *Pagans and Christians*, "So many overlapping and coexisting cultures make general descriptions of 'paganisms' extremely difficult. Indeed, there is a merit in studying pagan cults only on a small, regional scale, not least to bring out their variety and, by implication, their contrast with the more uniform religion of Jewish and Christian contemporaries."[13] Paganism was a religion of cult acts, as it is today, not a question of religious faith or creeds. Similarly, Grey Cat (pen name of a Tennessee writer), in her book *Deepening Witchcraft*, prefers *pagan* for ancient polytheistic religions, on the grounds that they used the term themselves, while employing *Pagan* as synonymous with *Neo-Pagan*.[14] Michael York, author of *Pagan Theology*, keeps small-*p pagan* when describing a variety of religious expression, as opposed to a self-conscious new religion.[15] But I prefer to stress the commonalities between the ancient Paganisms, although they were usually more ethnically and geographically limited, and today's varieties.

Even the origins of the word *pagan* are somewhat disputed. Most authorities do derive it from *paganus*, a country district or locale. "The word first appears in Christian inscriptions of the early fourth century and remained colloquial, never entering the Latin translations of the Bible. In everyday use, it meant either a civilian or a rustic," writes Fox. Unfortunately for contemporary Pagans' veneration of the country over the city (at least in theory), the slang meaning of *paganus* used by early Christians was that of "civilians," someone "not enlisted through baptism as soldiers of Christ."[16] Although contemporary Pagans' affection for the term is informed by its perceived association with nonurban life and thus a connection with the Gaian form of nature religion, *Pagan* as a descriptor apparently owes more to militant Christianity and its attitude of "you are with us or against us."

Much of the credit for the popularization of *Pagan* and *Neo-Pagan* goes to the Church of All Worlds (CAW). (For more on the Church of All Worlds, see chapter 6.) In a tract published in the 1970s, "Neo-Paganism: An Old Religion for a New Age," Tim Zell, who was also chief CAW spokesman, makes all the popular, if sometimes historically inaccurate, arguments that characterized the movement at the time:

- That *Pagan*, derived from the word for peasant, is, when capitalized, the correct term for "natural, indigenous folk religions" and embraces the categories of animism, totemism, and pantheism as well.

- That the "faeries" of British folklore were an earlier people forced by the Saxons onto the heath lands, hence *heathens*, and that these faeries were the victims of a church propaganda campaign to convince the world that they had never existed.[17]
- That nine million Pagans were killed in a "long-drawn-out conflict" with Christianity during the so-called Burning Times, the period of witch trials.
- That Pagan religions exist in contrast to "philosophical" (revealed) religions founded by a prophet. Zell also admired historian Lynn White Jr.'s 1967 essay, "The Historical Roots of Our Ecological Crisis," blaming ecological disaster on the Judeo-Christian tradition, and paraphrases it here, while reprinting the entire White essay as another CAW tract.[18]
- That Neo-Paganism in America began with the Transcendentalist movement and other antebellum utopian groups, and that it was influenced by the arrival of Zen from the East and existentialism from Europe, plus the Beat and hippie movements, to be joined by Wicca, "the last surviving Old Religion of Europe."
- That modern Neo-Pagan religions are "many and diverse," although he names only two others beyond Wicca and CAW: Feraferia and the Church of the Eternal Source, both headquartered in the Los Angeles area with some overlapping membership.

In summary, Zell writes, "Neo-Pagans have outgrown egotistical and temperamental gods, and expect no intervention from Big Daddy in the Sky to solve the problems of our times. Instead, we look to Nature (through the clear glass of ecology) for inspiration and direction, and to ourselves as the instrumentality for all that needs to be done. Thou art God!"[19] Other *Green Egg* contributors took the same line: another Church of All Worlds member, Kenneth Cohen, begins an article on Pagan theology and Judaism with the observation that *Pagan* "refers to the people, customs, and artifacts of folk or rural cultures," moving then to link Pagan theology with concepts of divinity manifest in Nature and in sexual polarity.[20]

In an ad for *Green Egg* printed within another 1970s CAW pamphlet ("The Gods of Nature, the Nature of Gods"), we read,

Paganism! What does it mean to you? Witches weaving gentle magick by the light of the full Moon? Druids and Wizards conjuring ancient entities by arcane spells? Naked dancers and the throb of drums in the dark forest? Nymphs and satyrs in Bacchanalian revels? All this and a bridge to our time. The old religions reawakened as an affirmation of the thrill of life in a world preoccupied with death!

By the early 1970s, with *Green Egg* serving as the official journal of the Council of Earth Religions—a brief successor to an earlier pan-Pagan group, the Council of Themis—the utility of *Pagan* and *Neo-Pagan* as umbrella terms had become well established. Writers such as Zell and Isaac Bonewits, who led one of the revived Druidic groups (then called the Schismatic Druids of North America)[21] were playfully "Paganizing" old folk songs in its pages, with, for instance, "House of the Rising Sun" given a new set of lyrics: "There is a sylvan wilderness/That greets the rising sun./It's been a home for many a heart/Where freedom has been won!"[22] Songwriter Gwydion Pend-derwen spoke for his group, Nemeton: "We are Pagans who have joined together. We believe in many Gods, many ways. Some of us are witches."[23] Holzer, at the time turning out a book a year on Neo-Pagans, titled his 1973 work *The Witchcraft Report*, but its cover blurb read, "An up-to-the-minute report on Pagan groups in America by the author of *Ghost Hunter, ESP and You,* and *Charismatics.*"

The word *Pagan*, with its overtones of nature religion, was a good fit for these groups, and it rapidly shouldered aside its only competition, *Aquarian* (as in "Age of Aquarius"), which had been chiefly used in the title of the Aquarian Anti-Defamation League (AADL), the first of a series of small, un-derfunded groups seeking to defend the religious rights of Pagan Americans.[24] In 1974, for example, a *Green Egg* writer discussing Wiccan use of high or ceremonial magic felt obliged to defend the nominally Christian coloration of the Order of the Golden Dawn (a British magical group begun in the 1880s), by pointing out that one of his sources, William Gray, was a professed Pagan, thus worth taking seriously.[25] Thus, for the members of a variety of covens, Druid groves, and temples of ceremonial magicians, or followers of reconstructed ethnic religions of Greece or Egypt, *Pagan* provided a common identity set in opposition to the Abrahamic religions. Zell would make that last point explicit in a latter pamphlet, "The Other People," in which he used the two creation stories from Genesis to argue that these other people were the Pagans who were not of Yahweh's creation, and that the story of Adam and Eve and the Garden of Eden did not apply to them. "Neither heaven nor hell is our destination in the afterlife; we have our own various arrangements with our own various deities. The Bible is not our story."[26]

Witch

For thousands of years, until the twentieth century, a witch was an antisocial evildoer, usually personified as female. The witch's offense was not following the "wrong" religion but her potential to hurt her neighbors. A countertra-dition of the good witch existed, but it was chiefly a literary invention, although possibly influenced by nineteenth-century feminism. During the nineteenth century, the French writer Jules Michelet had theorized a connection between the earlier witch trials, social tensions, and the oppression of women.[27] By the end of that century, Charles Godfrey Leland's research into folklore in Tuscany had led him to theorize a survival of classical Paganism among ostensibly Catholic witches. In the 1920s, as described earlier, Margaret Murray asserted a new etymological definition of *witch*, that it was related to the Old English verb *wit*, "to know," and linked that assertion to the claim that "when examining the records of the mediaeval witches, we are dealing with the remains of a pagan religion which survived, in England at least, till the 18th century."[28]

Following Murray in his redefinition of *witch*, Gerald Gardner rode two horses at once, like a circus performer. A witch was a follower of the Old Religion; a witch was any magic worker. In one paragraph of *Witchcraft Today*, he says that intellectuals and "bright young things" of bygone days were attracted to the witch cult, plus "the village wise-woman with her cures and curses," and, to round out the social scale, "the inmates of the castles and great houses."[29]

Contemporary Witches would find themselves having to make a sharper distinction, given an audience that had been raised on all the wicked witches of traditional children's books, the good and bad witches of Frank Baum's Oz stories,[30] the stage witches of *Bell, Book and Candle*, and their television sisters in such 1960s and 1970s serials as *Bewitched, Dark Shadows*, and *Tucker's Witch*.[31] In addition, Pagan Witches attending university anthropology classes were confronted with the commonplace of translating a given culture's word for "illicit or evil magic-worker, whether real or imaginary" into the English word "witch." Malcolm Brenner, a Wiccan journalist then working in Shiprock, New Mexico, on the Navajo reservation, writes of the terminological barrier after watching an all-night ceremony, a *Ye'ii-bi-chei*, "Having been the object of divine possession, I must be one of a very few Anglos to intuitively understand what I was witnessing. Yet I couldn't share my Wiccan experiences with the Navajos. That terrible 'W' word stood in the way," adding, "admitting any knowledge of [anthropological] witchcraft is tantamount [among Navajos] to admitting you practice it, because somebody who didn't know anything about it would be too frightened to talk about it."[32]

Other writers during the 1960s and 1970s also attempted to ride those two horses, claiming a connection with the victims of the witch trials while still asserting that the definition of those times—evil magic workers making pacts with the Christian Devil—was no longer operative.

- In 1964, *Pentagram*, probably the first modern Craft publication (price two shillings, "For private circulation only"), speaks editorially of "the Craft of the Wise, or the tradition of White Witchcraft, as it is commonly known." The editor, following the Murrayite line, also described it as the Old Religion, a *British* tradition, "which has come down to us from ancient times as Witchcraft" (note the capitalization).[33]
- Raymond Buckland, who with his wife Rosemary headed Gardnerian Wicca in the United States during the 1970s, writes of "witches" (lowercase), affirming, "It has been said, repeatedly, that witchcraft is a religion . . . a religion very close to nature in its origins."[34] In his 1971 book *Witchcraft from the Inside*, Buckland variously speaks of "the Craft," a "Mystery Religion," and "Wica" with one *c*. To Buckland, at this point in his writing career, there is only one authentic Old Religion, Wica, passed on in an initiatory chain.
- In 1973, Gwydion Pendderwen, who also edited the magazine *Nemeton*, scornfully reprints one of the many ads that appear in supermarket tabloids and magazine like *Fate*, Sister Paula's witchcraft courses. ("Be the center of attraction. People will flock to you. Become a certified witch.")
- Less-religious witches also spoke out: one was Louise Huebner, "the official witch of Los Angeles," who proclaims, "There is no such thing as black magic and white magic, evil spirits and good spirits. There is only energy." But the writer quoting her, Martin Ebon, assigned Huebner to the minority category, noting that the witchcraft he encountered seemed to be more "related to traditional religious concepts."[35]
- Sybil Leek, an English witch who moved to the United States, claimed to be initiated in a different tradition than Gardner's. Nevertheless, she begins her 1968 book *Diary of a Witch* with a similar definition: "A witch is a practitioner of witchcraft—the ancient pre-Christian occult religion which in Europe was called wicca [*sic*], an Anglo-Saxon word meaning 'the craft of the wise.'"[36]

Attempting to sort out the changing definitions, Margot Adler, writing at the end of the 1970s, observes that the "revivalist" Pagan Witches she interviewed were downplaying magic in favor of religion: "Some [Witches] regard [*witch*] as a word to be reclaimed, much as militant lesbians have reclaimed the word *dyke*. But others dislike the word. 'It has a rather bad press,' one Witch told me."[37] Others among her interviewees preferred the word *Craft* because it seemed more linked to an occult technology, a way of making things happen.

To further complicate things, some Satanists were using the word as well: Anton LaVey, the highly visible head of the Church of Satan, published a how-to book titled *The Compleat Witch* in 1970,[38] and another regular on the pop-occult tour of America, Herb Sloane of Our Lady of Endor, a Satanic congregation in Toledo, Ohio, also described himself as a "witch."

Given these negative connotations of *witch*, many Pagan Witches from the 1960s onward attempted to refute them by advancing their own etymologies. Granted, the etymology of the word *witch* is vague. The *American Heritage Dictionary* ("a woman who practices sorcery or is believed to have dealings with the devil") derives it from the Proto-Indo-European (PIE) root *weik-*, a word "connected with magic and religious notions" and related to *guile*, *wile*, and *victim*, in the sense of a sacrificial animal.[39] *Wit* and *wise* are shown as having a different root, which linguist Mario Pei derives from the PIE root *w(e)di*, "to see," and which underlies the Sanskrit *Veda*, the Greek *idea*, such Latin-derived words as *video*, *envy*, and *survey*, and the Germanic *wizard*, *wise*, and even *twit*, probably shortened from *nitwit*, "not wise."[40] Thus, from the point of view of the history of the English language, *witchcraft* cannot be said to mean the "craft of the wise."

Old English had grammatical gender, a feature that disappeared during the Middle Ages. The *Oxford English Dictionary* (OED) suggests that the masculine form, *wicca* (pronounced "witch-uh"), and the feminine *wicce* could have derived from the verb *wiccian*, "to bewitch," but that leaves us more or less where we were. *Witch* seems to mean "witch," not a wise person and not, as some hopeful Pagan Witches propose, a "bender of fate." Certainly none of the OED's citations from literature put a positive interpretation on the word: throughout the Middle Ages, they speak of binding and smiting witches, rhyme *wycche* with *bycche*, and speak of cursing and wasting by witches. The first citation of *witch* as meaning a beautiful and alluring young woman comes in the eighteenth century.

This somewhat tentative history of the word did not meet the emotional needs of many contemporary witches, who preferred to derive *witch* from other roots:

- WISE, hence *witchcraft* would be the "craft of the wise." The phrase "craft of the wise" is so appealing, however, that it lives on: the contemporary Pagan band Inkubus Sukkubus has a song by that name with the lines, "Across a thousand nations/And forty thousand years/The teachers and the healers,/We are the Craft of the Wise." A Web search on the phrase will turn up numerous pages making similar assertions to this: "The Craft of the Wise is otherwise known as 'Witchcraft'—a word that frightens some religious authorities. . . . It teaches spiritual ways of working in tune with nature."[41]

- TO BEND, hence to be able to change and control fate or natural forces. This is the "witch" of *witch hazel*, a combination of *wych*, meaning a type of elm tree, plus *hazel*. The false similarity comes from another PIE root, *wiek*, meaning to bend or wind, which also gave us *wicker*, *weak* ("bendable"), and *vetch*, a twining plant.

The "witch as bender" etymology was publicized by and probably invented by Isaac Bonewits. Here, with a nod to Jeffrey Burton Russell, a leading historian of medieval witch trials, Bonewits writes, "I seem to have been the first modern occultist to point out [that *wicce* and *wicca*] are based on the Old English root *wic-*." Following the untrustworthy principle that if two words sound the same, then they must mean the same thing, Bonewits merges two of the five PIE *weik-* roots and announces that "it is fairly obvious that those practicing *wiccian* or (*wigle*) were considered to be magicians and/or benders of reality."[42]

This new rhetorical definition of *wicca/wicce*, although not attested anywhere in Old English literature, appealed to the new Pagan Witches and rapidly became an accepted truth. In 1975, for example, a writer in *Green Egg*, skipping the etymology, would confidently explain, "A witch is a channel of nature forces. The word itself is derived from a root meaning 'wise,' or 'to bend, twist, turn, control, change.' Witchcraft is the 'art of change,' another form of technology."[43]

Despite eight decades of attempted redefinition (counting from Margaret Murray's first publication), *witch* remains a troublesome term. Contemporary Pagan Witches often refer to it humorously as "the W-word," and many, at least in public discourse, replace it with another twentieth-century coinage, *Wiccan*. In print, it may be capitalized to mean a follower of the new religion of Pagan Witchcraft or left lowercase to signify its anthropological sense or the witches of horror fiction and children's books.

Wicca

As stated earlier, *Wicca* is the Old English masculine singular noun meaning "witch" and a thousand years ago was pronounced "witch-uh." In its appearances since the 1950s, however, it has sometimes been spelled with one *c* and sometimes with two, and, except among a tiny minority of practitioners who insist on linguistic correctness, is invariably pronounced "wick-uh." (During the 1970s, the Wiccan writer Leo Louis Martello wrote a column in *Gnostica* magazine called "Wicca Basket," punning on *wicker*.) *Wicca*, with its hard *c*s, seems to pop out of nowhere. Margaret Murray, who did the most to popularize the notion of an "Old Religion" surviving underground from pre-Christian times, writes of capital-*p* Pagans and small-*w* witches, but she does not use the term *Wicca*. Her predecessor in postulating an Old Religion, Charles Leland, was at least aware of the term, although he connected it with the idea of "wisdom" also:

> As the English word witch, Anglo-Saxon Wicca, comes from a root implying wisdom, so the pure Slavonian word *vjestica*, Bulgarian, *vjescirica* (masculine, *viestae*), meant originally the one knowing or well informed, and it has preserved the same power in allied languages, as *Veaa* (New Slovenish), knowledge, *Vedavica*, a fortune-teller by cards, *Viedma* (Russian) a witch, and *Vedwin*, fatidicus.[44]

Gerald Gardner's novel *High Magic's Aid*, first published in 1949, features both ceremonial magicians and men and women who belong to "the brotherhood" or "the witch cult," but the word *Wicca* does not appear. In his 1954 book *Witchcraft Today*, however, he speaks of "the people who call themselves the Wica, the 'wise people,' who practice the age-old rites."[45]

Likewise, the 1960 biography of Gardner quotes him as hearing the word *Wica* for the first time during his alleged 1939 initiation, but that begs the question, how did he know what it meant when he heard it? If we accept the biography at face value, which we probably should not do, either he had already learned the word, perhaps in preliminary conversations with the New Forest witches, or else it was explained to him in the ritual circle. But if we accept an alternate chronology, as proposed by Ronald Hutton, then Gardner himself researched the word and applied it to the religion that he cocreated circa 1951. That biography, attributed to Jack Bracelin, is itself a suspect document. Hutton notes that it was "written, in reality, by the well-known author on Sufism, Idries Shah; but, as Gardner himself was the source of virtually all its information, it is effectively autobiographical."[46] And as Hutton has suggested, the 1939 initiation might itself be fictitious; we have no other firsthand source for its occurrence. If there was no Wicca until 1951 or thereabouts, the term's omission from his earlier novel of witchcraft makes perfect sense.

Wicca also appears in the Craft Laws, a collection of about 160 rules that Gardner created in 1956, according to his covener Doreen Valiente, which were "couched in mock-archaic language and ornamented with awesome threats of 'So be it ardane' (meaning 'ordained') and invocations of 'the Curse of the Goddess' upon anyone who dared to transgress them."[47] Versions of these Craft laws appeared in June Johns' 1969 book *King of the Witches*,[48] a highly embellished biography of another English witch, Alex Sanders, and four years later in *The Book of Shadows*,[49] a version of the Gardnerian ritual book published by Jessie Wicker Bell (1921–2002) under her Craft name, Lady Sheba.

Gardner was indeed fond of "mock-archaic language," as are many witches, Pagans, and ceremonial magicians, although he usually achieved at best a sixteenth-century (Early Modern English) flavor. True Old English, the language of Anglo-Saxon England through the eleventh century, would be unintelligible to modern ears, and even Middle English, the common speech of medieval times—Chaucer's English is its later form—is difficult. His Craft laws do employ a scant handful of Middle English terms, but these are in the unabridged dictionary and are themselves no guarantee of antiquity. Likewise, it is possible to envision him searching an Old English lexicon and discovering *Wicca* while ignoring the section on pronunciation rules of Old English. As for the different spellings, Gardner, although a fluent writer, had little formal education and tended to spell phonetically, which could explain the variations.[50]

If Gardner indeed reclaimed the word *Wicca* for his own use—thus far I have not been able to discover an earlier citation with its modern meaning— then that would be another piece of evidence to throw on the scales in the long-standing debate over whether he and his associates invented Wicca or merely publicized and updated an existing mystery religion. That debate, of course, involves events that took place in England from the 1930s through the 1950s in particular, and it stands outside the scope of this book. However, some of the positions in it could be summarized as follows.

One view is that Gardner and his friends were creative religious innovators, as much as are the founders of any new world religion (Wicca certainly can be called a world religion now, although a small one). Like many religious innovators, he presented himself as a reformer of something that already existed, but in fact he created a great deal that was new. Such was the position set by Aidan Kelly, one of the first Pagan scholars of religion to approach the question. Kelly was hampered by doing his work in the United States, without access to the archives used by British historians, but he began with something to which he did have equal access: the "Craft Laws" and other parts of the *Book of Shadows* that had been brought to North America. In fact, many of Gardner's personal notebooks ended up in the Ripley's International Museum in Toronto after the firm purchased the contents of Gardner's witchcraft museum that he had operated on the Isle of Man. Kelly applied to the Craft Laws and other Wiccan texts the same methods of

Figure 3.2.   Aidan Kelly about 1990. With a doctorate in religious studies, he was the first "insider" scholar to examine American Paganism. Photo by Malcolm J. Brenner/Eyes Open.

textual criticism that had been applied to the books of the Bible and claimed to be able to sort out different layers and threads of composition. While some of his specific conclusions, such as his suggestion that Gardner was sexually excited by flagellation ("the English vice"), have been challenged,[51] his essential conclusion is worth considering:

In emphasizing that the Craft is a new religion, and not the survival of an old religion, I am not "debunking" it. Rather, I am insisting on its ontological equality with every other religion, because—and this is the current scholarly consensus—all religions begin as new religions, which then survive only because they continue to evolve and adapt themselves to changing circumstances.[52]

More recently, in *Wiccan Roots: Gerald Gardner and the Modern Witchcraft Revival* and a sequel, *Gerald Gardner and the Cauldron of Inspiration*, the English author Philip Heselton argues the more traditional Wiccan view that there was a preexisting coven of witches in southern England that initiated a "seeker" named Gerald Gardner in 1939 or 1940 after first getting to know him through a metaphysically oriented amateur theatrical group, the Rosicrucian Theatre of Christchurch, Hampshire.[53] Through interviews, research in public records, newspaper accounts of the theater, and other sources, Heselton claims to have identified more of Gardner's associates than were previously known and links them to local traditions of witchcraft. Heselton, however, provides no earlier use of the word *Wicca* than in Gardner's writings, nor can he definitively show that a previous group considered itself to be an autonomous Pagan mystery religion, although such ideas were certainly "in the air" among British occultists of the 1930s. In addition, his second book records Gardner's brief experiences with other occult and esoteric groups during the 1940s, collecting initiations, a record that casts doubt on Gardner's claim that in 1939 he had found what he had always sought.

Unlike Kelly and Heselton, Ronald Hutton, in *The Triumph of the Moon: A History of Modern Pagan Witchcraft*, regards the very existence of the New Forest coven as "unconfirmed." While accepting the possibility that the traditional story of Gardner meeting some English witches immediately before the war might be true, Hutton suggests another possibility, which in his considered opinion accounts for all the chronological and textual problems posed by the other accounts, a post–World War II starting date:

[After the war], from 1946 onward [Gardner] determinedly sought a leading role in ritual magic, acquiring the perfect setting for a working group near London and then approaching England's leading ritual magician [Aleister Crowley] for advice and authorization. Having obtained both, he attempted to revive the OTO [Ordo Templi Orientis, a European magical order] in England as a vehicle for his plans, and having failed to do so, turned at once to reviving the ancient religion of pagan witchcraft, as described by Margaret Murray but in a form suited to his own tastes and experience, instead. This time he succeeded, spectacularly, and so won his place in history.[54]

Philip Heselton, who prefers the 1939 date, nevertheless furnishes evidence that during the 1940s, Gardner was involved with two other esoteric groups in addition to Crowley's magical order, whereas such involvement ceases after 1950.[55] To me, the search of the 1940s suggests either that Gardner had not yet found Wicca, or, more likely, that it did not yet exist under that name as a self-conscious Pagan mystery religion. Gardnerian Wicca appears to be a post–World War II creation.

In other words, everything else before the early 1950s was chiefly Gardner's smokescreen about the religion's origins. One way out of the origins question, Hutton suggests, would be a theological reading: "It would not be wholly just to describe him as having 'invented' or 'made up' modern pagan witchcraft. In religious terms, it might be said that [Gardner] was contacted by a divine force which had been manifesting with increasing strength during the previous two hundred years, and that it worked through him to remarkable effect." From a secular standpoint, one could speak of "cultural forces" that become embodied in certain historical figures. But in the end, "the old rascal is still in charge of the early history of his movement."[56] As for the word *Wicca*, Hutton suggests a specific source for it: *Chambers's Dictionary of Scots-English*, where it is spelled with one *c* and means "wise."[57]

In America, Raymond and Rosemary Buckland, English immigrants living in Long Island, were recent initiates of one of Gardner's priestesses, Monique Wilson.[58] By 1970, Ray Buckland was ready with his own book, *Witchcraft from the Inside*, part of the 1969–1970 boom in witchcraft books.[59] To a large extent, Buckland repeated the Murray-Gardner party line: Witchcraft was the Old Religion, dead for nearly four hundred years, which "had lain hidden, feigning death, awaiting the chance to once more come out and practise openly and unafraid."[60] It had arisen out of man's awe at the powers of nature: "Animism—the most potent factor in the evolution of religion."[61] The word *witch* came, said Buckland, following Gardner, "from the Anglo-Saxon *wica* (or *wicca*), meaning 'the wise one.' . . . *Wica* was the name originally given only to the priests of the Old Religion but, at a later stage, to all its adherents. Like the Druids the Wica were truly Wise Ones."[62]

In *Witchcraft from the Inside*, as in his earlier self-published book *Witchcraft . . . The Religion*, Buckland had emphasized *Witchcraft* over *Wica*. But in a very short time, *Wicca* would gain popularity as many American Pagans used it as shorthand for "the contemporary Pagan (or Neo-Pagan) religion of Witchcraft," a usage that left some Gardnerian purists fuming but that continues to gain ground today. As a neologism for a new religion, *Wicca* would prove to be neutral and free of unpleasant connotation, and it could be defined pretty much as the user wished, complete with at least three different etymologies that suited different circumstances. Its popularity reflected the popularity of Gardner's transformation of folk magic, ceremonial magic, and literary Paganism into a reborn Pagan religion even while the word itself quickly escaped the clutches of Gardner's line of initiates.

Throughout the 1960s and 1970s, non-Gardnerian American Witches generally spoke of themselves as practicing "the Craft" (originally a slang term for Freemasonry), the "Old Religion," or simply Witchcraft. One early appropriation of the word from the Gardnerians was the 1968 foundation of the Church (also School) of Wicca. Its founders, Gavin Frost, a British-born aerospace engineer, and his American wife, Yvonne, whose background was in Spiritualism, offered various correspondence courses in a rather nontheistic form of Witchcraft (they resisted using the word *Pagan* until the late 1970s), arguing that unlike such middle-class methods of transmission as books and Pagan festivals, their correspondence school reached a wider spectrum of society, necessary if the Craft would ever become a "strong religious force."[63]

Likewise, the word *Wicca* hardly appears in the first journalistic surveys of American Paganism, such as Holzer's *The Truth about Witchcraft* or Roberts' *Witches U.S.A.*, but by 1972, Holzer is dropping it into his latest work, *The New Pagans*, and using it interchangeably with *Old Religion* and *the Craft* or indeed for any sort of witchcraft.[64] Admittedly, Holzer is not the best of sources: his books are gossipy and occasionally vindictive. For example, after *The New Pagans* received a poor review in the Pagan journal *Green Egg*, his treatment of *Green Egg's* parent organization, the Church of All Worlds, then based in St. Louis, changed markedly. Now the magazine's content was, if not

Figure 3.3.   Yvonne and Gavin Frost, founders of the Church of Wicca, photographed in 1978. Photo by Chas S. Clifton.

"boring," then "downright embarrassing," and, furthermore, "the Church of All Worlds has been the center of controversy ever since it went on the war path against me for spelling Pagan with a small p and not giving it enough space in [The New Pagans]."[65]

Susan Roberts, a journalist then about fifty years old, followed a similar cross-country itinerary to Holzer's and included some of the same stops when writing Witches U.S.A., such as Our Lady of Endor, an independent Satanic church founded by Herb Sloane and housed in a converted barbershop decorated with photos of faded burlesque stars. Ironically, it is Sloane the Satanist who uses the word Wicca, "meaning WISDOM," in his discussion of his own heavily Gnostic theology.[66] Interestingly enough, Sloane buttressed his version of Satanism by reference to Margaret Murray's book The God of the Witches.

In the early 1970s, Wicca was gaining ground. It began a slow transformation from meaning the initiatory mystery religion promulgated by Gerald Gardner to meaning Neo-Pagan Witchcraft in general. This transformation and expansion of the term has not been welcomed by all Gardnerians or by some Witches of other traditions. For instance, one member of the Reclaiming tradition, which arose in the San Francisco Bay Area in the 1970s, contrasts her Craft with Wicca by describing it as nonhierarchical, eclectic, politically informed, not requiring formal initiation, and nonsecretive.

> Some people who are not British traditionals [i.e., not Gardnerian, Alexandrian, or otherwise rooted in Britain] called themselves Wiccans because the term is less loaded than Witch. Or they may be described themselves as practitioners of the Old Religion or Nature Religion. Or as Pagans or Neopagans. To me, this is retreating from our potential. I believe people use these terms because they are less loaded than the term Witchcraft, which comes complete with centuries of bad press. They are more respectable. I want respect for my spiritual practices from the rest of society, but I don't necessarily want respectability.[67]

A year after The New Pagans, the indefatigable Holzer published a new survey of the American Pagan scene, The Witchcraft Report, reporting that Wicca or Wica was employed by numerous and disparate groups and individuals as synonymous with the religion of Witchcraft. "I want to learn more about Wicca," wrote a reader of his earlier works, identified as "Marcia K . . . a recreation major at a Midwestern university."[68] Leo Louis Martello, a follower of "Sicilian Strega" and a leading figure on the New York City Craft scene, was publishing the Wica Newsletter while telling Holzer that he would rather be a Roman Catholic than a Gardnerian Witch.[69] Another group of

Boston-area university students maintained "a regular Wicca group"—and so on.[70] The term had outgrown the preference of the Gardnerian initiates and become the name of a new Pagan religion, decentralized and with no designated leadership, a condition that persists today.

The Covenant of the Goddess, founded in 1975, a national association of covens formed to issue ministerial credentials and to see other forms of legal recognition, listed its membership requirements for covens as

- at least six months of monthly-or-more-frequent meetings,
- that the [Wiccan] Goddess be the focus of thealogy and liturgy, and
- that the coveners be committed to "the Wicca/Craft community as their primary identification (i.e., not Druids or Egyptians [reconstructionists] or other neo-Pagans who also practice a bit of Witchcraft on the side.)"[71]

The *Covenant of the Goddess Newsletter* also reprinted articles about Wicca from the popular press, and the same 1982 issue quoted above included a piece from the *Boston Globe* in which Andras Corban, a well-known figure in the New England Wiccan community, explains to reporter Anne Wyman that going public for him and others "reflects a desire to reclaim the word 'witch' from stereotypes that have plagued the craft since the 15th century Inquisition [*sic*], when hundreds of thousands of people were killed in a holy war against unbelievers—or believers in what Corban, [Deirdre] Pulgrum, and some 30,000 to 40,000 other Americans see as more ancient and benign than organized religion."[72]

By shifting their public name increasingly from "Witchcraft" to a generic "Wicca," American Wiccans gained a relatively distinct identity. Wicca could be described as the underground Old Religion, but even as that version of its origins faded among its better-read adherents, it still offered a fresh, uncontaminated name, one that could not be confused with either contemporary Satanism or with alleged medieval Devil worship. It was clean, life affirming, youthful, and, by the 1990s, almost fashionable among young adults seeking alternative lifestyles.

Adoption of the term *Wicca* serves another goal: it separates the notion of a religion from that of a magical practice. "Witches" are expected, at least by outsiders, to be able to "make things happen." Since the 1970s at least, it has been a commonplace for Wiccan group leaders to insist that persons who become interested in the Craft because of their desire to cast spells must be reeducated to understand that it is first and foremost a religion, even while they admit that the perception of the witch as spell caster, which continues to be reinforced in popular culture, brings many newcomers to the coven stead's doors. Thus the debate continues: will *witch*, with its connotations of darkness, sexuality, and social rebellion, remain a self-description, or will it be replaced by the blander term *Wicca*, the name of a nature religion practiced by persons who see their religion as not only closer to the earth than its monotheistic rivals but (despite the objections of historians) as carrying on a tradition rooted in the Stone Age?

Notes

1. Here I follow Carsten Colpe, "Syncretism and Secularization: Complementary and Antithetical Trends in New Religious Movements," *History of Religion* 17, no. 2 (1977), 165.

2. Gwydion Pendderwen, *The Faerie Shaman* (Ukiah, Calif.: Nemeton Records, 1983).

3. Devyn Gillette and Lewis Stead, "The Pentagram and the Hammer," Raven Online, www.webcom.com/~lstead/wicatru.html (accessed January 25, 2006).

4. Margaret Murray, *The Witch-Cult in Western Europe* (Oxford: Oxford University Press, 1921).

5. Ronald Hutton, *The Triumph of the Moon* (Oxford: Oxford University Press, 1999), 362–63.

6. Gerald Gardner, *Witchcraft Today* (Secaucus, New Jersey: Citadel, 1973), 31.

7. Ed Fitch, June 6, 1997.

8. Jonathan Z. Smith, ed., *The HarperCollins Dictionary of Religion* (New York: HarperCollins, 1995), s.v. "Pagan."

9. Hans Holzer, *The New Pagans* (Garden City, N.Y.: Doubleday, 1972), vii.

10. Ibid., ix–x.

11. Ibid., vi.

12. C. R. F. Seymour, *The Forgotten Mage* (Wellingborogh, Northamptonshire: Aquarian Press, 1986), 149.

13. Robin Lane Fox, *Pagans and Christians* (New York: Knopf, 1987), 33.

14. Grey-Cat, *Deepening Witchcraft* (Toronto: ECW Press, 2002), 39n1.

15. Michael York, *Pagan Theology* (New York: New York University, 2003). Michael York, "Paganism as Root-Religion," *The Pomegrante: The International Journal of Pagan Studies* 16, no. 1 (2004).

16. Fox, *Pagans and Christians*, 30–31.

17. This theory about "faeries" was advanced in the 1890s by the British folklorist David MacRitchie and taken up by Gerald Gardner. For more discussion, see Sabina Magliocco, *Witching Culture: Folklore and Neo-Paganism in America*, ed. Kirin Narayan and Paul Stoller, *Contemporary Ethnography* (Philadelphia: University of Pennsylvania Press, 2004), 191.

18. Lynn White Jr., "The Historical Roots of Our Ecological Crisis," *Science* 155 (1967).

19. Tim Zell, "Neo-Paganism: An Old Religion for a New Age," (St. Louis: Church of All Worlds, n.d.).

20. Kenneth Cohen, "Pagan Theology and Judaism," *Green Egg*, September 21, 1975.

21. Bonewits's website is www.neopagan.net (accessed January 25, 2006).

22. Tim Zell and P. E. I. Bonewits, "Paganized Songs," Green Egg, Oimelc, February 1 1974.

23. Hans Holzer, *The Witchcraft Report* (New York: Ace Books, 1973), 135.

24. *Aquarian* was favored in the pages of *Gnostica*, the magazine-catalog of Llewellyn Publications, in the 1970s. AADL founder Isaac Bonewits also worked for a time as editor of *Gnostica*, where he may have picked up the usage from company president Carl Weschcke, who used it at the time.

25. The Wanderer, "Wiccan High Magick," *Green Egg*, Ostara, March 21, 1974. Gray, in fact, was more a Neoplatonic ceremonial magician than a Pagan. For more information, see Alan Richardson and Marcus Claridge, *The Old Sod* (London: Ignotus Press, 2003).

26. Oberon Zell, *The Other People* (Index, Washington: Pathfinder Press, 1998).

27. Jules Michelet, *The Sorceress: A Study in Middle-Age Superstition*, trans. A. R. Allison (1862; repr., Paris: C. Carrington, 1904).

28. Margaret Murray, "Witchcraft," *Encyclopaedia Britannica* (1929).

29. Gardner, *Witchcraft Today*, 41.

30. It may be no coincidence that Baum's mother-in-law was Matilda Jocelyn Gage (1826–1898), the pioneering feminist whose 1897 book *Women, Church and State* presented the myth of the "nine million" women killed by witch-hunters.

31. *Tucker's Witch*, in fact, was partially the creation of Paul Huson, whose *Mastering Witchcraft* (1970) was one of the leading how-to-be-a-witch books of the era. Huson was part of the British ceremonial magic world before immigrating to the United States in 1968.

32. Malcolm Brenner, "A Witch among the Navajos," *Gnosis*, Summer 1998.

33. Pentagram, "Before Gardner—What?" *Pentagram*, November 1964.

34. Raymond Buckland, *Witchcraft from the Inside* (St. Paul, Minn.: Llewellyn, 1971), 57–58.

35. Martin Ebon, ed., *Witchcraft Today* (New York: New American Library, 1971), 18–19.

36. Sybil Leek, *Diary of a Witch* (New York: Prentice-Hall, 1968), 9–10.

37. Margot Adler, *Drawing Down the Moon* (New York: Viking Press, 1979), 42–43.

38. Anton LaVey, *The Compleat Witch* (New York: Dodd, Mead & Co., 1970).

39. *American Heritage Dictionary of the English Language* (New York: American Heritage Publishing, 1969) s.v. "Witch."

40. Mario Pei, *The Families of Words* (New York: St. Martin's Press, 1962), 228.

41. Jani Farrell-Roberts, An Introduction to the Craft of the Wise, http://inquirer .gn.apc.org/craft-intro.html (accessed January 25, 2006).

42. P. E. I. Bonewits, *Real Magic* (Berkeley, Calif.: Creative Arts Book Company, 1971), 104–5.

43. Leliah Corby, "How to Form Your Own Coven," *Green Egg*, November 5, 1975.

44. Charles Godfrey Leland, *Gypsy Sorcery and Fortune Telling* (London: T. Fisher Unwin, 1891), 66.

45. Gardner, *Witchcraft Today*, 102.

46. Hutton, *The Triumph of the Moon*, 205.

47. Doreen Valiente, *The Rebirth of Witchcraft* (London: Robert Hale, 1989), 70.

48. June Johns, *King of the Witches: The World of Alex Sanders* (New York: Coward-McCann, 1969).

49. Lady Sheba, *The Book of Shadows* (St. Paul, Minn.: Llewellyn, 1971).

50. Philip Heselton, *Wiccan Roots* (Freshfields, Berkshire: Capall Bann, 2000), 10.

51. Donald Frew, "Methodological Flews in Recent Studies of Historical and Modern Witchcraft," *Ethnologies* 20, no. 1 (1998).

52. Aidan A. Kelly, *Crafting the Art of Magic: A History of Modern Witchcraft 1939–1964* (St. Paul, Minn.: Llewellyn, 1991), 2.

53. Heselton, Wiccan Roots; Philip Heselton, *Gerald Gardner and the Cauldron of Inspiration* (Milverton, Somerset: Capall Bann, 2003).

54. Hutton, *The Triumph of the Moon*, 239.

55. Heselton, *Gerald Gardner and the Cauldron of Inspiration*.

56. Hutton, *The Triumph of the Moon*, 239–40.

57. Ibid., 241.

58. Ibid., 250.

59. Buckland, *Witchcraft from the Inside*.

60. Ibid., xii.

61. Ibid., 2.

62. Ibid., 18.

63. Gavin Frost and Yvonne Frost, *Advanced Celtic Witchcraft and Shamanism* (New Bern, N.C.: School of Wicca, n.d.), 9.

64. Holzer, *The New Pagans*, 1–60 passim.

65. Holzer, *The Witchcraft Report*, 178.

66. Ibid., 200.

67. M. Macha NightMare, *The "W" Word, or Why We Call Ourselves Witches* (1998), www.machanightmare.com/W_word.html (accessed January 25, 2006).

68. Holzer, *The Witchcraft Report*, 15.

69. Ibid., 39.

70. Ibid., 59.

71. *Covenant of the Goddess Newsletter*, "Covenant of the Goddess Membership Requirements and Procedures," October 31, 1982.

72. Anne Wyman, "New Life Infuses and Old Religion as Witches, Pagans Join Ranks," *Boston Globe*, October 7, 1982.

☾

CHAPTER FOUR

The Playboy and the Witch: Wicca and Popular Culture

The image of the witch as extrasexy and rebellious received a powerful boost during the so-called sexual revolution of the 1960s, as ideas of rebellion and outrageous behavior were taken up in the popular culture of journalism, television, and the movies. The 1970s ended with the publication of two significant books on contemporary Paganism—Margot Adler's *Drawing Down the Moon*[1] and Starhawk's *The Spiral Dance*[2]—but both of those books were not so much pioneering works as they were outstanding examples of two genres that were already well represented: the Witchcraft survey book and the Witchcraft how-to book. *Drawing Down the Moon*, for example, while more detailed, better written, and more analytically dense than its predecessors, followed the "I go among the witches" path already trodden by American authors such as Hans Holzer, Susan Roberts, and Brad Steiger, not to mention Stewart Farrar (another professional journalist) and June Johns in Britain. Adler puts in at some of the same ports of call as Holzer's *The New Pagans*, published seven years earlier, not to mention many others. *The Spiral Dance*, likewise, stands on the shoulders of a great many "how to be a witch" books, right down to the inclusion of spells for attracting money and love.

What is important to understand is that these earlier works of popular journalism and how-to texts served, for all their faults, as a means for the new Pagans and would-be Pagans of the time not only to learn about Wicca and other forms of Paganism, but also, in many cases, to locate one another as members of a tiny, nearly invisible religious minority.

Sociologist Marcello Truzzi, writing about 1971, reflects that the "revival of interest in the occult and the supernatural is a current example of religious events that some have seen as being of great cultural significance and as reflecting serious social conflicts and strains of macroscopic importance." Counting entries in *Books in Print* under the headings "Psychology: Occult Sciences," "Parapsychology," and "Astrology," Truzzi sees increases of more than 100 percent annually during the late 1960s. In addition, the sale of Ouija boards outpaced those of the classic board game Monopoly.[3] Publishers large and small began adding books on Witchcraft, the Tarot, ceremonial magic, extrasensory perception, and similar matters to their lists. The occult thriller novels of Dennis Wheatley, first published in the early 1950s, were brought out again in new paperback editions. Doubleday, for example, instituted its Universe Book Club, specializing in occult and popular metaphysical nonfiction titles. Likewise, Hollywood studios, always sniffing the cultural winds, moved "the occult" from the B-movie range into such mainstream releases as *Rosemary's Baby* (1968, director Roman Polanski) and *The Exorcist* (1971, director William Peter Blatty).

Paul Huson (b. 1942), discussed in chapter 2, an English screenwriter, had a foot in both worlds: he was a Witch writing books on Witchcraft, and he was also a screenwriter who would help create a series, *Tucker's Witch*, that would help inject these ideas into popular culture. Huson, son of a writer and of a motion-picture costume designer, had attended the Slade School of Fine Art in London and had then worked as an art director in British film and television studios. Preferring the "expansiveness and generosity of the States," he emigrated in 1966 but had trouble initially finding work in his field. So he decided to write a book, and as he had studied with two well-known British esoteric groups, the Society of the Inner Light and another hermetic offshoot of the earlier Order of the Golden Dawn, he decided to write about Witchcraft. He was also well acquainted with Gardnerian Wicca and with the magical heirs of Robert Cochrane. Offering an outline and two sample chapters to a friend's agent, he in fairly short order received an offer from the publishing house of G. P. Putnam's Sons, and his book *Mastering Witchcraft* was published in 1970. "What had previously been the territory of Llewellyn, [and] Weiser [in the USA], and Aquarian Press in the UK, now became mainstream fare," he wrote in 2003. To Huson, the rise of interest in "things witchy" in the 1960s paralleled the rise of Spiritualism in the mid-nineteenth century—an alternative to the "bleak materialist worldviews of science."[4]

Publication of the Gardnerian *Book of Shadows*—the original Wiccan ritual manual—as a trade paperback by Llewellyn Publications in 1971 under the title *Lady Sheba's Book of Shadows* serves as a significant historical marker.

Figure 4.1.   Paul Huson in 1970, the year of publication of *Mastering Witchcraft*. Photo by William Bast.

For Llewellyn's president, Carl Weschcke, its publication marked the point at which his interest in Pagan and Wiccan publishing became more intensely personal, because after eleven years of ownership of Llewellyn Publications, he joined the Craft himself, and Lady Sheba (Jessie Wicker Bell [1920–2002]), was his high priestess.[5] Publishing the *Book of Shadows* would not endear Weschcke to conservative Gardnerian Witches, who were horrified and disgusted that key esoteric texts of their tradition, previously copied by students "in their own hand of write," were now available in bookstores for $2.95. (Portions of the same material would appear in other books of the era in Britain and the United States as well.)

Even *The Book of Shadows*, however, was the successor to other works that not only served to tell Americans about the existence of Pagan and Witch-craft groups but also helped seekers to find those groups and sometimes the groups to find one another. Instead of the one significant title, what came in-stead was a flood of books written chiefly to exploit a reawakened fascination with magic and witchcraft. Popular media also marked this renewed interest in magical religion: By 1971, the mass-circulation weekly *Look* headlined, "Witches are Rising," although the magazine's cover bore a photo of Anton LaVey, founder of the San Francisco-based Church of Satan and undoubtedly America's most-interviewed and visible occultist.[6] In the following year, the newsweekly *Time*'s issue of June 19, 1972, carried a cover story on "the oc-cult" as a "substitute faith."[7]

The publishing surge reached a crest in the period between roughly 1965 and 1975. R. L. Gault, who compiled an annotated online bibliography of key occult, countercultural, parapsychological, science-fiction, and fantasy books published in the 1960s and 1970s, speaks of "many survey books on the occult which appeared in great numbers in this period" and "the glut of quirky books on the occult."[8] In 1967, C. H. Wallace, author of *Witchcraft in the World Today*, observed, "Occult book suppliers and book clubs specializ-ing in the mystic have doubled in number in the last few years," citing sor-cery, herbal lore, extrasensory perception, and witchcraft among the subject areas.[9] From a different perspective, Roberta Blankenship, the twenty-something author of a Christian potboiler, *Escape from Witchcraft*, wrote, "Occultism has even worked its way into rural areas and the smallest towns. In a drugstore in our tiny Mt. Airy [North Carolina] I counted between fifty and sixty books dealing with some form of occultism."[10] (Blankenship's "witchcraft" consisted of a few teenage experiments with divination.)

Anthropologist Jay Courtney Fikes, author of *Carlos Castaneda, Academic Opportunism, and the Psychedelic Sixties*, in assessing the works of Castaneda and other authors portraying alleged traditional shamanism, suggested that "a huge audience participating in the psychedelic movement was looking for a compass and maps to guide them in the remote realms they inhabited during their altered states of consciousness."[11] Fikes's comments would tend to see a relationship be-tween this glut of books and the experience of psychedelic or entheogenic chemicals, which having been underground and somewhat elitist in the 1950s and early 1960s, were widely available by the late 1960s.

"The Sixties"

"The Sixties" have long been a contested decade and probably will remain so until no one who was alive at that time is still living. As Robert Ellwood noted in the preface to his own study, *The Sixties Spiritual Awakening*, "The Sixties are a period on which any number of defining perspectives on religious life, as on political and social life, are possible and no doubt defensible."[12] In the socially conservative version of history, the 1960s introduced the breakdown of society and an eruption of irrationality and unreason. Authority was questioned, gender relations were thrown into disarray, and the systematic alteration of consciousness was made respectable. To social conservatives, every decade since then has been marked by the struggle to regain the equilibrium that the 1960s disrupted, when, in the words of historian Allan Carlson, "the old social pathologies came roaring back" after the statistically abnormal 1950s—the divorce rate rose while birth rates fell.

> Attendance at religious services plummeted. A broad feeling of conformity gave way to a celebration of the abnormal. Ideologies long dormant in America (e.g., feminism, militant atheism, Malthusianism, and sexual libertarianism) combined with novel challenges such as the New Left and the counterculture in a broad assault on the existing order.[13]

To a different group of Americans, the 1960s were the decade of new forms and experiments in art, society, personal relationships, and religion. "Society was newly open, popular culture newly experimental, religious institutions (in the words of one contemporary observer) 'newly irenic.'"[14] To partisans of "the counterculture," such as Theodore Roszak, whose book *The Making of a Counterculture* was published in 1969, young people (or rather, that minority of American young people who participated in the counterculture) were resisting empty authority, dehumanizing technology, and a loss of intimate social scale. Their ephemeral families-by-choice in communal houses; their "tribes"; and, for our purposes, their covens, temples, and groves were an optimistic response to the times that blended the best of old and new. Ellwood also credits the diffused effects of the Human Potential Movement into larger society with giving 1960s intellectual life its characteristic tone, citing such "Esalen gurus as Abraham Maslow and Fritz Perls of gestalt therapy [and the Esalen center's] influential and controversial techniques."[15]

As an era, "the Sixties" is an elastic term. In popular use, the term *the Sixties* extends beyond the numerical boundaries of the decade. The decade's first five years included the ongoing Cold War, the Cuban Missile Crisis and the Berlin Crisis of 1961, the assassination of President John F. Kennedy in 1963, and the crest of the civil rights movement, culminating in the passage of the federal Civil Rights Act of 1964 and the subsequent Voting Rights Act (1965) and Fair Housing Act (1968). However, "The Sixties" might also be defined as coinciding with American military involvement in Vietnam and neighboring countries, beginning in 1961, when President Kennedy sent military "advisers" to Vietnam and Laos. These "advisers" numbered more than 16,000 in 1965, when President Lyndon Johnson sent larger units of American combat troops to fight on behalf of the Republic of South Vietnam. America's direct, large-scale involvement ended in 1973—one possible endpoint—and South Vietnam capitulated to the North in 1975—another. Finally, other endpoints to "the Sixties" might be the Organization of Petroleum Exporting Countries' (OPEC) oil embargo of 1973, and the election of President Jimmy Carter in 1976, marking a time when bills from the Vietnam War came due, both literally and metaphorically. By the mid-1970s, the era of war-fueled economic expansion and antiwar protest, when miniskirted "Cosmo girls" and natty followers of the Playboy philosophy were introduced to "free love" and the "psychedelic experience," began to feel passé. "The Sixties" had definitely ended.

As Amanda Porterfield describes the era in her book *The Transformation of American Religion*, "A torrent of countercultural protest, expression, and experiment erupted and dominated music, art, fashion, academic life, and various forms of spiritual expression for some time to come." Porterfield traces this eruption to America's heritage of Puritan protest as well as to sociologist Max Weber's tension between "prophetic" and "priestly" religion, mixed with the critique of social conformity that developed in the 1950s and was epitomized by Arthur Miller's play *The Crucible*—a standby of high school and college drama departments—among other influences (the "prophetic" theologies of Paul Tillich and H. Richard Niebuhr also are credited).[16] When we turn to the influences on American Paganism and Witchcraft, we see these movements, too, transformed by this era of social critique and prophesy. What had come from England as a socially radical but politically quiescent mystery religion would develop a political dimension that is still contested within the movement today, thanks to such leftist Wiccan writers as Margot Adler and Starhawk, both raised as "progressive" secular Jews (Adler describes her upbringing as "atheist, semi-Marxist, non-Jewish, Jewish"[17]).

Wicca, which had quietly celebrated sexuality, would also fit well with the so-called Sexual Revolution, the blanket term given to the re-visioning of sexual behavior that developed in the 1960s concurrent with the easier availability and acceptance of contraception. Folk witchcraft had a long association with sexuality, never better stated than by the fifteenth-century German witch-hunters Heinrich Krämer and Jakob Spenger in their handbook, *Malleus Maleficarum* ("The Hammer of [female] Evildoers"): "All witchcraft comes from carnal lust, which in women is insatiable."[18] This connection in the popular mind persisted into the 1960s and 1970s. Introducing "Swinging Covens," chapter 7 in a forgettable 1970 survey of American occultism called *Witchcraft in America Today*, writer Emile C. Schurmacher muses, "Sociologists might well ponder to what degree relaxation of American sexual mores in the 1960s has encouraged the resurgence of interest and practice of witchcraft." Schurmacher goes on to quote a psychiatrist, Mortimer McNaughton, who proclaims, "There can be little doubt that some of our modern covens basically serve both as an outlet for female release of sexual inhibitions and determination to achieve equality with the male."[19] Witchcraft, therefore, was sexy, and sexiness was suddenly "in," a cult with its own high priest, the magazine publisher Hugh Hefner, founder of *Playboy* magazine and its subsequent chain of nightclubs and casinos.

Other researchers have scoured popular culture for events that signal a resurgence in interest in witchcraft and magical religion. Robert Ellwood suggests that a daily television soap opera, *Dark Shadows*, which ran on ABC from 1966 to 1971, played a part in popularizing "occult" elements of the 1960s' spiritual counterculture. Its central characters, the Collins family, "did astrology, the Tarot cards, witchcraft, the *I Ching*. The show featured supernatural characters: witches, werewolves, and a family vampire called Barnabas Collins."[20] And of course the television comedy *Bewitched*, which ran from 1964 to 1972 on ABC, could be seen as "spreading the witchcraft word, albeit in a fantasy, situation-comedy manner," as C. H. Wallace observes, adding, "The significant point about this program, however, is that not so many years ago no television network would have dared consider it. Witchcraft, as a theme for mass media, would have been unthinkable."[21]

Sex and the Single Witch

By the late 1960s, two popular magazines had so influenced the social identities of their eighteen-to-thirty-five-year-old readers that their names became commonplaces: the *Cosmo* girl and the *Playboy* man. *Playboy*, founded in 1953 by Chicago entrepreneur Hugh Hefner, was a midcentury exemplar of publishing success with its mixture of "girl next door" nudes, serious journalism, interviews with opinion makers, and contemporary fiction—plus the all-important lifestyle-advice columns that taught *Playboy* readers what they needed to know about neckties, sports cars, stereo systems, mixed drinks, and the all-important changing etiquette of the Sexual Revolution. In 1962, Helen Gurley Brown, forty-two, published one of the decade's totemic lifestyle books, *Sex and the Single Girl*. While mocked by many reviewers, *Sex and the Single Girl* sold two million copies in three weeks, and by 1965 its success and those of its successors (such as *Lessons in Love*, 1963, and *Sex and the Office*, 1964) propelled Brown to the editorship of Hearst Publications' *Cosmopolitan* magazine, which she proceeded to redesign in her own image. Drawing on Brown's own years as a single secretary and advertising copywriter (she had married at thirty-seven), *Sex and the Single Girl* offered its readers advice not just on premarital sex but on low-budget urban living, dress and personal appearance, and gaining upward mobility through dating and marrying successful men.[22] As Brown herself explained in a 1968 interview, while some "girls" were not interested in "more than one man or one dress at a time . . . a sable coat or Paris for the weekend . . . my 'girl' wants it. She is on the make. Her nose is pressed to the glass and she does get my message. These girls are like my children all over the country. Oh, I have so much advice for them."[23]

It comes as no surprise, then, that some popular do-it-yourself witchcraft books copied the format of *Sex and the Single Girl*, while others took the tone of *Playboy*'s advice column, which could be summarized as, "This stuff is out there; there might or might not be anything to it, but at least you might meet some swinging chicks at the Sabbat."

Bringing the *Cosmo* girl spirit to how-to occult books, writer Gay-Darlene Bidart, "the beautiful and brainy witch you've probably seen on television," offers instruction on sensual meals, massage, and various lovemaking techniques in her book *The Naked Witch*. (Bidart, from Honduras, earned a master of fine arts degree at Yale University and is considered one of her Central American nation's recognized painters.) Writing in the early 1970s, she explains that "Modern standards of sexual morality leave the individual free to express himself sexually. Therefore, an orgy is no longer a necessary part of the Black Mass."[24] Most of *The Naked Witch* is devoted to sex and sex magic, for as the cover blurb proclaims, dropping the names of two prominent sexologists of the 1960s and 1970s, the book is "for all those who didn't get what they wanted from Doctors Masters & Johnson, Comfort and Reuben." Bidart's presumably female readers learn how to "Use your body as an altar of delight," "Bind love with ligature," and perform the "6 a.m. spell: Arise, kneel, and lick your lover's phallus to deliver him from devils that depress his desire for you." Oddly, although she identifies some of the men whom she quotes as homosexual, Bidart advises her readers to "avoid taboo sex," which apparently includes homosexuality, as well as group sex and sex with minors. Sex with spirits is all right, however. In fact, not only do some of her proposed practices seem to come straight from the tortured testimony of Renaissance and early modern witch trials, but her chapter "Thirteen Ways to Make Love Like a Witch" opens with the infamous "carnal lust" line from the *Malleus Maleficarum*.

Certainly Bidart's spells for binding one's lover cover well-trodden paths of folk magic, involving food, flowers, knots, candles, wine, sexual fluids, and other traditional ingredients, although she pushes the boundary in some respects. Surpassing "the majority of American women," who are content merely with palm reading, Bidart offers instruction on divining from a man's penis and scrotum; for example, "The bearer of stars on the scrotum is a born leader." Conversely, moles on a woman's nipples mean that she will attract celebrity lovers. (It is hard at times to tell how firmly her tongue is placed in her cheek.) A jewelry-based sex-magic spell requires the witch to "place a chain around your lover's neck, you can draw him away from his involvement with all other things so that you become the center point of his passions. . . . Kiss the chain each time you are in his arms and you will strengthen your bonds of communication."[25]

Hans Holzer, a prolific popular writer on parapsychology and magical religion (see chapter 3)—and ghost-hunting associate of the immigrant English Witch Sybil Leek—created a Wiccan *Cosmo* girl in "Heather P.," protagonist of *Confessions of a Witch*, a putative work of nonfiction written in "as-told-to" style.[26] Heather leaves Landowski, Ohio, for Cleveland and eventually New York City after her love affair with her high school principal is uncovered and her father suggests, "I think it would be best if you took a job rather than going on to college."[27] *Cosmo* girls generally entered "pink-collar" jobs and clerical positions requiring no college education, but since they often worked around college-educated men, they were encouraged to conceal their working-class origins and to appropriate "cultural signifiers of class, particularly European cuisine, art, foreign languages and good books."[28] The description fits Heather P. perfectly, as, nose pressed firmly to the glass, she enters into love affairs with various executives in her glamorous new field, television broadcasting. One boyfriend, a network vice president dropping in on the Cleveland station's Christmas party, takes her to New York to work for him. She meets "Linda," another network employee, who suggests that combining Heather's psychic talents with sex with the boss is the fast road to success. But in the long run she will end up with "Harold Tussman," a commercial artist and the high priest of Linda's Greenwich Village coven. Of course, practicing Witchcraft changes a young woman's fashion sense. "I went in for many black-and-purple outfits, usually cut in old-fashioned patterns; lots of silver jewelry."

Despite Holzer's claim that Heather P. approached him after a lecture in Hollywood and that he is only her "spokesman," the book cannot be verified as nonfiction. The text lacks consistency in places, to name just one problem. For example, on page forty-eight, Heather declares that Linda's apartment "on Commerce Street in Greenwich Village was a dream of an apartment. I wondered how she could afford it." But, on page 115, some weeks later in the narrative, "For the first time, I visited Linda at her apartment. It turned out to be a modest walk-up on the upper East Side, impeccably kept and tastefully furnished in a modern style." Able to afford two New York apartments on her clerical salary, "Linda" evidently could have given lessons to Helen Gurley Brown.

The elegantly bohemian Greenwich Village coven verged on being a literary cliché. Brad Steiger, another author of numerous books on occult and New Age topics, describes a 1960s Satanic coven somewhere in Greenwich Village in his 1969 book *Sex and Satanism*. While his last chapter makes the obligatory distinction between the Satanist and Pagan definitions of witch and quotes such figures of the 1960s Pagan revival as Sybil Leek, Ray Buckland, and Robert Cochrane, much of the book is in this vein:

> That night, the witch-parents of a teenaged girl were sponsoring her initiation into the coven. Peter watched wide-eyed and open-mouthed as they removed the loose-fitting black robe from the girl's shoulders and exposed her delicate nakedness to the High Priest. She was about sixteen, slender, with boyishly cropped blonde hair.[29]

While *The Naked Witch* is only one of many how-to witchcraft books of the period, Steiger's *Sex and Satanism* offers the typical cafeteria approach followed by such "outsider" authors as Susan Roberts (*Witches U.S.A.*, 1971); Martin Ebon (*Witchcraft Today*, 1963); Marika Kriss (*Witchcraft: Past and Present*, 1970); Alan Landsburg (*In Search of Magic and Witchcraft*, 1977); and, as mentioned, Hans Holzer, author of *The Truth about Witchcraft* (1969), *The New Pagans* (1972), and *The Witchcraft Report* (1973), among others. Holzer also served as one of the producers of the *In Search of Ancient Mysteries* television program, developed by Alan Landsburg. Anton LaVey, founder of the Church of Satan, added to the terminological muddle with his own how-to book, *The Compleat Witch, or What to Do When Virtue Fails*.

Witchcraft insiders contributed their own surveys of the occult and magical scene, including Sybil Leek (*Diary of a Witch*, 1968; *My Life in Astrology*, 1972; *The Complete Art of Witchcraft*, 1973; and others); Leo Louis Martello (*Weird Ways of Witchcraft*, 1969); and Ray Buckland (*Ancient and Modern Witchcraft*, 1970, and *Witchcraft from the Inside*, 1971). These books had been matched, and in some cases preceded, by others in Great Britain, where the Pagan Witchcraft revival had begun; Sybil Leek (1917?–1982) and Ray Buckland served as culture bearers, since they immigrated with their families to the United States in the 1960s. (For Buckland's contribution in particular, see chapter 1.)

Surveys—the *Playboy*-lifestyle pattern of broad and shallow knowledge—followed a predictable pattern. Typically, after a historical introduction, the writer begins in New York City and its suburbs, with "Julia Bryant . . . a personable career girl"[30] or "Mimi . . . a New York East Village-type witch, twenty-two, pretty, believes in demons, is married to a male witch and likes to dabble in the occult in general."[31] The writer might visit America's best-known Gardnerian Witches, Ray and Rosemary Buckland, then married and living on Long Island, or some of their initiates, such as Mary Nesnick, founder of the "Algard" (Alexandrian-Gardnerian) tradition. A visit to a bodega, a magical supply shop, in Spanish Harlem might be in order also. The author breathlessly announces that Witches are everywhere and establishes his or her authorial ethos with such statements as, "Some of my best friends are witches."[32]

Then the reader is off on a cross-country whirlwind tour of Witchcraft and sorcery. Not surprisingly, the interviewees usually have certain things in common: they are writers themselves or they own bookstores or occult-supply shops, and they are publicity conscious. Regardless of whether the writer seeks to differentiate Witchcraft and Satanism or considers them all part of the same thing, all roads lead to San Francisco and the Russian Hill home of Anton LaVey (1930–1997), the "black pope of San Francisco."[33] Even Margot Adler, writing in the late 1970s, herself a Gardnerian Witch and more knowledgeable about the Pagan community than any of her literary predecessors, discusses an anthropological study of the Church of Satan in *Drawing Down the Moon*, although she feels no need to interview its self-aggrandizing founder personally. When I created a simple spreadsheet comparing the interview subjects of seven survey-type mass-market paperbacks on Witchcraft in America, all published between 1969 and 1977, LaVey appeared in every one of them. His nearest rivals for ink were Sybil Leek; Sara Cunningham; the Bucklands; Leo Martello; Louise Huebner; the Toledo, Ohio, Satanist named Herb Sloane; Fred and Svetlana Adams, founders of Feraferia in Pasadena, California; and Frederic de Arechaga, founder of the Sabaean Religious Order in Chicago, which, like Feraferia, essentially represented one man's unique, unreplicated religious vision (the order also maintained an occult-supply shop, then called Sabarumel, as its public face[34]). All of these people except Sloan and Cunningham were themselves published authors during the period under consideration.

Granted, three of the seven books were written by the prolific Hans Holzer, and he served as a consultant to another, Alan Landsburg's *In Search of Magic and Witchcraft.*[35] In addition, Holzer, a hypnotist, developed entire chapters by hypnotizing certain persons, regressing them to alleged lives as witches of earlier times, and transcribing these purported past-life memories. Holzer also appointed himself ethnographer, ambassador, and matchmaker between teachers, covens, and would-be Witches. In his 1973 survey, *The Witchcraft Report,* he announces that the book will serve several purposes: "giving for the first time [*sic*] detailed accounts of currently working covens or communities, in some instances their addresses; and secondly, allowing those interested to practice some of the spells and incantations used by initiates and recorded by me for that purpose."[36] He also manages a put-down of his rival on the Witchcraft trail, Susan Roberts, "who seems to have developed a personal interest in Witchcraft as well."[37]

"Why People Want to Become Witches"

For all their inadequacies, books such as Holzer's and Roberts's offer a snapshot of Pagan history circa 1970. It may be a blurry snapshot, but it is one of very few from the period. In addition, Holzer was correct when he suggested that his books would serve people seeking Pagan groups and teachers. Even today, in the age of e-mail and the World Wide Web, with the explosive growth of American Paganism from the low thousands in the early 1970s to estimates of close to a million in 2000 and growing rapidly, the majority are still solitary practitioners. More than one contemporary Pagan has described how important a book such as *The New Pagans* could be when there was nothing else to go by.

"I found *The New Pagans* in a metaphysical bookstore in 1974, the year after it was published," recollects Phil Stanhope, a Witch living in northern Colorado. "Although I had intellectually adopted Paganism a year or so before, my first full-blown solo ritual—before I had had the chance to meet a single other person who thought as I did—was the Pagan Way's self-blessing ritual, which Holzer included in that book. That evening, alone in the living room of my little apartment on [Denver's] Capitol Hill, was a defining moment. To perform the ritual, I had to confront all my buried fears about 'magic' and 'witchcraft.' After that, there was no looking back. So even though I think that Holzer was a little sleazy sometimes, I have to thank him for that book."[38]

Phil Stanhope might well have joined "Diane M., a disillusioned former Episcopalian who spends a lot of time outdoors" or "Kim S.," grandson of a "conjure man" and aware of his own latent psychic abilities, or the many other such seekers whose letters Holzer paraphrased in his subsequent books.

"Ever since I wrote *The Truth about Witchcraft*, hundreds of people have approached me to show them the way to the nearest coven." Since we lack much else, we must turn to them to see who the new Pagans of the late 1960s and early 1970s were. In many cases, they were not necessarily the psychedelic explorers that Jay Fikes described—although a minority certainly were—but they were as likely to be persons who had always been fascinated with "magic" or extrasensory perception. They were less interested in serving "clients" and more interested in a unifying religious path. Susan Roberts' interviewees told her, whether in truth or for public consumption, "'Acid [LSD] and speed [methamphetamine] visions have no place in witchcraft . . . poor substitutes for the real thing.' . . . None of the witches I know will accept a candidate for training no matter how qualified he may be until he has been off acid for a year. . . . I have yet to meet a hippie witch."[39] That there were indeed hippie Witches—or, as Pagan writer Aidan Kelly put it, "Hippie Commie Beatnik Witches"[40]—does not materially affect the fact that these writers found a great number of Witches who were not.

The Pagans and Witches of the time took what they could get. As Mike Nichols of Kansas City, who entered the Craft in 1970, wrote, "There were no Starhawks or Margot Adlers back then—no one to nearly organize and systematize the beliefs of Pagans. There were instead books by Hans Holzer and Louise Huebner (at worst). And there were the historical tomes of Murray, Thorndike, Robbins, and others, as well as the disorganized 'linking' work of Gardner, [Charles G.] Leland, and a few more. And there was no one to tell you which book was worthwhile and which wasn't—so you read them *all.*"[41] Nichols's comments illustrate the importance of even mass-market paperbacks to American Pagans in the late 1960s and early 1970s. More than one person has told me of beginning with *Everyday Witchcraft*, a Dell[42] pocket book of the type sold at supermarket checkout stands.

As historical texts, these survey and how-to books document, for instance, a gradual shift from Witchcraft as magic to magical religion to—after the first Earth Day in 1970—nature religion. "We worship nature," a Witch from Philadelphia named Jane coincidentally tells writer Susan Roberts as they and two companions are stuck in Manhattan traffic, the ironic result of the first Earth Day celebration in Central Park that year. And by 1973, Holzer casually tosses out the phrase "nature religion" in describing the preference of Diane M., mentioned above. Even books such as *The Naked Witch*, for all that it seems to have been something of a spoof on one level, could have been liberating for the right reader, letting her feel her body as a "wild" and self-generating magical temple rather than as something only to be controlled and manipulated in *Cosmo*-girl style. Most of all, for those Pagans of the time who could sift through the authors' lurid mélange of Paganism, Satanism, Obeah, Wicca, hypnosis, necrophilia, fraud, self-glorification, rehashed historic witch trials, ghost hunting, Black Masses, and other topics, they offered assurance that there were others out there like themselves—and sometimes a key to finding them.

Notes

1. Margot Adler, *Drawing Down the Moon* (New York: Viking Press, 1979).
2. Starhawk, *The Spiral Dance* (San Francisco: Harper & Row, 1979).
3. Marcello Truzzi, "The Occult Revival as Popular Culture: Some Random Observations on the Old and Nouveau Witch," *Sociological Quarterly* 13, no. 1 (1972).
4. Paul Huson, January 2, 2003.
5. Carl Weschcke, pers. comm., November 8, 2002.
6. B. Vachon, "Witches Are Rising," *Look*, August 24, 1971.
7. *Time*, "Occult: A Substitute Faith," June 19, 1972.
8. R. K. Gault, *1969*, www.cafes.net/ditch/F69.htm (accessed January 25, 2006).
9. C. H. Wallace, *Witchcraft in the World Today* (New York: Award Books, 1967), 93.
10. Roberta Blankenship, *Escape from Witchcraft* (Grand Rapids, Mich.: Zondervan, 1972), 107.
11. Jay Courtney Fikes, *Carlos Castaneda, Academic Opportunism, and the Psychedelic Sixties* (Victoria, British Columbia: Millenia Press, 1993), 99.
12. Robert S. Ellwood, *The Sixties Spiritual Awakening* (New Brunswick, N.J.: Rutgers University Press, 1973), vii.
13. Allan Carlson, "How Did the '50s Ever Beget the '60s?" *The American Enterprise*, May–June 1997.
14. Bruce Bawer, "The Other Sixties," *The Wilson Quarterly*, Spring 2004.
15. Robert S. Ellwood, *The Sixties Spiritual Awakening* (New Brunswick, N.J.: Rutgers University Press, 1994), 192–93.
16. Amanda Porterfield, *The Transformation of American Religion* (Oxford: Oxford University Press, 2001), 93–94.
17. Margot Adler, *Heretic's Heart: A Journey through Spirit and Revolution* (Boston: Beacon Press, 1997), 42.
18. Heinrich Krämer and Jakob Spenger, *The Malleus Maleficarum*, trans. Montague Summers (1486, 1928), www.malleusmaleficarum.org/part_I/mm01_06b.html (accessed March 6, 2006).
19. Emile Schurmacher, *Witchcraft in America Today* (New York: Paperback Library, 1970), 53.
20. Ellwood, *The Sixties Spiritual Awakening*, 202.
21. Wallace, *Witchcraft in the World Today*, 96.
22. Laurie Ouellette, "Inventing the Cosmo Girl: Class Identity and Girl-Style American Dreams," *Media, Culture & Society* 21, no. 3 (1999).

23. Ibid.

24. Gay-Darlene Bidart, *The Naked Witch* (New York: Pinnacle Books, 1975).

25. Ibid.

26. Hans Holzer, *Confessions of a Witch* (London: W. H. Allen, 1975).

27. Ibid.

28. Ouellette, "Inventing the Cosmo Girl."

29. Brad Steiger, *Sex and Satanism* (New York: Ace Books, 1969).

30. Schurmacher, *Witchcraft in America Today*.

31. Hans Holzer, *The Truth about Witchcraft* (1969; repr., New York: Pocket Books, 1971).

32. Susan Roberts, *Witches U.S.A.* (New York: Dell, 1971).

33. After LaVey's death, the Church of Satan website was changed to debunk many details of his biography, which LaVey had fed to numerous interviewers, e.g., that he had been a circus lion tamer and a San Francisco police photographer, that he knew Marilyn Monroe before she became famous, and that he served as technical adviser for the 1968 film *Rosemary's Baby*. See Zeena LaVey and Nikolas Schreck, *Anton LaVey: Legend and Reality* (Church of Satan, 1998), www.churchofsatan.org/aslv.html (accessed January 25, 2006).

34. Adler, *Drawing Down the Moon*.

35. Alan Landsburg, *In Search of Magic and Witchcraft* (New York: Bantam Books, 1977).

36. Hans Holzer, *The Witchcraft Report* (New York: Ace Books, 1973).

37. Ibid.

38. Philip Stanhope, letter to the author, June 13, 2002.

39. Roberts, *Witches U.S.A.*

40. Aidan A. Kelly, *Hippie Commie Beatnik Witches: A History of the Craft in California, 1967–1977* (Canoga Park, Calif.: Art Magical Publications, 1993).

41. Mike Nichols, *Reflections on Old Guard Paganism*, www.geocities.com/Athens/Forum/7280/oldgard.html (accessed January 25, 2006).

42. Dell also published fantasy/science-fiction writer Evelyn E. Smith (1927–2000) under the pen name Delphine C. Lyons, who also wrote *Love Spells* under the same name.

☾

CHAPTER FIVE

West Coast Wicca, Self-Invention, and the "Gardnerian Magnet"

British Wicca came to America both as text and in person in the early 1960s. While its personal representatives, Ray and Rosemary Buckland, remained on Long Island during that decade (see chapter 1), the texts leaped across the country, where they were taken up by other, mostly young people who were creating new forms of Pagan religions. One of these groups, based in San Francisco, was the New Reformed Orthodox Order of the Golden Dawn (NROOGD),[1] which despite its self-consciously grandiose name, was actually another manifestation of Pagan Witchcraft. What makes NROOGD distinctive is its openness about the process of self-invention. Perhaps this is due in part to the fact that it, like the Reformed Druids described in chapter 6, developed in the environment of higher education—San Francisco State College, as it was then called (now San Francisco State University)—and academic life teaches the value of acknowledging one's sources and avoiding plagiarism. Also, one founder of NROOGD was Aidan Kelly (b. 1940), a writer who worked in the publishing industry before pursuing a doctorate in religious studies, which action placed him among the first "insider" scholars writing on the origins of contemporary Paganism during the 1980s. In the history of NROOGD, intellectual exploration and spiritual inspiration were paired with a typically American "do-it-yourself" attitude toward religion to produce a living tradition now in its second generation.

In 1993, Kelly self-published a short book called *Hippie Commie Beatnik Witches: A History of the Craft in California, 1967–1977*, an invaluable source for understanding contemporary Pagan origins in Northern California.

Through Kelly's narrative, we can see how original impulses, book research, and then personal experience created a Witchcraft tradition where none had been before. But we can also see how these particular 1960s Californians felt unsure of themselves in regard to the more established Anglo-American Witches, until—maturing and owning and deepening their own experience—they realized that they did not need anyone else's blessing; they were Witches, and that was that. Whereupon, firmly in the American tradition of self-creation, some of them took the next step of forming ecumenical Pagan organizations—chiefly the Covenant of the Goddess, a credentialing and interfaith organization for Pagan Witches founded in 1974 and still in existence today.[2]

When his interest in Witchcraft surfaced, Kelly himself was a bright, lonely teenager, recently returned to the United States after living as an "Army brat" in Germany in the early 1950s. Intellectually rejecting the "Thomist-catechist world" of his Roman Catholic upbringing, "and it was just as frightening as the portrait James Joyce paints of it," the teenaged Kelly bounced from Freud to Bertrand Russell to Marx in his reading, experiencing spontaneous mystical moments interspersed with depression. Visiting the public library in Mill Valley, California, he chanced across Theda Kenyon's *Witches Still Live*,[3] "a Neo-Frazerian hodgepodge of folk beliefs" but containing a summary of Charles Leland's 1898 *Aradia: Or the Gospel of the Witches*.[4]

> From it I learned of pagan traditions, older than Christianity, that had survived into modern times in spite of the atrocities the Church had committed against them—a gory bit of history I'd never heard mentioned in any sermon or catechism lesson! . . . They had believed not in a god, but a goddess, Diana, who had created the universe, and in a female messiah, Aradia, who had brought mankind a gospel of magic, of naked meetings under the full moon, of sexual love, of rebellion against oppressors. This was pretty heady stuff for a badly repressed 14-year-old, and I filed it all behind my left ear for future exploration.[5]

Future exploration in the mid-1950s was impossible, however. There was no way, for instance, that Kelly would have known of any nascent Pagan groups such as Feraferia, or even, closer to his home, the American presence of the Fellowship of the Four Jewels, which had been founded in 1916 in Ireland by Ella Young, William Butler Yeats, Maude Gonne, and others, who envisioned a ceremonial magical group whose workings would empower Irish nationalism.[6] (Yeats himself was also a member of the London-based Order of the Golden Dawn, the most influential magical order of the early twentieth century.) Ella Young in turn had moved to America and transformed the Irish group into the Fellowship of Shasta (named for Mount Shasta, a prominent extinct volcano in northern California), which celebrated the four Celtic feasts of the cross-quarter days. One member of the new American group was the celebrated San Francisco astrologer Gavin Arthur, who had known Young since the 1930s and who inherited Young's papers. These in turn would be bequeathed to NROOGD in the early 1970s, and they included "apparently unpublished essays by Maud Gonne, Red Hugh O'Donnell, and other Irish writers on the Four Feasts."

Making that connection was still in the distant future for Kelly, however, who enrolled at the University of California's Berkeley campus, planning on a PhD in mathematics, only to drop out and eventually transfer to San Francisco State. By then, Gerald Gardner's *Witchcraft Today* had been published, and Kelly encountered it in the San Francisco Public Library: "I recognized that this was witchcraft of the same general type as in the *Aradia*, and I was intrigued by Gardner's claims that it had survived from the Middle Ages into this century, and that he had been initiated into one of the last surviving English covens in September 1939. I took careful notes at the time on all the fragments of information about what was done in rituals."[7] Likewise, as the decade turned into the 1960s, he read Margaret Murray's *God of the Witches*, Robert Graves's *The White Goddess*, and Elliot Rose's refutation of Murray's work, *A Razor for a Goat*.[8] By the mid-1960s, reading William Blake, Norman O. Brown, Alan Watts, and other writers on mysticism, Kelly notes that he was consciously contemplating forming a new religion, but that his explorations at time were purely intellectual and theoretical.

The catalytic factor was the gay Dionysian poet and filmmaker James Broughton (1913–1999), who in 1967 was teaching at San Francisco State College, where Kelly had returned for a master's degree in creative writing. Broughton had a long-standing interest in ritual, and he had given his students in a class on ritual in society an assignment to create one. In *Hippie Commie Beatnik Witches*, Kelly recreates his October 1967 conversation with his friend Sarah T., Broughton's student, who approached him in the college commons with a request for his help with the assignment: "[Broughton] says the only way you can learn anything important about rituals is doing them. . . . So thinking about what I'd like to do, I remembered all the conversations we used to have about *The White Goddess* and about maybe doing a Witches' Sabbath."[9]

Kelly hit the books. A few years earlier, he had helped to script a "Goddess wedding" for friends in a loose-knit group who were already celebrating the equinoxes and solstices in a somewhat Pagan way. To that he added his notes from Murray, Graves, T. C. Lethbridge, and others—"after three days I had an outline of a plausible, basic ritual for worshippers of the Goddess."[10]

James Broughton approved the outline, and a dozen or so friends, planning the ritual performance, decided that they needed a name. Inspired by William Yeats, they arrive at the "New, Reformed, Orthodox Order of the Golden Dawn," which Sarah T. glossed as "new, because we aren't the old one . . . reformed, since we're trying to operate on different principles . . . orthodox because we're trying to cast back to principles that are much older than [the original Golden Dawn's], and do it right."[11]

The group performed the ritual at the Muir Beach Lodge to enthusiastic approval from Broughton's class and the instructor himself, but the participants felt let down: there were "no unusual changes in our perceptions either during it or after it." (That they expected perceptual changes suggests that they were not unfamiliar with mescaline, LSD, or other entheogenic drugs, unlike Susan Roberts' interviewees.) Nevertheless, they stayed together, becoming first an occult study group, combing books for information, trying new forms of ritual, and then becoming more practiced ritualists, until by the following August, aided by drummers, a larger group, "three or four dozen strong," met and experienced a rushing of ecstatic energy. As Judy F. later commented to Kelly, "When Marx said, 'Religion is the opium of the people,' he never imagined that someday people would say, 'Groovy! Let's get stoned!'"[12]

A year later, Kelly relates, the central group of participants felt a need to recognize themselves for their effort. They chose to award themselves white cords to wear at rituals—but did that mean they were Witches? There was no "real coven." Kelly was reluctant to promote the group as real Wicca, but his friend Joe argued, "The authority for doing something comes from doing it, but not from just sitting around and bullshitting about it. . . . Do we need someone else's permission [to keep on lifting ourselves by our bootstraps]?" Kelly demurred, afraid that the "real Gardnerians," whom they would meet someday surely, would not recognize them as real Witches. And, indeed, at that time, most Gardnerians would not have so recognized them, for a great deal of ink and energy was being expended in the Pagan press and elsewhere over who was a "real Witch." Raymond Buckland, still at that time the chief public spokesman for Gardnerian Wicca in the United States, would soon afterwards lambaste "latter-day 'witches' [who] have usually read, or heard of, at least two books—Gardner's *Witchcraft Today* and Leland's *Aradia*. From these they pick out as much information as they feel is valid and make up whatever is missing."[13]

As mentioned earlier, Buckland would soon reverse himself. His *Complete Book of Witchcraft*, published in 1986 and affectionately known for its large format and blue cover as "Big Blue," would include a complete self-initiation ritual, involving a self-anointing with consecrated oil and the choosing of a new magical identity:

> As a sign of my rebirth I take unto myself a new name.
> Henceforth I shall be known as (Name),
> For my life within the Craft.
> So mote it be![14]

At the time, however, the issue of acceptance by "real Witches" preoccupied NROOGD, as it would many other self-created traditions. But by 1971, when the group began to connect more with other varieties of Witchcraft, its members had their own history and more self-assurance; some had even appeared, skyclad, when two local photographers, Jack and Betty Cheatham, photographed their Beltane ritual that year, resulting in publications in *Look* and *Time* magazines.[15] Kelly re-creates a conversation between himself and his then wife Alta as follows:

> AIDEN: "But beside the fact that we dig on being creative, and that it's definitely part of the Craft, being the gift of the Muse and all that, I think we'd have to take this kind of [self-created] approach to the Craft anyway. Because our society is now completely unlike any that existed in the past; so any religion that worked in the past isn't going to work for us, now or especially in the future."
> ALTA: "You mean that even if we had some hereditary or traditional information, we have to be nontraditional about it anyway?"
> AIDEN: Yeah, we'd still have to tinker around with it to get it to work for us. And that's what every other coven does, really, no matter how conservative they talk about their traditions."[16]

"Ancient Celtic Knowledge"

In many other cases, however, borrowings were not so clearly acknowledged. As Ed Fitch had observed with the Pagan Way materials, published texts had a way of resurfacing as "ancient Celtic knowledge" or some such thing. One example will serve as illustration: In 1979, a Georgia Witchcraft leader, William Wheeler, published what purported to be his own autobiography, *The Quest*, under his Craft name, Rhuddlwm Gawr. The story begins in a way reminiscent of Fitch's and Joseph Wilson's experience: in 1965, Wheeler goes to Europe as a civilian employed by an Air Force contractor. He meets an intriguing and sexy young woman who turns out to be "a 'Gwiddon'—a Welsh Witch . . . She was twenty-three, unmarried, and a priestess of the fifth

level."[17] Through her, he becomes a student of the "Gentle Folk," Welsh Pagans who, withholding their secrets from the common people, maintain a
rural mystery school complete with enormous underground library, containing, among other things, "several thousand volumes [that] were all that were
left when the ancient library on the isle of Anglesley was burned by the Ro-
mans."[18] Considering that classical sources insist that the Druids memorized
all their teachings, this textual survival is truly astounding. Finally, after
much training, William is brought to his first full moon ritual, where we find
the priest and priestess using the exact phrasing of Doreen Valiente's Gardnerian ritual published in book form by Lady Sheba (Jessie Wicker Bell) a
few years earlier: "Hear the words of the Great Mother, who was of old
called among men Artemis, Astarte, Dione, Melusine, Aphrodite, Cerridwen, Diane."

Wheeler's attempt to authenticate his Welsh Witchcraft tradition through
secret libraries is, however, all too typical of many American Pagan leaders
who sought in some idealized period of the past an actual "sacralized cosmos,"
to use Mircea Eliade's phrase.[19] Conscious of dwelling in a desacralized world,
they picked a previous cultural period and anointed it. For many Pagans, this
has involved something in the relatively recent category of "Celtic," those
people of Cornwall, Wales, Ireland, and Scotland seen as the Other to ex-
pansive seventeenth- and eighteenth-century England. This attitude is summarized by archaeologist Simon James as one in which "the Celtic peoples,
ancient and modern, were characterized as 'timeless' . . . and widely seen as
primitive, even barbaric. The alleged characteristics of the Celtic 'race(s)'
were associated with the feminine."[20] As Marion Bowman wryly observes in
her 1993 article "Reinventing the Celts," "Celts enjoy high status in some
New Age[21] circles. 'Celtic' applied to something or someone is an immensely
positive adjective; 'he's very Celtic' is praise indeed."[22] One Pagan author,
Joanna Hautin-Mayer, expresses some insider disgust in a *Gnosis* article sub-
titled "An Irreverent Peek into Neopagan Views of History":

> For [many Neo-Pagans and Wiccans], the belief that "mundane" history has
> little bearing on "us" Neopagans has degenerated into the notion that, because
> we don't like the history that we have—for whatever reason—we have every
> right to *create* a history for ourselves that we do like. Hence we don't need to
> document where we *really* come from and what has *really* happened to us; we
> can simply invent a history to suit ourselves. . . . The view is that spiritual mat-
> ters should not be judged from such a mundane perspective.[23]

Hautin-Mayer, incidentally, creates in this article a term that has gained
some currency in the Pagan community: the "potato trap," an error "which

either bespeaks a reprehensible ignorance of elementary botany or a total lack of research." In this original instance, the eponymous potato was cited by the author of a how-to book[24] on "Celtic Wicca" as the ancient Irish symbol of "fertility and of the Good Goddess of the Earth." Potatoes, of course, are not native to Ireland but to Peru and were introduced to the Irish in the late sixteenth century at the earliest.

Much popular Pagan writing continues to seek sacred time in history, leading to such blunders as potatoes in ancient Ireland. Similarly, much of the related Goddess movement seeks to place its golden age in a hypothesized "Old Europe" of six thousand years ago, before the arrival of "the patriarchal hordes responsible for the invention of rape and the subjugation of women."[25] In fact, these Pagan writers' treatment of history-as-they-tell-it moves it into Mircea Eliade's category of sacred time, periods that "have no part in the temporal duration that precedes and follow them, that have a wholly different structure and origin, for they are of a primordial time, sanctified by the gods and capable of being made present at the festival."[26] Thus, not only do Pagan festivals or those of the Society for Creative Anachronism, highly Pagan in its membership, interrupt "profane temporal duration," but the creation of Pagan and Wiccan identities has applied the same process to secular history, which is selectively pillaged to create the sense of spiritual continuity that many find to be missing. "The aim of most Neopagan scholars is to enrich ritual experiences . . . rather than to spread historical or cultural knowledge into the academic community," comments Sarah Pike in her study of Pagan festivals.[27]

The Society for Creative Anachronism (SCA)[28] historically parallels such Wiccan groups as the New Reformed Orthodox Order of the Golden Dawn. It began as a backyard party in 1966 at the home of Diana Paxton ("Diana Listmaker" in the SCA), a writer of sword-and-sorcery fantasy novels and not coincidentally a leading figure in the revival of Norse Paganism, particularly oracular *seidr*. The name Society for Creative Anachronism was coined by another early member, fantasy writer Marion Zimmer Bradley, whose wildly popular novel *Mists of Avalon* put a Goddess-worshipping Pagan twist on the King Arthur saga.[29] Since then, the SCA has grown to a membership of thousands of persons devoted to the re-creation and practice of the arts of the Middle Ages and Renaissance, such as combat with edged weapons, music-making, costuming, calligraphy, herbalism, medieval cooking, and more. Co-founder Paxton spoke explicitly of the time-bending function of the SCA in a 1966 article: "When we gathered for the first Tournament, a catalytic reaction [sic] occurred. The moment was magic, and no one wanted it to end. And suddenly we realized that it did not have to—if we did not like the world we had been born into, we had the power to change it and create one of our own."

Like the nudist groups to which Gerald Gardner belonged, the SCA, while officially nonreligious, has been not only a recruiting ground for Wiccan groups but sometimes something of a cloak for them. Judith Brownlee, a long-time high priestess in Denver, after thirty years of participation in the SCA, wrote in 1998, "I finally decided that SCA was recreation and Wicca was life, and that I would do better to put my time and energy into Wicca," but added that SCA activities remain "the best way to find the Pagan community in a new location."[30] On the other hand, it has come in for its share of criticism for encouraging an "otherworldliness" that works against Wicca's other favorite self-descriptor of "nature religion." Its titles of Baron, Baroness, Lord, Lady, and so forth have been criticized as reinforcing undesirable tendencies toward hierarchy and high-handedness on the part of some Wiccan leaders who hold high rank in the SCA. I will never forget the advice given a fellow covener by our high priest about approaching another female Wiccan leader in the same city: "Always call her 'Baroness.'"

Other Authenticities: Self-Creation and Inheritance

Raymond Buckland's abandonment of strict Gardnerian initiatory lineage and the New Reformed Orthodox Order of the Golden Dawn's "go it alone" (but with an eye on the Gardnerian model) approach to creating Pagan Witchcraft may stand as signs of similar changes that were occurring throughout the Wiccan community in the 1970s. A 1974 *Green Egg* article, "How to Form Your Own Coven," speaks of working collectively with "the one energy that the whole world is made out of and runs on" and describes the main work of Witchcraft as contact with the gods of nature, yet skips the question of lineage-based initiation altogether. After a quick survey of possible coven activities and a discussion of finding like-minded persons and of magical ethics, writer Leliah Corby concludes simply, "If you are supposed to be in the work, you will be."[31] But this possibility of self-proclamation as Witch does not mean that the idea of initiation vanished; rather, it was redefined to be less of a "laying on of hands" and more of a ceremonial recognition that one had embarked on (initiated) the Wiccan path, had completed a course of study, and/or had adopted the Witch's worldview. In her book *Persuasions of the Witch's Craft* (which in fact is devoted more to ceremonial magicians than to Wiccans), the anthropologist Tanya Luhrmann categorizes this adoption of a new outlook as occurring by a process of "'interpretive drift'—the slow, often unacknowledged shift in someone's manner of interpreting events as they become involved with a particular activity." In Lurhmann's view, magical practitioners do not mark this shift with any particular ceremony and have no sudden conversions or insights or transcendental experiences: "There is no clearly marked threshold, no singly persuasive incident, no new explanation of anomalous events, that catalyzes the movement away from some more commonly accepted manner of viewing the world."[32]

From the participants' viewpoints, however, initiation may even be the signal that "interpretive drift" has occurred.[33] Whereas in the magical society headed by Gareth Knight, which Luhrmann joined, the first initiatory degree marks the beginning of study, some Wiccan groups offer initiation only if, first, the candidate completes a period of study (traditionally "a year and a day," but the time span is often shorter) and, second, if the candidate is judged to be suitable. Three researchers working with the Ravenwood coven in Atlanta, Georgia, which has a fairly clearly defined hierarchy, in the early 1990s found that, "Asking for initiation is an individual matter. Typically each neophyte requests initiation, much as they request taking a Craft name. Apparently they are not told specifically how to do this in classes, so many seek advice from one of the senior members of the coven or from the High Priestess."[34] Of the Ravenwood Witches whom they studied, some said that transformative experiences *began* once they were initiated, while others regarded the step as dedication to the will of the Goddess. "Similar metaphors—of death and rebirth, of marriage, of journeys and home—appeared in each initiate's writing."[35]

The idea of initiation implies both an initiator and an initiate, and it is difficult to split that relationship from the idea of hierarchy: someone passing down power, authority, and recognition to someone else, or bringing the newly initiated person up to a higher level. In contrast, some Witches, notably self-described feminist Witches, have recast initiation as more of a recognition of what was there already. In yet another response to the issue of initiation, members of so-called "family traditions" claim that their authority came from their relatives, thus freeing them from any need for a newfangled study course.

In Cynthia Eller's words, "Feminists entered [1970s Pagan Witchcraft] in numbers large enough to make a real impact."[36] Already in 1968, a group of radical feminists calling themselves "WITCH," Women's International Terrorist Conspiracy from Hell, which used street theater to mock such institutions of patriarchy and capitalism as the New York Stock Exchange, had seized the image of the witch as angry, outsider, and female and had issued a manifesto that included the words, "You are a Witch by being female."

"Women identified with the medieval witches of Western Europe: the poisoners and healers, the abortionists and midwives. Powerful, independent, ugly, vengeful, the witch became *the* symbol of female rebellion."[37] WITCH's manifesto, which included the "nine million burned" claim first floated by the nineteenth-century feminist Matilda Joselyn Gage, announced, "WITCH is an all-woman everything. It's theatre, revolution, magic, terror, joy, garlic, flowers, spells."

WITCH was not religious, yet as Eller and, before her, Margot Adler note, it was a small step from the intense, intimate feminist consciousness-raising discussion group of the early 1970s to the Witches' coven.[38] Adler quotes Morgan McFarland, cofounder of one type of Dianic Craft, as saying, "I have begun to see a resurgence of women returning to the Goddess, seeing themselves as Her daughters, finding Paganism on their own within a very feminist context. . . . Paganism has been, for all practical purposes, antiestablishment spirituality."[39] Only a few Second Wave feminists embraced Paganism, of course. Some whose philosophical roots drew on Marxism distrusted all organized religion and any form of supernaturalism, while others stayed within their birth religions and tried to bring a greater sense of gender equality into them, with varying results. "Words like 'embodiment,' 'nurturance,' and 'connectedness' became part of the lingua franca of women's spirituality, Christian and Pagan alike," writes Carol LeMasters. "In fact, the values associated with the Goddess tended at times to overshadow the Goddess herself, with Pagan feminists sometimes appearing closer to Christian feminists than to Wiccans and Neopagans who did not share the same political goals."[40]

Certainly the firebrand of 1970s feminist Witchcraft was Zsuzsanna Budapest (b. 1940), better known as Z, who left Hungary after the failed 1956 rebellion against the Soviet Union and adopted the name of her native city as her surname. She claimed to have inherited an eight-hundred-year-old lineage of Hungarian witchcraft from her mother, Masika Szilagyi, an artist and psychic medium. After university study in Austria, where many Hungarian refugees fled, Budapest immigrated to the United States in 1959. She attended the University of Chicago, married, and had two sons. In 1970, after the breakup of her marriage, she moved to California and became a strong advocate for women's rights.[41]

Founding the Susan B. Anthony Coven No. 1 in 1971, Budapest opened a shop and mail-order Witchcraft supply store, the Feminist Wicca, offering "herbs, oils, candles, spell books, Tarot, incense. Send 25¢ for brochure." She produced her own *Feminist Book of Lights and Shadows*, which more traditional Wiccans considered to be merely a revision of the Gardnerian Book of

Shadows with all male references removed. Her slogan "Hands off women's religion" was put to the test in 1975 when she was arrested for violating Los Angeles' anti-fortune-telling ordinance by reading Tarot cards for an undercover policewoman. Budapest (as did several other Wiccans of the period) attempted to fight the charge on the grounds, in effect, that she was providing the pastoral counseling service typical of her religion, an argument that the state supreme court eventually rejected.[42]

Budapest's arrest and legal battle divided the Wiccan community: the fledgling Aquarian Anti-Defamation League refused to help her, and *Green Egg*'s "Forum" letters pages erupted in a flurry of position-taking about radical feminism. "I have long considered myself a feminist (although I'm a people-ist above all other 'ists') but I'm as sick of female chauvinist bigotry as I am of the male variety," said one Ravenwolf. "Z Budapest is a right-on lady," countered Corby Ingold of Seattle in the same issue, echoing another pro-Budapest writer. "Glad to see that someone out there among those supposedly 'magnanimous' and 'big-hearted' Pagans could stop quarrelling about whose system is the 'One True Way' long enough to say something generous about a brave and beleaguered woman."[43]

When Penny Novack, a leader in the East Coast Pagan Way network, said that Budapest "turned her off" because "she came across in her letters as someone whose primary purpose was a politically separatist one," Budapest herself riposted that Novack was "lost in [a] cushy middle-class bedroom dilemma, when one of my feet is dangerously close to jail, the other firmly planted in [female separatist] Dianic circles."[44] In another East-versus-West-Coast battle, New York City occult-supply-shop owner Herman Slater accused Budapest of cloaking political radicalism in Witchcraft;[45] numerous West Coast Witches wrote back to support her. When the dust settled, one thing was clear: Dianic Witches were now part of the national Wiccan scene, even though *Green Egg* editor Tim Zell, enthusiastic as he might be about outré speculation, could not buy Budapest's claims of "the matriarchal ideal in which the Craft began and flourished for sixty thousand years."[46]

Budapest and the other feminist Wiccan figures who appeared in the 1970s had noticeable effects on American Pagan Witchcraft. From feminist conscious-raising circles, they brought the idea that "the personal *is* political" into Paganism (as in Budapest's attack on her one critic's middle-class lifestyle), exalting the fully committed, politically radical Witch against those who compartmentalized their lives into a bland, mundane identity on one hand and a secret, Wiccan identity on the other. They exposed the glossed-over sexism of some male Wiccan leaders, making it at least a topic of discussion if not removing it all together; unfortunately, a side effect of that exposure may have been that the lives of some significant male figures, such as Gerald Gardner, have been too cheaply devalued by those who came after, armed with the slogan "Destroy the patriarchy." One reads a more poignant feminist awakening in Doreen Valiente's *The Rebirth of Witchcraft*. Despite her high priestess status in the 1950s and 1960s, Valiente writes in the 1980s, "For instance, I had always thought of myself as being an upholder of women's rights; but it took a contemporary feminist book, Robin Morgan's *Going Too Far*, suddenly to hit me with the truth of what she was saying; namely, that women have no names. . . . We have status only as the appendage of some man."[47] Citing the appearance of a feminist current in Witchcraft, she observes, "In spite of the fact that modern witchcraft has priestesses, in fact they started off playing the role that men such as Gerald Gardner designed for them. We were allowed to call ourselves High Priestesses, Witch Queens, and similar fancy titles; but we were still in the position of having men running things and women doing as the men directed. As soon as the women started seeking real power, trouble was brewing."[48]

It would be fair to say that England gave Wicca to the United States, but the United States then exported feminist Witchcraft back to the rest of the world. We hear the trans-Atlantic admiration in Valiente's approval of Starhawk's 1979 book *The Spiral Dance* (Starhawk having been briefly a student of Budapest's): "The concept of powerful women, women who have power in themselves, is what seems to me to be new about feminist witchcraft."[49]

Two other legacies of the feminist Witchcraft of the 1970s are the concept of consensus-based decision making and, as noted above, a free-form approach to history and mythology that valued "empowerment" over documentation. The consensus decision-making process, already familiar to Quakers and to political anarchists, and modeled in some instances on tribal practices, offered a challenge to hierarchal coven structure and lineages. (On the other hand, people who have studied with *famous* feminist Witches such as Starhawk or Budapest usually manage to work that fact into their conversations.) Occasional critics of the consensus process will note that strong individuals seem to get their way even through consensus-based decision making, but the model of more egalitarian, fluid leadership is now firmly in place in many Wiccan circles.

Adler and others cite the well-known passage by Monique Wittig about mythology that ends, "Make an effort to remember. Or, failing that, invent," as guiding feminist Witches to design their own reality.[50] Academic historians of Paganism such as Ronald Hutton, who admits to great admiration for Starhawk's prose style, flinch at her unquestioning recycling of "the concept of witchcraft as the Old Religion of Europe, re-emerging after centuries of persecution, and embodying features of prehistoric matriarchy," when scholars of the witch-trial period find no evidence for a broad, long-lasting Old Religion. "Had Starhawk carried out any actual archival work to prove her [Marxist-influenced] assertions, she would have needed to show that the trials were driven on by new-style merchant capitalists, enclosing landlords, and professional doctors, or else took place especially in areas affected by the processes which they represented. . . . There is absolutely no evidence to support either possibility."[51] In Hutton's view, although 1960s British Wiccans had tended to affiliate with the political right, subsequent adherents tended to be more leftist and more anti-intellectual, and thus receptive to what he disdainfully labels "the California Cosmology," the whole brew of leftist radical politics, a sense of political and spiritual mission, freewheeling mythology, and "witchcraft as a system of personal and group development, self-discovery, and liberation, for women above all"—as exemplified in the 1980s and subsequently by Starhawk and other members of the Reclaiming Witchcraft tradition. Its ideas, he says, influenced the "whole radical British counterculture of the 1980s, and became part of its folklore."[52]

Much the same thing could be said in the United States, with this difference, or perhaps this clarification: the other forms of Wicca are still there. For every nuclear-power-plant-protesting Reclaiming Witch, we can find one Republican Witch who fully supported President George W. Bush's war on Iraq, or one military Witch on active duty, regardless of political affiliation. For every vegetarian Pagan, there is another performing hunting magic and paying dues to the National Rifle Association. Undoubtedly the infusion of feminist Witches greatly increased the diversity of viewpoints in what was already a diverse religion, and they brought to the religion a keener sense of political awareness with concurrent attacks on bias and complacency, but neither the Dianic feminists nor the "orthodox" Gardnerians should be seen as representative. If there is a representative Wiccan approach, it is probably closer to the do-it-yourself-book beginnings of the New Reformed Orthodox Order of the Golden Dawn.

The Puzzle of Family Traditions

In a 1980s television commercial for a firm of stockbrokers, the veteran actor John Housman, evoking one of his earlier cinematic roles as a demanding professor at the Harvard Law School,[53] intoned, "We make money the old-fashioned way. We earn it." Likewise, while some contemporary Witches earn their status through a period of training, and while others more or less train themselves, one group has claimed a special authenticity, that of being descended from a family of Witches. In *Real Magic* and elsewhere, Isaac Bonewits separated out two categories, family traditions, or "fam-trads," and immigrant traditions, or "imm-trads," but in actual practice, the two frequently overlap, so I will treat them together.

In *Secrets, Gossip, and Gods*, a work about the changing face of the Afro-Brazilian religion of Candomblé, Paul Christopher Johnson defines the practice of "secretism" as "the milling of the pretense and reputation of secrecy; not that which cannot be spoken, but rather how the rule to not speak it goes around; not the contents of secrets, but rather secrecy as a discursive framing of power, a hermeneutic strategy, and as constitutive of social groups and authorities." In Johnson's view, as Candomblé moved from being truly secret—illegal, in fact—during Brazilian slavery times, to being quasi-illegal, to being less persecuted but nevertheless avoiding publicity until the early twentieth century, and finally to becoming public and even a "cipher of exotic" more recently, complete with a body of scholarly and popular books and Web sites, "secretism" has remained and even gained importance.[54] When Candomblé becomes more accessible and textual, as opposed to completely "mouth to ear" (in the Craft phrase) and initiatory, its adherents employ the discourse about secrets (their possession, not their content) "to forward and broker claims of prestige in the intrareligious competition among terreiros [centers of worship]."[55]

Despite the vast difference in culture and history between Candomblé and Wicca, a parallel exists.[56] In the area of intrareligious competition, Wiccans deploy claims of ancestry and roots in some European homeland (typically in the so-called Celtic fringe of Scotland, Ireland, Wales, and Brittany, but also elsewhere in Europe) as a means of gaining prestige. In the case of Lady Sheba, the claim was that the texts of Gardnerian Witchcraft—which can be demonstrated to have been created during the 1950s—were "handed down by word of mouth during the time of persecution." Yet a more recent edition of her book from the same publisher, Llewellyn Publications, attributes this indisputably Gardnerian material to a family witchcraft tradition from the hills of Kentucky.

Similarly, marketing material for a more recent Llewellyn book, *Grimoire for the Green Witch*, announces that it is "based on family traditions."[57] One skeptical reviewer, commenting on the book *Ways of the Strega*, which purported to update an Italian version of the Old Religion[58] for modern times, observes that, despite author Raven Grimassi's (a pseudonym) authoritative-sounding claim that "The Aridian Tradition [as in *Aradia*, presumably], originally established in North America as a branch of the Tanarra [given as a name for the Old Religion in 'central Italy'—the Romagna?], is based upon a blending of the Triad Traditions in an attempt to restore the original Tradition which Aradia had returned to the people," a close reading of Grimassi's books in fact reveals virtually no material that is not found either in Charles Leland's books from a century earlier or in a sort of generic, post-Gardnerian Wicca. Although Grimassi says that this "way of the strega" came to America with his relatives, he (unlike Leland translator Mario Pazzaglini[59]) never names them or interacts with them in print. Given Leland's concentration on Tuscan sources, the reviewer, Silvio Baldassare, concludes by saying of Grimassi's reworking of the older folklorist's books:

> One American scholar of new religions dismissed Grimassi's work as "Gardnerian Wicca with marinara sauce." But marinara sauce is typical of southern Italian cooking. Perhaps one should say instead, *Wicca alla Fiorentina* (Wicca Florentine-style).[60]

Nevertheless, examples are legion of Witchcraft teachers wrapping themselves in the prestige of "family" or "hereditary" lineages, using such language as "I am an initiate/elder of a Celtic Craft (not Wiccan, thank you very much) Trad[ition] that shows every sign of being derived from the hereditary practices of a Welsh extended family that came over to the US/Canada in the 1800s."[61] Compare the claim made by Heather Botting, at the time the Wiccan chaplain at the University of Victoria, British Columbia: "I have it direct from two individuals who are family traditionalists that their own memories take them back to discussion with pagans who called themselves 'the Wicca' as early as the 1870s and 1880s. Given that one was from the Bristol witches and the other from the Welsh, I take their word as more credible than that of any armchair speculator or 'historian' in the later part of the 20th century."[62] To put Botting's remarks in context, they were written shortly after the publication of *Triumph of the Moon*, and the so-called armchair historian under attack is Ronald Hutton, who writes rather skeptically about several icons of allegedly pre-Gardnerian British Witchcraft, such as Sybil Leek and George Pickingill, noting for example that "of all the educated and literate people who are supposed to have visited or entertained Pickingill [allegedly the head of numerous covens a century ago in southeastern England], not a single one left any written reference to him."[63]

Botting holds a doctorate in anthropology, and anthropologists usually strive to do fieldwork, although they, like historians, do read books, perhaps even in their armchairs. Yet Botting's claim has this in common with virtually every claim to family witchcraft status that I have encountered: it is what newspaper reporters call a "one-source story." Her claim is backed by neither fieldwork nor documentary sources. Hutton himself makes the same skeptical judgment about the Pickingill material, as presented through the 1970s and subsequently by the writer E. W. Liddell and others: "There are two classic means of vindicating a body of evidence. One is by independent witnesses, and the other is by supporting documentation. None of the former has emerged. . . . He [Liddell] is the sole source of testimony for [the Pickingill witches'] very existence. . . . The situation regarding documentary evidence is no better."[64]

What has happened is more of a reinterpretation than a continuation of family-based Witchcraft, which is always conveniently undocumented. Since the creation of the Gardnerian Craft, with its claim that Witchcraft is a Pagan religion rather than either miscellaneous spell casting or Satan worship, many contemporary Pagan Witches have sought to augment their prestige by embroidering some family connection to magic working, Spiritualism, Theosophy, divination, water witching (dowsing), astrology, or the like. For example, were I to claim to be a family-tradition witch, I would proceed on these lines: My grandmother, Metha Hillemann, grew up in a large, rural, German-immigrant family in southern Missouri. She was the seventh child, and she did claim that this gave her a sort of second sight. Certainly, when I was a footloose, rebellious teenager, she had a knack for coming through with a gift, for instance, of just enough money to buy a bus ticket when I needed to travel to another city. How seriously she took her "seventh-child" powers, I cannot say, and since she died in 1978, I cannot ask her. She came from a strict Missouri Synod Lutheran family but was not a regular churchgoer.

Were I to construct my "fam-trad" Witch identity, I would now have three elements in place. First would be the ethnic connection, which could be fleshed out with references to the rich tradition of German folk and ceremonial magic, notably such books as *Pows-Wows, or the Long-Lost Friend* (in German, *Der Lange Verborgene Freund*), written about 1819 by a German-American folk magician, John George Hohman. Hohman lived in Berks County, Pennsylvania, whereas the Hillemanns left their village in Lower Saxony, took ship in Hamburg, sailed to New Orleans, and then traveled up the Mississippi River to southeastern Missouri, but never mind. The second element would be Metha's avoidance of churchgoing, which although it might have had more to do with my Scots-English grandfather's similar attitude, could be reinterpreted as a sign of Pagan leanings. Third, there is the rural Missouri connection. While Metha Hillemann did not grow up precisely on the Ozark Plateau, she was not too very far away—just two counties to the east—and thus I could further support my claims by careful use of

Vance Randolph's *Ozark Magic and Folklore* (originally published as *Ozark Superstitions*).[65] And, were I to claim that my grandmother (who is not present to be questioned) taught me various folk practices while evidencing hostility to Christianity, I would be in the good company of other, better-known figures of the Pagan revival, such as Alex Sanders and Sybil Leek, both English witches who claimed to have been taught by their older relatives. The entirely spurious initiation-by-grandmother tale that Sanders spun for June Johns, an English journalist, in the 1960s gave birth to another bit of Pagan slang, "the grandmother story," and I have just created my own.

Actually, had he been possessed of a more Pagan sensibility and read Robert Graves, Vance Randolph (1892–1980) could well have been the Gerald Gardner of America. Born in eastern Kansas, he studied psychology at the graduate level but turned to fiction writing, folklore collecting, and musicology. (His wife, an English professor at the University of Arkansas, was also a folklore collector.) As a musicologist, he was an associate of the better-known folk song collector Alan Lomax; Randolph is credited with collecting and saving the song "May the Circle be Unbroken," now a standard in gospel, bluegrass, and "roots music" repertoires. In the preface to *Ozark Superstitions*, Randolph blazes the trail since followed by dozens of "fam-trad" Witches:

> It has been said that the Ozarker got his folklore from the Negro, but the fact is that Negroes were never numerous in the hill country, and there are many adults in the Ozarks today [1940s] who have never even seen a Negro. Another view is that the hillman's superstitions are largely of Indian origin, and there may be a measure of truth in this; the pioneers did mingle freely with the Indians, and some of our best Ozark families still boast of their Cherokee blood. My own feeling is that most of the hillman's folk beliefs came with his ancestors from England or Scotland. I believe that a comparison of my material with that recorded by British antiquarians will substantiate this opinion.[66]

Randolph's 1947 book is a collection of ghost stories; weather lore; tales relating to death and burial; ways of managing plant, animal, and human fertility; and superstitions about every area of rural life. His romantic love of all-but-forgotten lore, out-of-the-way places, tales of the supernatural and the sexual, and premodern ways of thinking make him an intellectual fellow traveler of Gardner or of Rudyard Kipling, parts of whose *Puck of Pook's Hill* have been passed off as genuine Pagan survivals. Indeed, all that is missing from Randolph's collection is a James Frazer– or Edward Tylor–style discussion of the survival of Pagan practices in the Ozark backwoods. But such a discussion is not necessary, for the same attitudes about Pagan survivals in the "fossilized" countryside that Hutton discusses in his "Finding a Folklore" chapter of *Drawing Down the Moon* took root in an attenuated form in the United States. Perhaps part of the credit indeed goes to musicologists who extolled the survival of old ballads (at least as old as the early eighteenth century) in the hills of Virginia or Kentucky, combined with the slightly overstated belief that I have often heard that somewhere "back in the hills" there are, or were until recently, persons speaking "pure Elizabethan English." Add to this the fact that the highland South has long been a fertile ground for self-proclaimed preachers and for the most Dionysian forms of Protestant Christianity: snake handlers who "take up serpents" (and periodically die of snakebite all the same) and "Holy Rollers," ecstatic Pentecostal Christians who speak in tongues and, "slain in the spirit," fall unconscious to the ground.[67] It is not coincidental that those "fam-trad" Witches who do not claim recent immigrant roots often, instead, emphasize their roots in the Southern mountains or the Ozark hills, Jessie Wicker "Lady Sheba" Bell being just the best known.

Randolph's discussion of Ozark witchcraft is fairly brief: his witches are usually women (otherwise, a "he-witch") "who had dealings with the Devil and thereby acquired some supernatural powers." These witches display some of the same powers described in earlier European witch trials, such as being able to draw fresh milk from a rag (the milk, of course, coming from a neighbor's cow). An injury done to an enormous cat, for example, might be followed by the discovery that a nearby woman suffered the identical injury. According to Randolph's informants—he does not say that he personally encountered such things—the necessary "conjure words and old sayin's must be learned from a member of the opposite sex. Another thing to be remembered is that the secret doctrines must pass only between blood relatives, or between persons who have been united in sexual intercourse. Thus it is that every [female] witch obtains her unholy wisdom either from a lover or from a male relative."[68]

This necessity for sexual initiation was seized upon by Aidan Kelly, who wrote informally in 2002 that Randolph's Ozark witches were one of only "four credible cases" of American traditional witchcraft that he had located, and that all four used sexual initiation.[69] (One of Kelly's four was Joe Wilson's experience with Sean/Mac in 1962, but Wilson does not mention a sexual initiation.)

Kelly's other two instances are intriguing, however. One involves a late-nineteenth-century magical order called the Order of the Magi, founded by Olney Richmond in Chicago in the 1890s. Richmond, according to one of his magical descendents, left three branches of students behind him, some of them blood kin and some of them not. Cat Chapin-Bishop, a psychologist who has researched Richmond, describes him as "a farmer's son who seems to have been highly intelligent but not extensively educated," with possible connections to the nineteenth-century utopian Spiritualist Andrew Jackson Davis. "He never wrote of himself as a witch, nor of his group as a coven," she writes, but his "temple" performed rituals with Masonic, Spiritualist, and astrological elements. From Richmond, the tradition passed to Thomas Giles, whom I mentioned earlier as one of the founders of the widely influential Pagan Way. Kelly describes Giles as "a Witch of a home-grown American Tradition that began with Olney Richmond . . . and passed on to [Giles] by his mentor, the Chicago bookseller Donald Nelson. In his own practice, Giles had begun blending the folk-magic practices of his own Tradition with the Gardnerian procedures coming to light, and moving more and more toward Gardnerianism because of its usefulness, as apparently all traditional American Witches did."[70]

What Chapin-Bishop correctly realizes is that such homegrown ceremonial/Masonic/Spiritualist/astrological practices were easily relabeled as Pagan Witchcraft *after* Gardner's writing and practices made such a labeling possible. Likewise, the sex-magic writing of another self-educated nineteenth-century American magician, Paschal Beverly Randolph, were reprinted and recycled by Pagans in the 1970s. "I suspect that a number of hereditary or family traditions reflect a similar synthesis of many occult elements, and especially those of astrology and Spiritualism. That is less because magic is not taught in families than because magickal practitioners love to learn, to borrow, and to create," Chapin-Bishop concludes. "As fashions shifted and changed in the occult (as they do), some of the heirs of these traditions began to speak and think of their work as witchcraft."[71] By contrast, ceremonial magicians such as Richmond were and are less likely to think of a Pagan-Christian divide than of an exoteric-esoteric distinction; thus, their original teaching might and could have been presented within an ostensibly Christian framework, even as Dion Fortune's Society of Inner Light would be a few decades later.

Besides the case of Olney Richmond and his magical heirs, who included some of the key figures in the Pagan Way, Kelly's fourth example is the Harpy Coven, supposedly active in the then-small logging and farming town of Bend, Oregon, in the 1930s (other sources[72] say Ashland, Oregon, which is roughly two hundred miles distant by road). "The coven was quite eclectic, mixing [Hawaiian] huna with varieties of folk magic more common in the continental United States."[73] The one source (thus far) on the Harpy Coven is Victor Anderson (1917–2001), certainly an influential figure in West

Coast Paganism. Born on a ranch near Clayton, in northeastern New Mexico, Anderson lost almost all of his eyesight in an accident when he was two years old.

"Years of surgery and treatment only further limited the tiny fragment of sight left to him," said Gwydion Pendderwen, who met Victor and Cora Anderson in 1959 in the Bay Area of California. He was thirteen at the time and got into a fight with the Andersons' son, Victor Elon, but as often happens with boys that age, the two ended as buddies, and young Tom (as he was then known) became a family friend. In my conversations with Pendderwen about his early visits with the Andersons, before the former's death in 1982, he described Victor as irascible, intriguing, and prone to answer a straight question with a seemingly nonsensical reply that threw the question back at the asker. In an unpublished essay, "Anatomy of a Witch," Pendderwen writes, "I do service to my teacher and whomsoever he wishes. I wash his pots and take dictation for him. I bring him food when he is sick; and he comforts me when I am depressed. I love him well, and he teaches me."

When he was a boy, Anderson's parents apparently moved to Bend, on the east side of the Cascade Range. In Oregon, he attended a school for the blind, and in 1944 he met his future wife, Cora, in Bend. In her memoir, *Fifty Years in the Feri Tradition*, which is chronologically vague, she writes of their early years:

> Besides working to earn a living we did rituals and worked on experiments and studied the history of Witchcraft. Most of what we found were bits and pieces from various books including the Bible and much hidden in poetry. . . . In the fifties we were able to get a few more books relating to the Craft. Victor received a letter from Gerald Gardner and they corresponded for awhile. We could see a pattern forming in the knowledge of the Craft. It was becoming more open.[74]

Victor Anderson was a man of small stature, but with a strong and resonant voice. He made his living as a musician, usually playing the accordion in dance bands. To Anderson, his short stature connected to his belief that "a small slender dark people" came from Africa thousands of years ago and spread throughout the world, becoming the literal race of little people known as *menehune* in Hawaii, fairies in Western Europe, and so on. "Fairy was originally spelled Feri which means the things of magic."[75] Thus Anderson's teaching, and the variants of it passed on to his students in different decades and subsequently modified by them in their own several ways,[76] is known as the Feri (or Fairy or Faerie) Tradition. Anderson's teachings rely a great deal on the Hawaiian *huna* magical system as it is described in the works of Max

Freedom Long, and in their writing, he and Cora freely move between British Wicca, Huna, Voudoun, and other terminologies, since they believed that all of them expressed an underlying unified system of Feri magic. "He was allied spiritually with all the indigenous traditions of the planet."[77]

A collection of Anderson's ecstatic, devotional, and humorous poetry, *Thorns of the Blood Rose*, was privately published in 1970 and reprinted by Gwydion Pendderwen in 1980. Pendderwen put some of Anderson's lyrics to music on his 1975 album, *Songs for the Old Religion*, arguably the first nationally played collection of Pagan music, and for many hearers, their first introduction to Anderson's work, since he rarely traveled. After Anderson's death, Penny Novack assessed his impact from her viewpoint on the East Coast:

> To us, our beloved copy of his book of poetry and the songs which were his from Gwydion's first album tied together a sense that our community to a future, national Pagan community could happen. . . . In the late sixties and seventies, these were the basis of much of what our children understood about the Old Religion though they were too shy to ask about the meaning of "Song to Mari." These are our history, but what we did not know was that much else which is our history and our culture flowed out from the work of Victor and Cora Anderson. In teaching, they created a huge pool of talented, intelligent Witches and Pagans whose huge body of work has deeply influenced the entire nation. . . . No other single source in this country has had the tremendous impact of Victor and Cora Anderson.[78]

In terms of research, however, nothing to my knowledge has been done on the Harpy Coven comparable to Philip Heselton's work on tracking down the possible members of the supposed New Forest Coven that he believes initiated Gerald Gardner in 1939.[79] Aidan Kelly published what he claimed were the names of several of its members in his 1991 study of Wiccan origins, based on research done by Valerie Voigt, another studious Bay Area Witch (she served in the 1980s as coordinator of the Pagan, Occult, and Witchcraft Special Interest Group for Mensa and as editor of its newsletter, *Pagana*). Certainly it would seem that of all the various claimants to a pre-Gardnerian Witchcraft tradition, the Harpy Coven and the Andersons offer one of the most promising possibilities. Other descriptions of pre-Gardnerian covens have been collected by J. Gordon Melton, director of the Institute for the Study of American Religion in Santa Barbara, California, and a noted scholar of new religious movements.

What seems to me unlikely is that any of these groups considered themselves to be following a self-described Pagan tradition, as opposed to a sort of

Gnostic counter-Christianity, or, as in the case of many ethnic magic workers, considered themselves to be good Christians who simply feel that God and the saints at times need a bit of encouragement or assistance (such people, as in the case of some Mexican-American *curanderas* I have encountered, may call themselves "witches" in a humorous-ironic way, but they do not encourage the term on others' lips). At this time, therefore, I am inclined to a parsimonious reading of the evidence, which would suggest that these magic workers who chose to identify themselves as Pagan, such as the Andersons, seamlessly modified their practices to mesh to some degree with the Gardnerian model, while perhaps retaining enough distinctions to support a separate identity. (Followers of the Feri Tradition are likely to be quite vocal about the fact that they are not "Wiccan.")

Reading between the lines of Cora Anderson's memoir, quoted above, I think that it is most likely that the Andersons read of Gardner's work in the 1950s, as did many other Americans, and wrote to him to learn more—although her version makes it sound almost as though Gardner first heard of and consulted her husband. In doing so, they would have followed what appears to have been the common pattern of using the Gardnerian model as a sort of "style guide," for from the 1950s through the 1970s, it was still invested with the glamour of being the Old Religion, as proclaimed with the authority of Margaret Murray, and it thus seemed to have the greatest prestige of all.

Despite Witches' affection for the myth of the lineage-based coven that takes students through extensive training and into initiation, a number of the significant figures in the rise of Pagan Witchcraft in America turn out to have been self-taught, inspired by written texts, or introduced to the idea of magic (but not necessarily "magical religion") through a variety of folk-magic practitioners—or some combination of the above. More than half were men (also true in revived Druidism, Ásatrú, and other reconstructionist Paganisms), and, in several significant instances, such as those of Joe Wilson and Ed Fitch, the United States Department of Defense played an unwitting part in the Pagan revival by supplying the logistics to put them in touch with their religious teachers.

Before the late 1950s, there were those persons who were called "witches" in the popular sense, particularly women who were fortune-tellers, Tarot card readers, spell casters, and the like. Contemporary Pagans who counted such a person in their ancestry could gain additional prestige in the new Pagan community by claiming to be a "hereditary" or "family tradition" Witch; however, there is no clear documentary evidence for Witchcraft as a self-consciously Pagan counterreligion to Christianity prior to the 1950s and the arrival of Gardner's writings on these shores. When Gardner's ideas did arrive, they carried the seductive glamour of Margaret Murray's theory of a widespread Western European Pagan "Old Religion," not to mention her professorial approval in print. Thus, like the magnet under the sheet of paper in the traditional demonstration of a magnetic field, Gardner's ideas caused all the iron filings scattered on top of the sheet of paper to align themselves in relationship to this "magnet."

In the mid- to late 1970s, a new form of Wicca arose, informed by Second Wave feminism and, in some cases, valuing all-female groups more than those of mixed gender. Despite some initial conflicts between "old" and "new" Wiccans once again, this feminist Wicca became a strong thread in the new weaving of contemporary Witchcraft. Exported back to Europe either through the books of Starhawk and Budapest or, in some instances, through their students, it attracted the notice of such Wiccan writers as Stewart Farrar and Doreen Valiente in the 1980s, and as Ronald Hutton writes, "Feminist witchcraft of the American sort . . . deeply permeated the whole radical British counterculture of the 1980s and became part of its folklore."[80] But not all American Pagans were keeping a wary eye on their British counterparts, who tended to be perceived as more rooted and authentic. Some, instead, had made entirely new beginnings that owed their inspiration to personal vision and unique responses to the impulse to create other forms of Paganism and nature religion.

Notes

1. NROOGD is often pronounced informally as "nah-ROO-gud." The organization still exists.

2. The Covenant of the Goddess website is www.cog.org (accessed January 25, 2006).

3. Theda Kenyon, *Witches Still Live: A Study of the Black Art Today* (New York: I. Washburn, 1929).

4. Charles Godfrey Leland, *Aradia, or the Gospel of the Witches*, trans. Mario Pazzaglini and Dina Pazzaglini (Blaine, Wash.: Phoenix Publishing, 1998). This centennial edition includes both Leland's original text, together with a retranslation of those portions written in Italian, and additional critical essays.

5. Aidan A. Kelly, *Hippie Commie Beatnik Witches: A History of the Craft in California, 1967–1977* (Canoga Park, Calif.: Art Magical Publications, 1993), 8. Much of *Hippie Commie Beatnik Witches* appeared first as articles in the NROOGD magazine, *The Witches' Trine*.

6. At that time, all of Ireland was part of the British Empire.

7. Kelly, *Hippie Commie Beatnik Witches*, 13.

8. Elliot Rose, A *Razor for a Goat: A Discussion of Certain Problems in the History of Witchcraft and Diabolism* (Toronto: University of Toronto Press, 1962).

9. Kelly, *Hippie Commie Beatnik Witches*, 27.

10. Ibid., 27.

11. Ibid., 29.

12. Ibid., 33.

13. Raymond Buckland, *Witchcraft from the Inside* (St. Paul, Minn.: Llewellyn 1971), 79.

14. Raymond Buckland, *Buckland's Complete Book of Witchcraft* (St. Paul, Minn.: Llewellyn, 1986), 45. "So mote it be" is another borrowing from Freemasonry.

15. *Time*, "Occult: A Substitute Faith," June 19, 1972; B. Vachon, "Witches Are Rising," *Look*, August 24, 1971.

16. Kelly, *Hippie Commie Beatnik Witches*, 44–45.

17. Rhuddlwm Gawr, *The Quest* (Smyrna, Ga.: Pagan Grove Press, 1979), 12.

18. Ibid., 15–16.

19. Mircea Eliade, *The Sacred and the Profane*, trans. Willard R. Trask (1957; repr., New York: Harcourt Brace Jovanovich, 1959), 17.

20. Simon James, *The Atlantic Celts: Ancient People or Modern Invention* (Madison: University of Wisconsin Press, 1999), 55.

21. Contemporary Pagans generally have an aversion to the term "New Age," which Bowman intends in a broader sense; however, the gist of her observation fits the Pagans perfectly as well.

22. Marion Bowman, "Reinventing the Celts," *Religion* 23 (1993).

23. Joann Hautin-Mayer, "When Is a Celt Not a Celt?" *Gnosis*, Summer 1998. Emphasis in the original.

24. Edain McCoy, *Witta: An Irish Pagan Tradition* (St. Paul, Minn.: Llewellyn, 1993).

25. Carol LeMasters, "The Goddess Movement Past and Present," *Gnosis*, Summer 1998. The language is that of Z Budapest, founder of the Susan B. Anthony Coven No. 1 in 1971.

26. Mircea Eliade, *The Sacred and the Profane*, trans. Willard R. Trask (New York: Harcourt Brace Jovanovich, 1959), 71.

27. Sarah Pike, *Earthly Bodies, Magical Selves: Contemporary Pagans and the Search for Community* (Berkeley: University of California Press, 2001), 133.

28. The Society for Creative Anachronism's official website is www.sca.org (accessed January 25, 2006).

29. Tony Ortega, "Sworded Behavior," *The New Times*, October 26, 1995.

30. Judith Brownlee, "Re: Food for Thought," ColoPagan mailing list, October 10, 1998.

31. Leliah Corby, "How to Form Your Own Coven," *Green Egg*, November 5, 1975, 7.

32. T. M. Luhrmann, *Persuasions of the Witch's Craft* (Cambridge, Mass.: Harvard University Press, 1989), 311–12.

33. Lurhmann herself worked as a type of participant-observer, but stopped at the threshold, so to speak, when she herself felt she had "drifted" so far as to lose her anthropological detachment. Had she written as an insider *and* a scholar, I suspect that her conclusions might have changed.

34. Allen Scarboro, et al., ed., *Living Witchcraft: A Contemporary American Coven* (Westport, Conn.: Praeger, 1994), 84.

35. Ibid., 86.

36. Cynthia Eller, "The Roots of Feminist Spirituality," in *Daughters of the Goddess*, ed. Wendy Griffin (Lanham, Md.: AltaMira Press, 2000), 37.

37. LeMasters, "The Goddess Movement Past and Present."

38. This idea is also developed in Wendy Griffin and Tanice G. Foltz, "Into the Darkness: An Ethnographic Study of Witchcraft and Death," *Qualitative Sociology* 13, no. 3 (1990): 211–34.

39. Margot Adler, *Drawing Down the Moon* (New York: Viking Press, 1979), 177.

40. LeMasters, "The Goddess Movement Past and Present," 45–48.

41. Shelley Rabinovitch and James Lewis, eds., *The Encyclopedia of Modern Witchcraft and Neo-Paganism* (New York: Kensington, 2002), s.v. "Budapest, Z."

42. The ordinance itself was repealed some years later.

43. Corby Lance Ingold, "Forum Letter," *Green Egg*, March 21, 1976.

44. Z Budapest, "Forum Letter," *Green Egg*, June 21, 1976.

45. This charge apparently arose because Z Budapest had led a memorial service for the radical women killed in a shootout between the tiny "Symbionese Liberation Army" and the police .

46. Z Budapest, "Forum Letter," *Green Egg*, September 21, 1975.

47. Doreen Valiente, *The Rebirth of Witchcraft* (London: Robert Hale, 1989), 180.

48. Ibid., 182.

49. Ibid., 187.

50. Adler, *Drawing Down the Moon*, 186.

51. Ronald Hutton, *The Triumph of the Moon* (Oxford: Oxford University Press, 1999), 348.

52. Ibid., 350, 365–66

53. The movie was 1973's *The Paper Chase*, in which Housman's character said much the same thing, substituting "grades" for "money." The brokerage was Smith Barney.

54. Paul Christopher Johnson, *Secrets, Gossip, and Gods: The Transformation of Brazilian Candomblé* (London: Oxford University Press, 2002), 23–34 passim.

55. Ibid., 19.

56. Another parallel could perhaps be discovered between the construction of "Celtic" identity in the eighteenth and nineteenth centuries and that of "Yoruba" identity in the nineteenth and twentieth. See Johnson, *Secrets, Gossip, and Gods*, 63–64.

57. *Llewellyn Trade Catalog, Fall 2003*, "Grimoire for the Green Witch," (St. Paul, Minn.: Llewellyn, 2003), 4.

58. It is actually quite likely that the twentieth-century Wiccan fondness for the term "Old Religion" owes much to Charles Leland's use of *La Vecchia Religione* in his books on Italian Pagan survivals, which were published at the close of the nineteenth century.

59. Leland, *Aradia, or the Gospel of the Witches.*

60. Silvio Baldassare, review of *Ways of the Strega*, by Raven Grimassi, *Songs of the Dayshift Foreman* 69 (1997).

61. E. Laurie, "Child Indoctrination," Nematon mailing list, December 17, 1994.

62. Heather Botting, "Reply re: Historical Depth of Wicca from Heather Botting to Sam [Wagar]," e-mail, September 30, 2000.

63. Hutton, *The Triumph of the Moon*, 295.

64. Ibid., 294.

65. Vance Randolph, *Ozark Superstitions* (New York: Columbia University Press, 1947).

66. Ibid., 4.

67. This religious tradition produces one of my favorite Southern expressions, that such-and-such a locale is "so far up in the hills that even the Episcopalians handle snakes." The Western equivalent, which I learned from my father, is "that the owls fly around in the daytime."

68. Randolph, *Ozark Superstitions*, 266.

69. Aidan Kelly, "Re: Sexual Initiation," Tradition_Witchcraft mailing list, May 18, 2002, http://groups.yahoo.com/group/tradition_witchcraft/message/1533.

70. Aidan A. Kelly, *The People of the Woods: Some History of the Pagan Way Tradition*, Art Magickal Publications (1994), www.oldways.org/paganway.htm.

71. Chapin-Bishop, *Right, Sure You're a Fam Trad* (2001) www.stepchildcoven.org/famtrad.html.

72. Aidan A. Kelly, *Crafting the Art of Magic: A History of Modern Witchcraft 1939–1964* (St. Paul, Minn.: Llewellyn, 1991), 21.

73. Ibid., 21.

74. Cora Anderson, *Fifty Years in the Feri Tradition* (San Leandro, Calif.: Cora Anderson, 1994), 2–4.

75. Ibid., 5.

76. Gwydion Pendderwen introduced a great deal of Welsh poetry and folklore, for example; while Starhawk, a decade later, incorporated much of the Andersons' material in her book *The Spiral Dance.*

77. Starhawk, "Eulogy for Victor H. Anderson," September 23, 2001, www.witchvox.com/passages/victoranderson.html (accessed January 25, 2006).

78. Penny Novack, "Belated Thoughts," September 23, 2001, www.witchvox.com/passages/victoranderson.html (accessed August 18, 2003).

79. As I have argued elsewhere, I interpret the evidence of Heselton's two books as showing that Gardnerian Wiccan came into existence about 1950 but was backdated by Gardner to a decade earlier.

80. Hutton, *The Triumph of the Moon*, 366.

☾

CHAPTER SIX

A Search for Paradise:
Other New Pagan Religions

Although this book focuses on Wicca as the largest and most active form of contemporary Paganism in America, other non-Wiccan forms of Paganism have originated in this country, beginning as early as 1938. While smaller in number of adherents, some of them have influenced the development of American Wiccan through two mechanisms. First, some individuals have been active both in Wiccan and in non-Wiccan Pagan groups, particularly those who go on to head one type or the other, leading to cross-fertilization between them. Secondly, outstanding individuals in the non-Wiccan groups have in several cases influenced the broader Pagan community through their writing and publishing endeavors, as was the case with Frederick Adams, Tim Zell, and Isaac Bonewits, to name just three. Through these processes, a group such as the Church of All Worlds, which never had a large membership, might exert a considerable intellectual effect. In another instance, a member of perhaps the first openly Pagan religious group in America, the Church of Aphrodite, moved across the country and became an influential elder in a new group, Feraferia.

These new Pagan religions may also be described as "excursus religion," for they represent a "going out" from a society's mainstream religions—in the United States, primarily Christianity—by spiritual seekers and social rebels. In his 1979 book *Alternative Altars: Unconventional and Eastern Spirituality in America*, Robert Ellwood employs the term *excursus religion* to describe the sort of religious life led outside the official "temple" of a given culture. In that spatial metaphor, the "temple" is opposed by the "cave"—Plato's cave—the religion of initiatory mystery. To it and from it come those who turn away from established religion: "In the bosom of kin and community, they feel not at home but in expressibly different, out of harmony. Their inner sails are set to a crosswind, they are fledgling swans amid ducklings."[1] Individually, but often following well-worn paths, these persons set out on their excursions of self-discovery, leaving the established temple of their community behind, for as Ellwood writes, "Excursus religion is a spiritual movement away from ordinary social and psychic structures alike, for a quest will steadily reassemble both as they impinge upon consciousness to mirror each other."

Ellwood's discussion of excursus religion, only briefly mentioning the new Pagan religions, ranges from Spiritualism to Christian Science to Zen Buddhism, but whether these excursus religions are imported or homegrown, he argues that they all partake of a spiritual vocabulary whose essence is American, based chiefly in Transcendentalism. In America, he notes, "such symbols as meditation, monism, feminine spiritual leadership, and orientation towards a distant and exotic culture have been among those signaling an excursus toward the emergent shore."[2]

Of his list above, all or some characteristics can be found in every Pagan group. Feminine leadership (even in groups founded originally by men) is considered desirable by virtually all Pagans except, perhaps, some reconstructionist groups such as Ásatrú, but the reconstructionists are themselves defined by their "distant and exotic cultures," those Celtic Irelands and Iron Age Scandinavias and Minoan Cretes as favorably imagined by today's practitioners. The item of monism is trickier: one Wiccan group, the Church of Wicca, does tend toward monism with its teaching that all "visible" gods are human creations, but most Wiccan traditions are either polytheistic or duotheistic.

In addition to those characteristics, all of which the new Pagan religions shared to some extent, we can add a turning away from scriptural or prophetic guidance in favor of seeking spiritual value in nature. Another distinctive character of these emergent groups is that they present themselves paradoxically as "older and deeper" than the established churches. Wiccans in particular have a long history of making that argument, both through their own readings of history and even through arguments based on creative etymology.

Although Wicca came to the United States from Britain, first as texts in the 1950s and then as immigrant Witches in the 1960s, certain native new Pagan groups preceded Wicca or developed independently. While not surveying all non-Wiccan Pagan groups, I have chosen to focus on those that in some way or other emphasized either Goddess worship or that might be described—or describe themselves—as nature religion. It is important to understand as well that boundaries between Wiccan and other Pagan groups are often quite porous. For instance, one might identify as a Witch but attend a seasonal ritual of Feraferia, affiliate in a Church of All Worlds nest, or participate in a ceremonial magical ritual of the Ordo Templi Astartes or any of a number of other ceremonial magic groups. In her own study of Witches and magicians in the United Kingdom during the early 1980s, anthropologist Tanya Luhrmann observes that such multiple involvement in different forms of magical religion "illustrates one of the important elements of the practice: being involved in magic is a general enterprise, not best defined as the practice of joining one particular group but as a practice whose ends can be met by joining some group, more than one group, or even no group at all. . . . But in the end, as many people told me, 'all paths are the same path.'"3

The Church of Aphrodite

If an unarticulated American nature religion was the soil onto which the seed of Wicca fell, it must also be understood that other forms of reconstructed Pagan religion sprouted here also. A significant example of a self-consciously Pagan new religion of the twentieth century was the Church of Aphrodite, formally announced by Russian immigrant Gleb Botkin in 1938. Through some of its later members, the Church of Aphrodite in turn connects to the "Neo-Pagan" revival of the 1960s. Botkin's own writings anticipate by a generation the sort of Goddess religion found later in the pages of *Green Egg* and elsewhere:

> The relationship between the Goddess and the visible world may once again be illustrated by that between a mother and her child. Having given birth to a child organically, a mother proceeds to take care of it with both her body and her mind. So the Goddess in Her relation with our world is both the Universal Cause and the Universal Mind.4

Born in 1900, Botkin spent his childhood in the Russian imperial household. His father, Evgeny, was the royal family's physician, and together with three other family retainers, he was gunned down in July 1918 with the Czar Nicholas II, his wife, his son, and his daughters in the basement of the Ipatiev house in Ekaterinburg, where the revolutionary Bolsheviks (Communists) had held them prisoner. A member of the "White" or anti-Bolshevik faction in the ongoing Russian civil war, Gleb Botkin eventually made his way out of Russia via Japan and came to America, where he worked as a commercial illustrator and wrote several novels and nonfiction books, including his own memoir of life with the royal family, *The Real Romanovs.*[5]

In addition to his memoir, Botkin's works included *Her Wanton Majesty,* a fictionalized biography of Catherine I of Russia (czarina to Peter the Great), whose cover blurb proclaimed it "a novel that thrills with risks and dangers, strong passions, and revelations of a court where exalted titles merely gave sanction to unbridled lust."[6] A more Pagan theme lies at the heart of *Immortal Woman,* which begins in prerevolutionary Russia, as did Botkin, and ends on Long Island, where Botkin himself lived at the time. It is the love story of Nikolai Dirin, a gifted composer who survives combat in World War I only to be hounded by the Communists, and of his childhood friend Arishka, who having been the mistress of various generals and warlords during the Russian Civil War of the 1920s, ultimately is reunited with him after both come to the United States. At the book's conclusion, when the lovers live on Long Island together with Dirin's father, the aged Father Aristarch (Russian Orthodox clergy may marry), the priest remarks, "Nikolai always tells me that the Supreme Deity must be a woman."[7] Again, the blurb writer tellingly describes "Arishka, beautiful and pagan as a divinity whom men could adore, and adoring—forget their God."[8]

The fictional Dirin at one point enters an Orthodox church in New York City, drawn by the music, but then begins "to pray fervently to Aphrodite—his beautiful and kind Goddess whom the Christian Church decried as the White She-Devil, whose worshipers the heads of the Christian Church have repeatedly anathematized."[9] Likewise, the protagonist of *The God Who Didn't Laugh* (1929), described by Wiccan journalist Margot Adler as Botkin's "most autobiographical" book, studies to become an Orthodox monk, receives a vision of Aphrodite, and abandons Christianity.[10]

On May 6, 1938, "the open worship of Aphrodite in the Christian world was restored" when Botkin founded the Church of Aphrodite in West Hempstead, New York. The church was "formally recognized [in other words, incorporated] by the State of New York through the grant of a charter to the first Aphrodisian congregation" on October 4, 1939.[11] Its headquarters (i.e., Botkin's home) were transferred later to Cassville, New Jersey, and in 1963 to Charlottesville, Virginia. The date of May 6, 1938, is now recognized by some contemporary Pagans as a significant historical date; for instance, several online Pagan calendars list it along with the alleged founding of the Bavarian Illuminati by Adam Weishaupt on May 1, 1776, or the birthday of Gerald Gardner on June 13, 1888.

According to Adler, the Church of Aphrodite had at most fifty members. Its temple room held a reproduction of the Venus de Medici standing in front of a purple tapestry and lit by nine candles.[12] Its theology and liturgy are laid out in *In Search of Reality*, published by the Church of Aphrodite two years before Botkin's death in 1969. *In Search of Reality*, a slim volume of forty pages, presents Aphrodite not as the Olympian deity of love and beauty—of "Virginal sweet-talk, lovers' smiles and deceits/And all the gentle pleasures of sex"—but as the sole Goddess of a somewhat Neoplatonic Pagan monotheism.[13] Botkin credits the fabled ancient singer Orpheus with bringing Aphrodite's worship to Greece but claims that the Greeks failed to realize the importance of worshiping Aphrodite alone. A parallel misunderstanding occurred in Palestine, he claims, where "the worship of Aphrodite—or Ashtoreth, as the Jews called the Goddess—aroused the bitter enmity of some influential religious leaders who felt that it constituted treason to Jehovah." Nevertheless, "peasants in remote villages and secret societies in urban centers" kept the worship alive, while the Christians appropriated the Goddess' symbols: "Christianity's chief Deity, the Holy Ghost, is but a pale and slightly distorted copy of Aphrodite, while the Dove which traditionally symbolizes the Holy Ghost is an exact replica of Aphrodite's Dove."[14]

Botkin's portrayal of the Great Goddess and her relationship with Judaism and Christianity resembles that laid out by British poet and novelist Robert Graves in his novels *King Jesus* and *Watch the North Wind Rise* and in his encyclopedia of poetic myth, *The White Goddess*. But unlike Graves, who avoided any sort of formal Goddess religion, saying that he served her best through his writing, Botkin developed a formal cult with such documents as the Aphrodisian Credo; the Twenty-One Aphrodisian Articles of Faith; an additional thirteen Basic Assertions of the Religion of Aphrodite ("1. The Supreme Deity and Creator of the cosmos is a Feminine Being Who creates, not arbitrarily, but organically."); and assorted hymns and liturgies. Perhaps the Church of Aphrodite resembles what Graves would have created had he chosen the path of religious creation instead of writing, but it is significant that Graves's utopian Pagan novel, *Watch the North Wind Rise* (also published as *A High Wind in New Crete*), ends with the Goddess assessing her utopian society, judging it to be stale and lacking savor, and destroying it in a wind storm.[15] Botkin, however, looked forward to a time "wherein all evil—which is but a remnant of the primordial chaos—will disappear and goodness and happiness reign supreme and unchallenged," as the Aphrodisian Credo states in its fifth article of faith:[16]

Aphrodite, the flower-faced, the sweetly smiling, the laughter-loving[17] Goddess of Love and Beauty, is the self-existent, eternal and Only Supreme Deity,

Creator and Mother of the cosmos, the Universal Cause, the Universal Mind, the Source of all life and all positive and creative forces of nature, the Fountainhead of all happiness and joy.[18]

Similar language would be used by Frederick and Svetlana Adams, the founders of Feraferia ("wilderness festival") but with an invocation of an idealized "wilderness" that was missing in the Church of Aphrodite. While the Adamses lived in Pasadena, California, and their new Pagan organization was not an offspring of Botkin's, a physical connection existed in the form of W. Holman Keith (c.1900–1992), a member of the Church of Aphrodite who became an elder of Feraferia.

Feraferia

Writing in the late 1970s, Margot Adler describes Feraferia as "the beautiful jewel that lies in its box." Obviously impressed by its founders, Frederick and Svetlana Adams, who welcomed her "with a short ritual in English and Greek . . . a drink that tasted of cinnamon and mint, and a dish of fresh raspberries," she also gave space to those Pagan critics who described the Adamses' vision as unrealistic and elitist.[19] Adler points out that Feraferia's influences included not just the utopian novels of Robert Graves and William Morris but also icons of American nature writing such as Henry David Thoreau and John Muir, along with archetypal psychologists (Jung, Neumann, and Kerényi) and naturist/nudist writers.

Feraferia emerged from a utopian California subculture of simple living, minimal clothing, and "natural" foods that predated the better-known 1960s counterculture by at least thirty years. In the mid-1950s, Frederick Adams lived on the Hesperian commune in California, where a group of families celebrated seasonal festivals, practiced nudism, and experimented with entheogens. (LSD had not yet been made illegal, and peyote cactus buttons could be ordered by mail from suppliers in Texas until the early 1960s.) His residence from 1955 to 1961 was a cabin in Sierra Madre Canyon, when the canyon "was a haven for an eccentric crew of artists" and other bohemians, as a local newspaper observed in May 2003, after the cabin's new owner tore down some paneling and found "murals of naked goddesses" that Adams had painted in the 1950s, "voluptuous maidens dancing across the walls, feasting on fruit and rejoicing beneath trees."[20]

In the late 1950s, Adams traveled to sacred Pagan sites in Europe and made some contact with British Pagan groups. As it developed, Feraferia's theology celebrated humans' erotic union with nature, expressed through an

Figure 6.1.   Feraferia founder
Frederick Adams, 2005. Photo
by Ed Fitch.

annual ritual cycle. The goddess of Feraferia embodied a cycle of three aspects: the erotic Maiden, the nurturing Mother, and the death-and-wisdom-
dealing Crone, as well as that of Demeter and Persephone. To Feraferia, however, the Maiden aspect was most important—*Kore Soteira*, the Holy Maiden
Savioress. This unique characteristic separated Feraferia, Adams wrote, from
other Pagan groups, with their "repugnantly brutish and primitive practices."
    Although not formally incorporated until August 2, 1967, Feraferia's gen-
esis occurred in 1956 when Adams, then a student at Los Angeles City College studying fine arts and anthropology, was walking across campus and experienced a mystical awakening, "a sense of the 'mysterium tremendum' in
feminine form" and realized that "the feminine is *a priori*."[21] From then on,
he considered himself to be a priest of Kore, a Greek word here signifying the
"Maiden Goddess of Wilderness."

Feraferia's vision was utopian and paradisiacal. The Adamses did not ro-manticize rural life; they were the furthest thing from those "back-to-the-landers" who wanted to re-create an improved version of nineteenth-century homesteading. The United States represented a "progressive" civilization, Svetlana Adams writes sarcastically, because it had destroyed most of its prairie grasslands in only a couple of centuries through the American mani-festation of the "cattle-battle" culture of warlike pastoral nomads. In the Fer-aferian vision, however, the warlike god Ares "has been transformed into a Divinity governing grassland—prairies, fields, meadows, etc.—as far as ecosystems are concerned [as well as] the following qualities: action, striving-without-strife, initiative, exhilaration, to name only a few." Consequently, Feraferia had no use for agrarian magic in the conventional sense: "Agricul-ture and animal husbandry are destructive and hence evil. . . . The only way to implement Paradise today, apart from writing about it, praying, and ritu-alizing, is to be sufficiently endowed to start a Paradisiacal Sanctuary in Wilderness."[22]

W. Holman Keith, a former member of Botkin's Church of Aphrodite, contributed articles to the Feraferian magazine, *Korythalia*, which often served to counterbalance Adams's almost stream-of-consciousness writing. In the early 1970s, Keith describes how "Modern religious Paganism . . . have as one of their [sic] goals attunement with Nature and an intensified sense of life awareness," but he rapidly moves on to the "cosmic religion of nature," not the "here & now" but the "there & then." Through the study of cosmology, Keith continues, we come to an understanding that "as human souls we are children of eternity as well as time, & that we are not alone, but are co-existents in a great cosmic consortium of sentient beings." Keith seamlessly blends Cosmic Nature with Erotic Nature, continuing that "religious ortho-doxy" rejects the Divine Feminine; "it excludes *eroticism* from any place in religious rite & thought. . . . The Divine for the Christian is not the Eternal & Divine Feminine as The Righteous Awakener & Sovereign of Desire, The Eternal Lure in early sex & romance, & in the supreme quest, adventure & romance that is religion."[23] It comes as no surprise that Keith would advocate female religious leadership in this qualified way, which does not seem to yet reflect the effects of Second Wave feminism: "There is only one major walk of life in which modern woman can supplant the supremacy of the man: that of religious leadership. In all others . . . women can be only compeers at best. But in the Neo-Pagan religion that is in the offing . . . the Priestess takes precedence over the Priest."[24]

By comparison, Adams's prose tends to be purpler, as in this passage from a "prophetic romance" in the same issue of *Korythalia*, in which two utopian lovers embrace: "Swell after swell of cosmic pleasure ripple up & down the curving slopes of their forms, igniting the color-flooded chakras. Bridges of energy begin to spurt between detonating whorls that both pierce & interlace their two torrents of flesh."[25] In both writers' visions, however, Cosmic Nature and Erotic Nature are joined: erotic union is a short cut to the constellations, and the Tree of Life grows among the trees of southern California.

Being in its own way as dogmatic as the Church of Aphrodite, Feraferia has never attained great size, although it still exists.[26] Its greatest effect on the emerging Pagan movement came in its articulation of an ecstatic theology of nature, based on a reenchanted version of the solar and lunar calendars, tied to the seasonal changes of the California landscape. Whether it will survive its founders remains to be seen. Holman Keith himself spent his last years in a welfare hotel, "a few decades too soon for the Goddess religions that he so wanted to be a part of."[27] In the 1970s, Svetlana Adams lamented, "We don't seem to attract people willing to put energy into the more mundane aspects of a functioning religious group. There is a plethora of creativity but material and other implementational help is lacking. We get tired, Fred and I, of doing it ourselves."[28]

The Church of All Worlds

The Church of All Worlds (CAW) is not numerically large, but its influence spread widely in the Pagan movement through its magazine, Green Egg, through other publications, and through the activities of the charismatic couple at the center of its priesthood during the 1970s and 1980s in particular: Tim and Morning Glory Zell. (Tim Zell is now known as Oberon Zell Ravenheart.) Although the interaction of science-fiction and fantasy literature with the Pagan revival is worth a book in itself, the Church of All Worlds remains the best-known example of that interaction—a religion launched by a novel that achieved near-scriptural status while remaining, in the end, a novel: Stranger in a Strange Land, by Robert A. Heinlein, a leading American science-fiction novelist. To borrow from the cover blurb of the 1968 edition (the thirty-sixth printing of this wildly popular signature 1960s novel), Stranger is "the story of Valentine Michael Smith, born and educated [by Martians] on Mars, who arrives on our planet super-human in abilities and ignorant of sex as we know it." Surely Smith's utopian and paradisiacal attitude toward sex was responsible for much of the book's popularity: Stranger was one of the first science-fiction novels to deal openly with sex, and beyond that, to advocate (through its characters) communal living and group marriage. As another of the novel's central characters summarizes

Figure 6.2.   American Druid Isaac Bonewits planting trees for a California Pagan forest-restoration group in 1979. Photo by Chas S. Clifton

Smith's "Church of All Worlds," in its teaching about sexuality, it "preaches that all living creatures are collectively God . . . which makes Mike and his disciples the only self-aware gods on this planet . . . which rates him a union card by all the rules for godding. Those rules *always* permit gods sexual freedom limited only by their own judgment" (ellipses in the original).[29]

Stranger in a Strange Land had not been long in print before a group of twenty-something Missourians decided to make it literally come true—not the expedition to Mars, but the communal "nests," the ritual of water sharing, the terminology ("Thou art God"), and the name of Michael Valentine

Smith's fictional Church of All Worlds, described in the text as "not a religion [but] a church, in every legal and moral sense. . . . We're not trying to save souls, souls can't be lost. We're not trying to get people to have faith, what we offer is not faith but truth—truth they can check."[30] A priestess of the fictional Church of All Worlds draped herself in a boa constrictor: very well, so did high priestess Morning Glory Zell. As Margot Adler describes it, the Church of All Worlds was "a religion from the future," and science fiction was its mythology.

At CAW's root was a group of bright, alienated, bookish high school students who read, for example, Ayn Rand's libertarian political philosophy and Abraham Maslow's psychology of self-actualization and thought that the two could be combined.[31] One of the group, Lance Christie, met Tim Zell (b. 1943) at Westminster College in Fulton, Missouri; after reading *Stranger*, they and their friends created a "water brotherhood" that became the seedbed for CAW (CAW's official birth date is April 7, 1962).[32] As Zell remembers, "*Stranger in a Strange Land* introduced me and a few friends to the ideas of Immanent Divinity ('Thou Art God'), Pantheism, ('all that groks is God'), Sacraments (water sharing), Priestesses, social nakedness, intimate extended families as a basis for community; and, of course, open, loving relationships without jealousy; and joyous expression of sexuality as divine union."[33] Robert Heinlein himself had been made aware of the literal Church of All Worlds that had sprouted from his novel. To judge from a letter he wrote to *Green Egg*, he viewed the organization with friendly detachment.

While Christie played an important part, the church "was Tim Zell's baby," and its structure of concentric circles of commitment had the Zells at its center.[34] Zell described CAW as "Pagan," and his vision of Paganism (or "Neo-Paganism," as he often described it) was strongly nature centered. As editor, publisher, and theologian, Zell would have enormous influence on shaping the new Pagan movement—CAW, Wicca, revived Druidism, and other manifestations. One vehicle for his and Pagan writers ideas was the CAW journal *Green Egg*, published initially from the early 1960s through 1976. In a more elaborate and short-lived scheme, *Green Egg* was the newsletter for the outer ring of CAW membership, while two other newsletters, *Scarlet Flame* and *Violet Void*, would be written for the middle and innermost rings respectively. That scheme, along with the plan of publishing according to a thirteen-month lunar calendar (introduced to the CAW by Frederick Adams of Feraferia) was abandoned as too elaborate. Only *Green Egg* survived of the three, published eight times a year at the quarter and cross-quarter days, and produced first by mimeograph and then on a Multilith offset duplicator.[35] The magazine, by then averaging close to sixty pages, died in 1976 when Tim and Morning Glory Zell moved from St. Louis to California, leaving another editor, Tom Williams, in charge, until he too felt the need to move west. (CAW's true life was wherever the Zells were.)

Green Egg was reborn in 1988, now edited by Otter G'Zell (Tim Zell's new name at that time), Morning Glory, and Diane Darling,[36] and upgraded to a full-size magazine published bimonthly with slick covers and a new subtitle: "A Journal of the Awakening Earth." Green Egg ceased publication in 2000, a casualty of persistent undercapitalization, of CAW's own struggles over the "routinization of charisma" as a new board of directors exercised more control in place of the charismatic founders, and, possibly, of the increasing importance of the World Wide Web as a venue for Pagan writing. In the next-to-last issue, the last editor, Maerian Morris, eulogizes Green Egg as "a publication that doesn't sell out, cater to white-bread Paganism [a concept that would not have existed in CAW's early days], censor Pagan thought and realities, or gloss over issues that others would prefer shoving into the shadows." These included, she continues, "Modern Primitives . . . S&M and B&D[37] and body modification . . . radical environmentalism, transgender and sex issues, and Pagan subcultures like Goths, Technopagans, etc. We get a surprising amount of flak from some segments of the community for being 'so out there.'"[38]

Green Egg was more than the CAW house organ; in its early days, it devoted some of its pages to other Pagan tradition newsletters, such as Khepera, published by the Burbank, California-based Egyptian reconstructionist Church of the Eternal Source, as well as Gardnerian Aspects, "newsletter of the Gardnerian Tradition [in America]," then edited by Tom Kneitel (aka Phoenix).

The Rise and Fall of the Council of Themis

During the first decades of the new Pagan movement, the Church of All Worlds' other most important contribution was Green Egg's letters section, which provided an impartial forum for all manner of groups. In his typical florid style, Frederick Adams of Feraferia praises Green Egg's contribution: "The whole community of PAGANA and the Eco-Psychic Revolution depend mainly on the network of intercommunications the EGG keeps in vital operation!"[39]

One of these was the short-lived (1969–1973) Psychedelic Venus Church. Not related to Gleb Botkin's Church of Aphrodite, the Psychedelic Venus Church, in the words of founder Jefferson F. Poland, worshipped "the sex goddess Venus-Aphrodite . . . in her psychedelic aspect. We see her presiding over nude orgies of fucking and sucking and cannabis: truly venereal religion."[40] Described by writer Michael Marinacci as "the ultimate hippie religion," the Psychedelic Venus Church fruited from the 1960s Sexual Freedom League and took literally the era's anti–Vietnam War slogan, "Make love, not war." In return for a five-dollar membership fee, Poland, also known as Jefferson Clitlick and other pseudonyms, mailed PVC members two cannabis cigarettes with the instructions, "Enclosed is a small sample of our holy religious sacrament, cannabis. . . . We hope it proves useful in your meditation." During the solstice and equinox rituals held in the San Francisco Bay Area, one male and one female member, the "sacrifices," would strip and lie blindfolded on a altar, their genitals smeared with honey. After invocations of Kali and Shiva, the worshippers licked off the honey as part of the celebration.[41] Occult journalist Hans Holzer sniffed that the Psychedelic Venus Church's rituals lacked "the spiritual element" and complained that Poland's group treated ritual sex as its own reward rather than as a form of psychic technology reserved for initiates.[42] Paid membership rose to about one thousand in the early 1970s and then fell off as the decade progressed.

It would be too easy to dismiss the Psychedelic Venus Church as just a short-term manifestation of the Psychedelic Era, the period from roughly 1966 to 1973 that coincided with the height of the Vietnam War and gained much of its "countercultural" energy from the opposition to that war as well as from such social developments as the birth control pill (giving women for the first time fairly secure control of their own reproduction) and the publicity over consciousness-changing drugs such as LSD that previously, in the 1950s, had been known only to an elite set of researchers and their friends. Another factor was the increasing, if superficial, awareness of Eastern religion in America: one of Poland's inspirations was a San Franciscan named Willie Minzey, who on a 1967 trip to India was impressed by the cannabis consumption of Shiva-worshiping "ascentics," leading him to set up the Shiva Fellowship when he returned to San Francisco. Minzey's fellowship, with its open-air cannabis smoking in Golden Gate park, ended in 1969 when he was charged with distributing marijuana to minors.[43] But what unites the Psychedelic Venus Church, the Church of All Worlds, Feraferia, and many other past and present Neo-Pagan groups is the idea of paradise on earth, a desire that in Christian terms has been expressed periodically by groups generically called "Adamites," those who wish to live as did Adam and Eve in the story of the Garden of Eden. They want paradise, and they want it now. The radical Adamites of the fifteenth and sixteen centuries (some associated with the Hussites in Bohemia) at times went naked to proclaim their sinless state and attacked the clergy and organized religion generally. Those Adamites claimed to have transcended the machinery of sin and redemption preached by the church; similarly, the Brotherhood of the Free Spirit in the fourteenth century (more an intellectual current than an actual organization) held that a person could reach a state beyond the category of "sin" in this life and be free from all obedience to the church, and significantly, for such a person, sexual intercourse was never sinful.

Likewise, Jefferson Poland (and others) saw sex and drugs as sacralized in the lives of the counterculture: in the words of writer Michael Marinacci, "a triple combination of drugs, sex, and pagan spirituality . . . would give the Woodstock Nation a Mother Church."[44] Like its secular counterpart, the Sexual Freedom League, and like the antiwar protestors in the streets, the Psychedelic Venus Church would provide a paradisiacal vision that could avert war, exploitation, and ecological disaster. In sponsoring nude dances, orgies, and cannabis smoke-ins, Psychedelic Venus was only slightly more literal than the Church of All Worlds, whose inner circle espoused nudity; sacramental drugs; and, following *Stranger in a Strange Land*, a form of group marriage. And, ironically, founder Poland was one of the first Pagans to advocate for the term *earth religion*.

The indisputably Pagan (in both the religious and generic sense) but controversial Psychedelic Venus Church created a problem for some members of the first American Pagan interfaith group, the Council of Themis, mentioned in chapter 3. Founded in 1968, the council took its name from Themis, a goddess described by the Greek mythographer Hesiod as a daughter of Earth but also a personification of justice. Although the idea of earth religion as an umbrella term for the new Pagan groups was not yet widely employed, Jefferson Poland, during the waning days of the Psychedelic Venus Church in 1974, would suggest its use in a letter to *Green Egg*: "This category, with its strong eco-flavor, opens much wider, perhaps too far, to include some who reject or ignore the polydeities."[45] Tim Zell, one of the council's founders, described the Council of Themis as "a universal Pagan umbrella organization that would be empowered to authorize delegates, representatives, spokespeople, etc.—as well as create and put out 'position statements.' . . . There needs, I feel, to be some 'club' to which we *all* belong!"[46] The new Pagans of the Church of All Worlds and other organizations felt the need for some common organization that could carry their voice into America's religious marketplace, but the Council of Themis, as well as its successors, the Council of Earth Religions (1972) and the American Council of Witches (1973), would not succeed. A more specifically Wiccan group, the Covenant of the Goddess, was founded in 1975 and has endured until the present.[47]

The Council of Themis's Greek name bespeaks the influence of Feraferia's Frederick Adams, and Feraferia and Church of All Worlds were among the council's initial members, CAW having adopted wholesale large parts of a Feraferian cosmology as it became more of a self-conscious Pagan religion and less of a book-discussion group.[48] Aside from the (then) St. Louis–based Church of All Worlds, the focus of the Council of Themis was in greater Los Angeles: members included Feraferia, the Church of the Eternal Source (a group based on ancient Egyptian Pagan religion), the Ordo Templi Astartes (a Pagan-oriented ceremonial magic lodge), and several others, now all vanished or mutated into other forms.

The Council of Themis adopted two "articles of faith": that all deities of polytheistic religion are aspects of "the female and male principles, the Goddess and God, divine lovers, from whose love all creation is derived," and that its members' worship would focus on "Goddess and God as divine lovers" however they chose to express that worship, "so long as their worship imposes no undue hardship on others."

Enter the Psychedelic Venus Church, whose presence would fracture the council. For years, Frederick Adams had created art and writing that featured youthful divine nymphs in cosmic rapture, while also participating himself in the nudist movement. Some members of the inner circle of the Church of All Worlds entered into group marriage based on Heinlein's literary vision in *Stranger in a Strange Land*. In the words of Jubal Harshaw, the grey-haired philosopher who serves as Heinlein's mouthpiece, "You told me this group was a plural marriage—a group theogamy, to be technical. . . . 'Ain't nobody here but us gods'—so how could anyone be offended?"[49] The pages of *Green Egg* were illustrated by many nude, voluptuous goddess figures (the tendency of mostly male Pagan artists to draw only young, shapely images of the divine would become an ongoing issue in the Pagan press during the 1970s and afterward). Even one of the magazine's sections carried a drug reference: the reviews column was titled "Dry Mouth Musings," referring to the "cottonmouth" sensation often experienced by cannabis smokers. But Jefferson Poland and the Psychedelic Venus Church would push the envelope too, despite advocacy of earth religion in the *Green Egg* readers' forum: "Ecology lends itself to ethics, philosophy, politics, and religion as readily as to 'pure' science."[50]

Looking back some thirty years later, Carroll Runyon, head of the Ordo Templi Astartes, recalls, "In 1971 Fred Adams and I took emergency action to expel Jefferson F__k Poland's Psychedelic Venus Church from the Council of Themis, in order to protect the nascent NeoPagan movement from radical political (drug and sex-perversion) exploitation blatantly instigated by a self-proclaimed professional agitator."[51] Allegedly, the crisis was a supposed merger of Psychedelic Venus with the Church of All Worlds, (about 1,000 people had sent in their five dollars to Psychedelic Venus at its peak membership level in 1971[52]). The Church of All Worlds' Tim Zell replied that PVC's membership would not change the flavor of the Church of All Worlds. Other Council of Themis members also challenged Runyon's and Adams's decision, and the organization broke apart, although some of the original members have held occasional reunion weekends in the 1980s and 1990s. Another organization, the Council of Earth Religions, with *Green Egg* as its official organ, rose from the ruins but, dependent on volunteer labor, lasted only a short time.[53]

The New Druids

The idea of the Druid as a Pagan philosopher adept in the laws of nature can be traced to Roman writers who never met a Druid. Those who did meet these priests of the Gauls and Britons, such as Julius Caesar, wished only to break their power during the Roman conquest of their lands some two millennia ago. The British archaeologist Stuart Piggott summarized textual and archaeological evidence for the Druids in his 1968 book, *The Druids*. The Druids, Piggot says, were a Celtic priesthood of whom all that is known comes from other cultures or later times: "The understanding of, and comments on, the barbarians around them by the classical *literati* were inevitably coloured by contemporary modes of thought and current philosophical schemes." But those accounts were just a part of an ongoing re-creation of the Druids, who were, at various times and places and to various writers, "barbarian sages, primeval Christians, champions of liberty, repositories of ancient wisdom."[54]

Stuart Piggott was aware of the popular *Asterisk the Druid* comic books but was unaware that a new Druidic group had formed in 1963 at an American college. That institution, Carleton College in Northfield, Minnesota, had been founded under the auspices of the Congregational Church (now United Church of Christ), although it was a nonsectarian institution by the 1960s. Still, Carleton, like many colleges of that era, retained an obligation that "attendance is required at the College Service of Worship or at the Sunday Evening Program or at any regularly organized service of public worship."[55] Even as a group of bright, disaffected college students were organizing the Church of All Worlds in Missouri, in the spring of 1963, a group of male students at Carleton decided to form their own religion to protest the college's

worship requirement. The leader of the group, and self-proclaimed Third Order Druid priest, was David Fisher, who later became an Episcopal priest; others included David Frangquist, Howard Cherniak, Jan Johnson, and Norman
Nelson. Calling themselves the Reformed Druids of North America
(RDNA), they presented a challenge to the administration of Carleton president John W. Nason in the form of the school's required "chapel slips," filled
out to indicate that they had attended Druidic services, which were held on
a small knoll beyond the athletic fields. As Nelson recalled, "The sole mo-
tive was to protest the requirement, not to try for alternatives for worship. . . .
There was never any intention to mock any religion; it was not intended that
RDNA should compete with or supplant any other faith. We tried to write a
service which could be attended 'in good faith' by anyone."

It is possible that the Carleton College Druids might have seen news photos of the British Druids of the era. The Order of the Universal Bond, also
known as the Ancient Druid Order, celebrated the summer solstice at Stone-
henge during the 1950s and 1960s. At the time, this Druidic order was the
chief survivor of several British revived Druidic groups, more fraternal than
religious, that sprang up in the eighteenth and nineteenth centuries, partly
rooted in Welsh cultural revival and partly in the blossoming of men's fraternal groups of the time.[56] But "the Druid" was also in American literary
consciousness (and these were students at a top-ranking liberal arts school,
hence better read than average), as the poet Philip Freneau had recorded in
the 1780s—the Druid as custodian of nature and follower of some sort of noble but non-Christian religion was part of the Romantic legacy shared by
both America and Britain. With this legacy to draw upon, the American
Druids would take their own developmental path.

From the Carleton student Druids' point of view, if the officially nonsectarian college administration refused their chapel slips as invalid, then the
administrators would be guilty of hypocrisy and "creedism." When Cherniak,
using the Minneapolis-St. Paul Yellow Pages, pointed out the wide variety of
religions available in southern Minnesota, he was told that the Druids lacked
a faculty advisor. Eventually, they acquired one, but meanwhile the administration faced the Druidic crisis by doing nothing. While the dean of men did
not accept their chapel slips (the dean of women did accept slips from the
two female RDNA members), no disciplinary action was taken either. In
fact, a year later, the board of trustees abolished the religious-attendance rule,
and President Nason and his wife themselves attended the final Druidic service of the academic year.[57]

The RDNA's original worship service was a pastiche of vaguely Protestant
liturgical language ("O Lord, forgive these three sins that are due to our

human limitations") and invocations of "the Earth-mother," who received the sacrifice of a living tree branch, followed by "communion" in the form of the "waters of life" (whiskey, as literally translated from the Gaelic) or "waters of sleep" (plain water), in the summer half and winter half of the year respectively. Hence the original student Druids' fears when the college president arrived at a June service: for students to serve alcohol was technically illegal—but President Nason wisely said nothing.

The Carleton Druids' story was a quintessential 1960s episode. All across the nation, in both higher education and in secondary schools, the social regulation of students was being shattered. Whether it was high school dress codes that regulated the lengths of girls' skirts (female students were generally not permitted to wear jeans or other pants at all) or the length of boys' hair, or university in loco parentis rules that set 10 p.m. curfews for female students living in dormitories or that required chapel attendance, students were discovering that these edifices of rules were actually quite brittle and that, at the time, administrators did not seem too inclined to defend them. (At this writing, in the early twenty-first century, the pendulum has swung partway back—we see public schools introducing uniforms for a "better learning environment," for instance, something unheard of in 1963.) The Carleton College Reformed Druids of 1963–1964 (who have continued to exist erratically as a student organization) discovered that a gentle push brought down the edifice. In their case, mass rallies, the occupation of college buildings, and other protest tactics were not required.

In addition, the Reformed Druids would soon face another challenge. When their members graduated or, in some cases, transferred to other colleges, they had the choice of leaving their Druidism behind or taking it with them. As David Fisher said in a letter to Norman Nelson in August 1964 while working at a Boy Scout camp in Wisconsin, where he found others interested in Reformed Druidism, "Here there were no restrictions against which to rebel, but only the desire to find truth in our own way." Nelson, attending graduate school at the University of South Dakota, reported the same transformation.[58] For Fisher, who had always said that his Druidism was compatible with his Christianity, Reformed Druidism was more of a philosophic approach to life: "Druidism has never claimed to be a religion," he wrote as he finished his time at Carleton. "As a [Druid] priest, I do not seek to consecrate the water to any use with my words, but rather think of my words as a common means for others, who watch and listen, to consecrate the water within themselves."[59]

The Druid Chronicles (Evolved), published in 1976, contains a footnote to Fisher's second statement about Druidism as a religion: "Others do, however." In that and in other editorial comments, we hear the voice of the man who did the most to change Reformed Druidism into the seedbed of several avowedly Pagan religions, Isaac Bonewits. Born in 1949, Philip Emmons Isaac Bonewits grew up in a Catholic household, living in Royal Oak, Michigan (whose name, he likes to say, holds special significance for an archdruid) and then in San Clemente, California. He entered a Catholic high school seminary in the ninth grade and rapidly realized that he was not cut out to be a Catholic priest, but his interest in the theory and mechanics of religious ritual and the history of magic only grew. As a student at the University of California at Berkeley, he met a Carleton College alumnus, Robert Larson, one of the Reformed Druids, who initiated him into the RDNA. They established a Berkeley RDNA "grove," where Bonewits was ordained a Druid priest in 1969. "The Berkeley grove was shaped as a Neopagan religion, unlike other RDNA groves, which considered the order a philosophy. The Neopagan groves became part of a branch called the New Reformed Druids of North America (NRDNA)."[60] In Bonewits, American Druidism found its most articulate and prolific voice.

Bonewits became a young Pagan celebrity upon graduation from the University of California in 1970 with a bachelor of arts degree "in magic." He had taken advantage of the university's individual-group study program to fashion his own degree in the academic study of magic, ritual, and thaumaturgy. Afterward, "administrators were so embarrassed over the publicity about the degree that magic, witchcraft and sorcery were banned from the individual-group study program."[61] That publicity greatly benefited Bonewits: his revised undergraduate thesis was published in 1971 as the book *Real Magic*. Subsequently further revised and updated, *Real Magic* was a milestone. Neither autobiography nor "I go among the witches" journalism, it represented a bright, brash insider's attempt to break down old categories such as "black" and "white" magic, to examine the structure of magical ritual in a cross-cultural way that was informed both by anthropology and by hands-on practice, and also to sort out the different individuals calling themselves "witches." His categories for the last—Classic, Gothic, Immigrant, and so on—have proved lasting and useful.

Moving to Minnesota, Bonewits edited *Gnostica*, a magazine produced by Llewellyn Publications, for a year and a half. There he established the Schismatic Druids of North America (SDNA), a splinter from the RDNA for the more Pagan faction, as well as the short-lived Aquarian Anti-Defamation League. From the SDNA and the NRDNA would grow Ár nDraíocht Féin (Irish: "Our Own Druidism"), or ADF.[62] Begun in 1983, ADF was designed as a fresh start in revived Pagan Druidism, "a new Neopagan religion . . . not

Figure 6.3. Morning Glory and Tim (Oberon) Zell of the Church of All Worlds in 1978. Photo by Chas S. Clifton.

just pan-Celtic but pan-European . . . based on the best scholarly research available, combined with what has been learned (about art, psychology, small group politics and economics) through the theory and practice of modern Neopaganism, and my own knowledge of (the polytheological and practical details) magical and religious phenomena."[63] This new creation would negate the tensions that had arisen within the scattered members of the RDNA and the NRDNA over just how Pagan to be, tensions that had driven Bonewits out of those organizations. Directed by Bonewits and his third wife, Deborah Lipp, the ADF became the largest Pagan Druidic group in North America. Bonewits, however, had to resign his leadership in 1996 for reasons of health, but he remains active as writer, speaker, and "archdruid emeritus."

After only three years, the ADF faced its own schism from members who felt that it "lacked mysticism" and that its public rituals, held in city parks and other open venues, were detrimental to "spiritual attainment," attract-ing as they did "casual gawkers and people not participating." In addition, the breakaway group did not share Bonewits' interest in the entire spectrum of pan-Indo-European Paganism; Bonewits followed Georges Dumézil in seeking common elements of pre-Christian religious practice and leadership. "Our studies convinced us that Druidism was a Celtic phenomenon while ADF embraced Druidism encompassing the entire Indo-European world," complained Tony Taylor, one of the five dissidents who taped a list of their concerns to Bonewits's van during the 1986 Pagan Spirit Gathering, an an-nual outdoor camping festival held in the Midwest. The list of concerns numbered thirteen, but feeling that the list would prove to be as pivotal within American Druidism as Martin Luther's Ninety-five Theses were to the Protestant Reformation, the dissidents numbered the list one through twelve followed by ninety-five. Ultimately the dissidents founded a new group, still in existence, called the Henge of Keltria.[64]

Independently created, these new Pagan groups would soon be influenced by—or would exert their influence upon—the new American Wicca that would arise in the late 1960s. And both would be eagerly described, interviewed, and photographed by authors and journalists who viewed this new Paganism as yet another manifestation of the rebellious, countercultural "Swinging Sixties."

Pagans: The New "Tribe"

In the 1970s, the British Pagan writer and communalist Tony Kelly promoted the idea that Neo-Paganism in its different forms was "tribal" rather than "dogmatic."[65] Kelly had written in his influential essay "Pagan Musings," "Our first work and our greatest wish is to come together, to be with each other in our tribe," and the words *tribe* and *tribal* carried a great deal of connotative force at the time, when countercultural youth considered themselves to be a "tribe" set apart from the mainstream. As a parallel example, the large "be-in," or festive gathering, held in San Francisco's Golden Gate Park in January 1967 was publicized as "The Gathering of the Tribes." Likewise, residents of and regular visitors to one Colorado Wiccan commune referred to it as "the rez," borrowing the American Indian slang term for *reservation*. In a 1975 article, CAW priest Lewis Shieber notes that "conversations with CAW members are studded with remarks indicating strong interest in Tribal/Tradition-based religions and religious practices."[66] The essence of the matter was that "tribal" religions were nondogmatic and did not make universal claims; they were not the One True Way. What mattered was *participation*: "Thus many sometimes contradictory beliefs may be held by individuals without harm to the religion as long as the *identification with the Tribe and tribal practices is strong*" (emphasis in the original). Only Feraferia, Shieber comments, had among Pagan religions veered toward the dogmatic pole by requiring acceptance of Frederick Adams's vision. As for CAW, Shieber outlines his own form of religious excursus: "We must assume that we are a 'guest people' in a possibly unfriendly nation and act accordingly. We must ever hope for a land or lands of our own."

In Feraferia, the Church of All Worlds, the new American Druidism, and even the Psychedelic Venus Church, we can see several common elements of contemporary Paganism arising. First, visionary individuals either created new religious organizations or, as in the case of Isaac Bonewits and Reformed Druidism, took them to a new level. At the same time, in keeping with the countercultural idealization of tribal societies, these new organizations tended to spread horizontally (for instance, the CAW's various "nests") rather than to organize themselves in vertical hierarchies. Second, they either perished with their visionary founders, as did Botkin's Church of Aphrodite, or members of a second organizational generation had to either move aside the founder (Church of All Worlds) or break away in order to realize their own ideas (as happened repeatedly in the Druid movement). Third, the growth of the largest Pagan movement, Wicca, which had no single visionary leader but was the most "horizontal" of all, would either force these other Pagan groups to remain aloof (Feraferia), to happily cross-fertilize with Wicca (Church of All Worlds), or to define themselves separately while often sharing members (Druidism).

Finally, all these groups saw sacred authority placed in what I defined earlier as the three levels of nature religion: the cosmic cycles, the land itself, and the human body. Feraferia in particular consecrated the calendar, but Frederick Adams's art and writing also emphasized the possibility of erotic paradise within a utopian, ecstatic relationship with the landscape of southern California itself. The Church of All Worlds looked to planet Earth itself—or rather, herself—as a primary deity, with humans, whales, and dolphins as her nervous system. And the first American Druids, too, took Nature as the source of all that was good, echoing both eighteenth-century Deists and the later Romantic, literary concept of the wise Druid philosophizing in the forest glen.

Notes

1. Robert S. Ellwood, *Alternative Altars: Unconventional and Eastern Spirituality in America*, ed. Martin E. Marty, *Chicago History of American Religion* (Chicago: University of Chicago Press, 1979).

2. Ibid., 21.

3. T. M. Luhrmann, *Persuasions of the Witch's Craft* (Cambridge, Mass.: Harvard University Press, 1989), 37.

4. Gleb Botkin, *In Search of Reality* (Charlottesville, Va.: Church of Aphrodite, 1967).

5. Gleb Botkin, *The Real Romanovs, as Revealed by the Late Czar's Physician and His Son* (New York: Fleming H. Revell, 1931).

6. Gleb Botkin, *Her Wanton Majesty* (London: Putnam, 1934).

7. Gleb Botkin, *Immortal Woman* (New York: Macaulay, 1933), 312.

8. Ibid.

9. Ibid., 197.

10. Margot Adler, *Drawing Down the Moon* (New York: Viking Press, 1979), 226.

11. Botkin, *In Search of Reality*, 32.

12. Adler, *Drawing Down the Moon*, 226.

13. Hesiod, *Theogany*, lines 205–6, trans. Stanley Lombardo (Indianapolis: Hackett Publishing, 1993), 67.

14. Botkin, *In Search of Reality*, 32.

15. Robert Graves, *Watch the North Wind Rise* (New York: Avon Books, 1963).

16. Ibid., 33.

17. This common epithet for Aphrodite (*philoommeides*), derived from Hesiod, may represent a bowdlerization of *philomedes*, "genital loving," suggests translator Stanley Lombardo, cited above.

18. Graves, *Watch the North Wind Rise*, 34.

19. Adler, *Drawing Down the Moon*, 240, 42.

20. Lisa Faught, "Goddesses Rejoice: Pagan Murals Reflect Area's Earthy Era," *San Gabriel Valley Tribune*, May 18, 2003.

21. Robert S. Ellwood, *Religious and Spiritual Groups in Modern America* (Englewood Cliffs, N.J.: Prentice-Hall, 1973), 195.

22. Svetlana Adams, letter to the author, late May 1976.

23. W. Holman Keith, "Thoughts on Eleusinian Thealogy of Kore, the Divine Maiden," *Korythalia*, 1977, 2.

24. W. Holman Keith, "The Priestess," *Green Egg*, February 1, 1974.

25. Frederick MacLaurin Adams, "The Cascades of Pegasus," *Korythalia*, 1977, 4.

26. At this writing, its website is www.phaedrus.dds.nl/fera.htm.

27. Ed Fitch, e-mail, November 14, 2002.

28. Svetlana Adams, letter to the author, late May 1976.

29. Robert A. Heinlein, *Stranger in a Strange Land* (New York: Berkeley, 1961), 350.

30. Ibid., 330.

31. Adler, *Drawing Down the Moon*, 271.

32. *Stranger in a Strange Land* has also been more darkly credited with inspiring Charles Manson's "family" of serial killers in the late 1960s. (Heinlein considered filing a libel suit against the newspaper that made the connection between his book and Manson, but he let the matter drop after his own lawyer interviewed Manson in prison, who professed no knowledge of the book.)

33. Oberon Zell, "Science Fiction, Double Feature," *Green Egg*, March–April 1997. See also chap. 6, "A Religion from the Future—the Church of All Worlds," in Margot Adler, *Drawing Down the Moon* (Boston: Beacon Press, 1979) as well as Robert S. Ellwood, *The Sixties: Spiritual Awakening* (New Brunswick, N.J.: Rutgers University Press, 1994): 183–85.

34. Adler, *Drawing Down the Moon*, 274.

35. Otter G'Zell, "An Editorial History," *Green Egg*, May 1, 1988.

36. Darling would go on to editorial posts at the Pagan magazines *Sagewoman* and *PanGaia*.

37. "Modern primitives" refers here to persons who ritually decorate their bodies with piercings, tattoos, and other adornments. "S&M" stands for consensual sadistic and masochistic sexual practices, while "B&D" likewise refers to consensual bondage and "master/slave" discipline.

38. Maerian Morris, "Letter to CAW and the Readership of Green Egg," *Green Egg*, September–October 2000, 37.

39. Frederick MacLaurin Adams, "Forum Letter," *Green Egg*, September 21, 1975.

40. R. Stuart, *Entheogenic Sects and Psychedelic Religions*, Multidisciplinary Association for Psychedelic Studies (2002), www.maps.org/news-letters/v12n1/12117stu.html (accessed January 25, 2006).

41. Michael Marianacci, *Sex, Drugs, and Hindu Gods: The Story of the Psychedelic Venus Church* (1998), http://pw1.netcom.com/~mikalm/psyven.htm (accessed January 25, 2006).

42. Hans Holzer, *The New Pagans* (Garden City, N.Y.: Doubleday, 1972), 67.

43. Marianacci, *Sex, Drugs, and Hindu Gods*.

44. Ibid.

45. Jefferson Clitlick, "Letter to the Editor," *Green Egg*, March 21, 1974.

46. Oberon Zell, November 18, 1999.

47. The Covenant of the Goddess's website is www.cog.org.

48. Adler, *Drawing Down the Moon*, 277–78.

49. Heinlein, *Stranger in a Strange Land*, 343.

50. Clitlick, "Letter to the Editor," 40.

51. Poland used various pseudonyms besides "Jefferson Clitlick," including "Jefferson Freedom Poland" and "Jefferson Fuck Poland."

52. Marianacci, *Sex, Drugs, and Hindu Gods*.

53. Harold Moss, personal e-mail, July 10, 2003.

54. Stuart Piggot, *The Druids* (Harmondsworth, Middlesex: Penguin Books, 1974), 2.

55. P. E. I. Bonewits, "The Book of Footnotes," in *The Druid Chronicles (Evolved)*, ed. P. E. I. Bonewits (Berkeley, Calif.: Berkeley Drunemeton Press, 1976).

56. Ronald Hutton, *Witches, Druids and King Arthur* (London: Hambledon & London, 2003), 240–41.

57. Bonewits, "The Book of Footnotes."

58. David Fisher, "The Epistle of David the Chronicler," in *The Druid Chronicles (Evolved)*, ed. P. E. I. Bonewits (Berkeley, Calif.: Berkeley Drunemeton Press, 1976).

59. David Fisher, "The Book of Faith," in *The Druid Chronicles (Evolved)*, ed. P. E. I. Bonewits (Berkeley, Calif.: Berkeley Drunemeton Press, 1976), verses 5, 10.

60. P. E. I. Bonewits, *A Brief Biography of Isaac Bonewits* (April 6, 2001), www.neopagan.net/IB_Bio.html (accessed January 25, 2006).

61. Ibid.

62. The Ár nDraíocht Féin website is www.adf.org (accessed January 25, 2006).

63. P. E. I. Bonewits, *The Origins of Ár Ndraíocht Féin* (April 10, 2001), www
.neopagan.net/OriginsADF.html.

64. Ellen Evert Hopman, *The Origins of the Henge of Keltria 1.1* (2001), www
.neopagan.net/OriginsKeltria.html.

65. Chas S. Clifton and Graham Harvey, eds., *The Paganism Reader* (London:
Routledge, 2004), 300.

66. Lewis Shieber, "The CAW and Tribalism," *Green Eggs*, December 21, 1975, 7.

☾

CHAPTER SEVEN

Final Thoughts

In 1980, the sociologist Marcello Truzzi, among the first social scientists to study contemporary Paganism, opined that "Witchcraft covens . . . are on the decline," suggesting that the next step for sociologists of religion would be to follow the members of these "volatile and somewhat ephemeral" covens into their next form of spiritual seeking.[1] In fact, while many covens are volatile and ephemeral, the organization described in the book to which Truzzi supplied a foreword, the New Reformed Orthodox Order of the Golden Dawn, still exists today, a generation later. Its original members from the 1960s and 1970s, who might then have been considered part of "youth culture," are now middle-aged, and, of course, the overall Pagan movement has exploded in size since 1980. To a Pagan historian, in fact, that year marks not a slump but rather the beginnings of the large-scale outdoor festival movement, with the Pan-Pagan festival, soon followed by many others, for example the Pagan Spirit Gathering and the Starwood festival, first held in 1981 near Butler, Pennsylvania[2] (both events are still ongoing at this writing). Through the festivals, American Pagans made new contacts, shared songs and rituals, and created a quasi-ethnic new identity.

Researchers of the time, such as Truzzi, Edward Tiryakian, and Andrew Greeley, tended to view the "occult revival" of the 1960s and 1970s as a search for meaning and identity among young people, a way of rejecting "the Establishment." Tiryakian, in particular, suggested that

Persons playing the role of witches, for example, are attacking some of the last cultural frontiers of Western psychic inhibitions; to engage in a role taking of parts formerly branded as odious and the object of extreme, social repression is, in a sense, to demonstrate the final liberation of Western man (and woman) from traditional cultural prohibitions dealing with the supernatural. The occult revival, at least in terms of the receptivity of witchcraft among segments of the middle class, could thus be seen as another step in the modernization of Western society, in this context as a secularization of the demonic. Such a perspective would be consonant with the secularization hypothesis concerning the relation of religion to modern society.[3]

While the "secularization hypothesis" has taken some battering in the last generation, I would prefer to note what Tiryakian left out and to explore briefly one point that he made. First, emphasizing "youth culture" in the 1960s and 1970s was a rhetorical commonplace; the demographic bulge of the baby boom,[4] combined with the rising economy of the 1960s and early 1970s, led to a great deal of focus on "young people"—their music, their work and spending habits, their lifestyles, and so on. But as that group passes into middle age, contemporary Paganism—Wicca in particular—continues to attract the newer generations, and the Internet has become the new conduit of information, topping small-circulation magazines and even festivals.[5] The how and why of that attraction deserves further academic study. Although the U.S. Census Bureau does not collect religious data and Pagan groups do not publish membership statistics, it is safe to say that the self-identified American Pagan population numbers between the high six figures (a conservative estimate) and the low millions (a more liberal one). Jim Lewis, for example, notes a memo from the bookstore chain Barnes & Noble describing a "Pagan buying audience" (not all necessarily active Pagans, of course) of 10 million. Like American Buddhists, many of whom—primarily those not of Asian Buddhist ancestry—connect to their tradition through solitary meditation, reading, and attendance at occasional lectures and multiday events, American Pagans are more widespread than realized.

For different reasons, both the Buddhists and the Pagans challenge traditional views of religious membership, even as governmental structures (tax codes, for instance, or the requirements of military or prison chaplaincies) force them into some sort of compromise with the dominant model of minister plus congregation plus regular meeting space. No longer a youth movement with a sprinkling of elders, contemporary Paganism is a multigenerational movement existing in tension with other American models and institutions of religious behavior. Its progression from "new religious movement" to an accepted part of the religious landscape has only begun, but it is ongoing.[6] Wicca and other Pagan traditions continue to challenge many assumptions about new religious movements, for they lack single charismatic leaders, apocalyptic messages, and rigid separations between "them" and "us."

In addition to its emphasis on "youth culture," such early study tended to overlook both the "nature religion" and the "Goddess religion" aspects of contemporary Paganism. When we place the new Pagan religions in the continuum of a European encounter with the "unspoiled" American continent, we can, as does Catherine Albanese, see them as participating in a long, tense encounter between earlier forms of Western religion[7] and philosophy and the voice of the new continent. (That the "unspoiled" landscape was to some extent the creation of its indigenous people is true, but I am dealing with the way the newer arrivals perceived it.) I have attempted to show that American Pagans rather unconsciously appropriated a particularly American discourse about the value of "being out in nature" and of learning from nature, even as the secular environmental movement was gaining strength. I have cited Regina Oboler's preliminary study of environmental attitudes and actions among American Pagans, but more scholarly work needs to be done in that area as well. Certainly to call Paganism the "spiritual wing of the environmental movement" would be doing a disservice to the environmental movement, which does not need to be saddled with a religious preference, and it would be misdescribing Paganism. (Nor is Paganism the "spiritual wing of the feminist movement.")

The origins of contemporary Pagan "nature religion" are found in a generally unarticulated American reverence for "nature" as a source of sacred value combined with a persistent Neoplatonic "cosmic nature"—itself a source of value—and revaluation of bodily wisdom and a sense of sacred eros. Now, more than a generation after new Pagans began saying that they practiced nature religion, the term is thoroughly embedded in both academic and popular description, not just in America but in other countries as well. For the former, consider the name of a 1995 British academic conference, "Nature Religion Today," whose focus was on "Western Paganism, Shamanism, and Esotericism in the 1990s," evidence that while Wicca had come to North America from England in the 1960s, there had been a subsequent flow back across the Atlantic of nature religion, earth religion, and core shamanism,[8] all essentially American developments. For just one of many evidences of continued acceptance of the term among Pagans, a recent article in the journal *PanGaia* uses "Earth-based spiritual community" as synonymous with the American Pagan community.[9]

Future research needs to be done on the demographics of American Paganism. Because the United States does not collect religious-affiliation information during our national census, it is difficult to gauge the number of

American Pagans, although various observers have called it "America's fastest-growing religion."[10]

James Lewis compared statistics on new religious movements in New Zealand, Australia, the United Kingdom, Canada (all through census data), and the United States (telephone surveys). In New Zealand, the number of followers of "earth-based religion" (excluding the native Maoris) grew more than 500 percent from 1991 to 1996 and nearly tripled again between 1996 and 2001. In Australia between 1996 and 2001, "religions in the Neopagan categories experienced the most rapid rate from growth—an average 250% increase." Total membership in the categories of Wiccan, Pagan, Druid, and Heathen in the United Kingdom far outnumbered such better-studied new religious movements as Eckankar, Scientology, Hare Krishna, or the Unification Church. Similar figures were obtained in Canada. Finally, in the United States, increasing numbers of self-reported Pagans, Wiccans, and Druids from the 1990 National Survey of Religious Identification to the 2001 American Religious Identification Survey (both carried out by the City University of New York) forced the addition of new categories to report responses—and led Lewis to speak of the "meteoric growth of Neopaganism."[11]

With growth come growing pains. American Pagans are struggling to cope with both the influx of newcomers and the concurrent demand for religious services: rituals for life passages (marriages, burials, etc.); military and prison chaplaincies; and the like. Several virtual seminaries make use of the World Wide Web to provide training in pastoral counseling, large-group ritual, and other services unheard of in the Wiccan community forty years ago.[12] More than anything, growth threatens the self-identification of many Pagans, Wiccans in particular. Since its inception in the 1950s, Pagan Witchcraft has been a "religion of clergy." In the Gardnerian tradition, for example, a person initiated into the first of its three degrees is declared to be "priestess (or priest) and witch." Now, while some Wiccan leaders struggle with adapting an intimate, small-scale mystery religion both to larger numbers of persons and to the bureaucratic requirements of being a "real religion," other Wiccans grumble that a small-scale mystery religion is all that they wanted. Other Pagans appear to be looking forward to the creation of a congregational form of organization, in which the initiates will be the new clergy— ideally with salaries. Here again researchers on religion will be able to see a new movement transform itself—or transmogrify itself—as it meets the demands of new members and increased public visibility.

If—or when—planet Earth faces increasing environmental disruption, the self-proclaimed "nature religions" may find themselves shoved even more onto center stage. Michael York, author of *Pagan Theology*, suggests that Paganism, shorn of specific traditions (Wiccan or otherwise) may well become more globally politicized and may give birth to a new global civil religion, "impersonal yet animated, pantheistic yet animistic," emerging from environmental catastrophe.[13] Certainly any movement in that direction would transform the small-scale Paganisms discussed here beyond recognition, and as well would incite a backlash from the monotheistic religious traditions. The story of the "hidden children of the Goddess," then, has more chapters yet to be told.

Notes

1. Gini Graham Scott, *Cult and Countercult: A Study of a Spiritual Growth Group and a Witchcraft Order*, ed. Don Martindale, *Contributions in Sociology* (Westport, Conn.: Greenwood Press, 1980), x–xi.

2. The definitive study of Pagan festivals remains Sarah Pike, *Earthly Bodies, Magical Selves: Contemporary Pagans and the Search for Community* (Berkeley, Calif.: University of California Press, 2001).

3. Edward A. Tiryakian, "Toward the Sociology of Esoteric Culture," *American Journal of Sociology* 78, no. 3 (1972).

4. "Baby boom" described the children born immediately after World War II, beginning in 1946 and continuing, depending on who you ask, at least through the 1950s, as well as those born in the early 1960s.

5. Based on my own observation, many isolated Wiccans and others have their first interactions over the Internet; then, when they learn of a local festival and gather courage to attend it, that act becomes a virtual self-initiation.

6. As regards the academic study of religion, the first official program unit at the American Academy of Religion's annual meeting was added in 2005.

7. Sadly, we know quite little about the encounter between the partly Christianized Norse and the New World, not even the extent of their settlement, only that they were unable to sustain it.

8. *Core shamanism* is the cross-cultural term used by Michael Harner and the Foundation for Shamanic Studies, now well diffused into esoteric culture. See Michael Harner, *The Way of the Shaman: A Guide to Power and Healing* (San Francisco: Harper & Row, 1980).

9. Archer, "Bumps Along the Pagan Path," *PanGaia*, August–October 2004.

10. The same claim, however, is made about Islam, and Muslims are easier to count, as they have more formal religious organizations.

11. James Lewis, "New Religion Adherents: An Overview of Anglophone Census and Survey Data," *Marburg Journal of Religion*, 9, no. 1 (September 2004).

12. The leading contender seems to be Cherry Hill Seminary, whose website is http://www.cherryhillseminary.org.

13. Michael York, "Civil Religion Aspects of Neo-Paganism," *The Pomegranate: The International Journal of Pagan Studies* 6, no. 2 (2004).

☾
Glossary

ADLER MARGOT (1946–): A journalist for National Public Radio and a Gardnerian Witch, Adler is the author of *Drawing Down the Moon* (1979), an important survey of American Paganism, and of an autobiography, *Heretic's Heart* (1997). She lives in New York City.

ÁR NDRAÍOCHT FÉIN: American Druidic organization. See Bonewits, Philip Emmon Isaac.

BODHISATTVA: In Buddhism, a person who achieves enlightenment but remains in this world to help others achieve Nirvana or deliverance.

BONEWITS, PHILIP EMMON ISAAC (1949–): A leading intellectual figure in American Paganism, Bonewits graduated from the University of California with a self-created interdisciplinary degree in magic in 1970. His subsequent book, *Real Magic*, has gone through several editions. Bonewits served as an editor at Llewellyn Publications in the 1970s and headed the short-lived Aquarian Anti-Defamation League. Involved in revived Druidism since the 1970s, in the 1980s he helped to form Ár nDraíocht Féin ("Our Own Druidism") and served as its first archdruid. Bonewits lives in New York state.

BOTKIN, GLEB (1900–1968): Son of the physician who attended to the Russian Royal Family, Botkin left Russia after the Communist victory in the postrevolutionary civil war, settling in New York City, where he became a commercial artist. In 1939, he founded the Church of Aphrodite, believed to be the first consciously Pagan religious body in twentieth-century America.

CHURCH OF APHRODITE: See Botkin, Gleb.

CHURCH OF ALL WORLDS: An America Pagan organization formed in 1962 by Tim Zell and other students at Westminster College in Missouri and inspired by Robert Heinlein's science-fiction novel, *Stranger in a Strange Land*. Local groups are called nests or protonests. Website: www.caw.org.

DHARMA: Originally a Hindu and Buddhist term for cosmic law, now sometimes extended to include the teaching of that law.

EROS: The force of love or desire, whether sexual or for beauty, often personified as a Greek god, the son of Aphrodite.

ESOTERIC: Any teaching or religious practice intended for a select group of suitable people. The opposite term is *exoteric*.

EXCURSUS RELIGION: Those religious movements that attract people who find that their spiritual needs are not met in their society's mainstream. They may or may not have authoritarian leadership structures, but generally they offer complex symbologies and a sense of "lineage," or the passing down of spiritual authority in their own channels.

FERAFERIA: A Pagan religion founded by Frederick and Svetlana Adams in 1967. The name means "wilderness celebration." Feraferia seeks to celebrate wilderness mysteries and the sacred cosmos, and describes itself as a synthesis of cult, culture, and cultivation in devotion to nature.

GAIA (or GAEA): Planet Earth personified as a goddess.

GAIAN HYPOTHESIS: Developed by the British biochemist James Lovelock, the idea that Earth's living creatures, near-surface rocks, and atmosphere act as a single, self-regulating system to maintain the conditions that are suitable for life. Lovelock saw his view of "Gaia" as a way to unify religion and physical science. His book *Gaia: A New Look at Life on Earth*, was first published in 1979. A more mystical "Gaea hypothesis," that Earth was a living being with humans, whales, and porpoises as her nervous system, had been offered slightly earlier by Pagan thealogian Tim Zell.

GARDNER, GERALD (1884–1964): Born into a wealthy family in Liverpool, Gardner spent much of his adult life working as a tea plantation manager and customs official in what were then British colonies in the Far East. He retired in England in his fifties, just before World War II. Involved in a number of mystical and esoteric religious groups before and during the war, he and several associates created the new mystery religion of Wicca (Pagan Witchcraft) around 1950–1951, although Gardner insisted that he had merely discovered a tiny group of existing Wiccans in 1939, just before the war. Gardner wrote several books, gave numerous interviews to journalists, and operated a museum on the Isle of Man, all to help publicize the new religion of Wicca.

GRAVES, ROBERT (1895–1985): British poet and novelist, his examination of "poetic myth," *The White Goddess* (1948), was a powerful incentive to the new Pagan movement. In the 1960s, Graves claimed to have been asked to lead a British Wiccan group, but he refused, saying that he served his Muse Goddess through writing.

KACHINA: A deified ancestor or deity of the Pueblo Indian people, or a masked dancer or doll personifying one of the kachinas.

MESMERISM: A form of spiritual healing developed by Franz Anton Mesmer in the eighteenth century that incorporated what is now called hypnotism.

MONISM: The notion that all reality is "one thing," not separated into spiritual and material dimensions.

MUDRA: In Hinduism and Buddhism, a hand gesture with a religious significance, often seen in portrayals of gods, holy persons, and in East Indian classical dance.

MURRAY, MARGARET (1863–1963): A pioneering British archaeologist—one of the first women to work in that field—Murray was primarily an Egyptologist, but she also published three books arguing for the survival of pre-Christian Pagan religion in Western Europe up until at least the seventeenth century. Although her ideas were well received in the 1920s, further research into the historic witch trials caused scholars to reject almost all her ideas about the so-called Old Religion. Meanwhile, however, her works inspired the creators of twentieth-century Wicca: she supplied an introduction to Gerald Gardner's *Witchcraft Today* (1954) that gave it a veneer of academic approval. Murray's ideas of Pagan survival, sometimes called the "Murrayite hypothesis," are still echoed by some Pagan writers today.

NEO-PAGANISM (also NEOPAGANISM): A term popularized by the Church of All Worlds' *Green Egg* magazine in the 1970s, to distinguish contemporary Pagan religions from the idea of "pagan" as irreligious and from older, pre-Christian religions. The term is now losing favor, however, replaced by simple Paganism.

PAGANISM: A form of religion that allows the sacred dimension of life, or deity, to manifest in the material world—in natural phenomena, animals, human beings, or human creations—as well as "supernaturally." Pagan religions see humanity as part of nature rather than seeing the natural world created for the exclusive use of human beings, and they also tend to see divine energy assuming multiple forms (polytheism).

PANTHEON: A group or family of gods particular to a given culture—from the Greek, meaning "all the gods." Some scholars suggest that the idea of a fixed Norse, Roman, or other pantheon developed only as a reaction to Christianity.

RECONSTRUCTIONISM, RECONSTRUCTIONIST PAGANISM: Any new Pagan religion that seeks its inspiration in literary or historical accounts of pre-Christian religion but attempts to modify them to fit today's society. Examples include revived Egyptian, Canaanite, Greek, Roman, Celtic, German, Scandinavian, Lithuanian, and Russian religions. Reconstructionists often emphasize learning the language used by earlier practitioners, for instance, Old Norse or Classical Greek.

SWEDENBORGIANISM: The teachings of Emmanuel Swedenborg (1688–1772), a Swedish scientist and mystical theologian, including an elaborate scheme of the afterlife and the idea that people can learn much about God by observing nature. Swedenborg's followers founded the Church of the New Jerusalem, or "New Church."

THEOSOPHY: The teachings of the Theosophical Society, founded in 1875 in New York City, which acquainted many Westerners for the first time with certain Buddhist and Hindu teachings, including reincarnation, karma, and spiritual evolution.

TRANSCENDENTALISM: A literary and philosophical movement in early nineteenth-century America whose favored ideas included finding spiritual meaning in nature and seeking truth through creativity and intuition. Famous Transcendentalists included Ralph Waldo Emerson, Margaret Fuller, and Henry David Thoreau.

WICCA: (1) an initiatory Pagan religion developed by Gerald B. Gardner and others around 1950–1951 in England. (2) Any new Pagan religion inspired by, similar to, or developed from "Gardnerian" Wicca, generally including invocation of a male and female deity in a ritual circle marked by four quarter points, and following a ritual calendar with eight holy days ("Sabbats").

ZELL, TIM (1942–): Founder of the Church of All Worlds, first editor of *Green Egg*, and leading Pagan "thealogian" (from *thealogy*, to give a Goddess emphasis) from the 1960s to the 1980s. He and his partner and coeditor, Morning Glory Zell, were frequently interviewed as spokespeople for the Pagan movement. Now known as Oberon G'Zell Ravenheart, he lives in northern California.

❨

Bibliography

Adams, Frederick MacLaurin. "Forum Letter." *Green Egg*, September 21, 1975, 35.
————. "The Cascades of Pegasus." *Korythalia* 1977.
Adler, Margot. *Drawing Down the Moon*. New York: Viking Press, 1979.
————. *Heretic's Heart: A Journey through Spirit and Revolution*. Boston: Beacon Press, 1997.
Albanese, Catherine. *America: Religion and Religions*. Belmont, Calif.: Wadsworth Publishing, 1981.
————. *Nature Religion in America*. Chicago History of American Religion, edited by Martin E. Marty. Chicago: University of Chicago Press, 1990.
————. *Reconsidering Nature Religion*. Rockwell Lecture Series, edited by Gerald P. McKenny. Harrisburg, Pa.: Trinity International Press, 2002.
Anderson, Cora. *Fifty Years in the Feri Tradition*. San Leandro, Calif.: Cora Anderson, 1994.
Archer. "Bumps Along the Pagan Path." *PanGaia*, August–October 2004, 22–28.
Asher, Rhiannon. "When Sex Is a Sacrament." In *Living between Two Worlds*, edited by Chas S Clifton, 165–87. St. Paul, Minn.: Llewellyn, 1996.
Baldassare, Silvio. Review of *Ways of the Strega*, by Raven Grimassi. *Songs of the Dayshift Foreman* 1997, 12–16.
Bawer, Bruce. "The Other Sixties." *The Wilson Quarterly*, Spring 2004, 64–85.
Benet, Rosemary, and Stephen Vincent Benet. *A Book of Americans*. New York: Holt, 1961.
Berman, Morris. *Coming to Our Senses: Body and Spirit in the Hidden History of the West*. New York: Simon & Schuster, 1989.
Beston, Henry. *The Book of Gallant Vagabonds*. New York: George H. Doran, 1925.
Bidart, Gay-Darlene. *The Naked Witch*. New York: Pinnacle Books, 1975.

Blacksun. "The Earth Altar." *Panegyria*, November 1, 1994, 1.

Blankenship, Roberta. *Escape from Witchcraft*. Grand Rapids, Mich.: Zondervan, 1972.

Bonewits, P. E. I. *Real Magic*. Berkeley, Calif.: Creative Arts Book Company, 1971.

———. "The Book of Footnotes." In *The Druid Chronicles (Evolved)*, edited by P. E. I. Bonewits. Berkeley, Calif.: Berkeley Drunemeton Press, 1976.

———. "Official Report of the President to the Board of Directors on His Investigation into the John Todd/Lane Collins Affair in Dayton, Ohio." *Green Egg*, March 20, 1976, 49.

———. "Letter to the Editor." *Green Egg*, June 21, 1976, 41.

———. *A Brief Biography of Isaac Bonewits*. April 6, 2001. www.neopagan.net/IB_Bio.html (accessed January 25, 2006).

———. *The Origins of Ár Ndraíocht Féin*. April 10, 2001. www.neopagan.net/Origins ADF.html (accessed January 25, 2006).

Botkin, Gleb. *The Real Romanovs, as Revealed by the Late Czar's Physician and His Son*. New York: Fleming H. Revell, 1931.

———. *Immortal Woman*. New York: Macaulay, 1933.

———. *Her Wanton Majesty*. London: Putnam, 1934.

———. *In Search of Reality*. Charlottesville, Va.: Church of Aphrodite, 1967.

Bowman, Marion. "Reinventing the Celts." *Religion* 23 (1993): 147–57.

Bracelin, Jack. *Gerald Gardner: Witch*. London: Octagon, 1960.

Brandon, George. *Santeria from Africa to the New World, Blacks in the Diaspora*. Bloomington: Indiana University Press, 1993.

Brenner, Malcolm. "A Witch among the Navajos." *Gnosis*, Summer 1998, 36–43.

Buckland, Raymond. *Witchcraft from the Inside*. St. Paul, Minn.: Llewellyn Publications, 1971.

———. *The Tree*. York Beach, Maine: Samuel Weiser, 1974.

———. *Buckland's Complete Book of Witchcraft*. St. Paul, Minn.: Llewellyn, 1986.

Budapest, Z. "Forum Letter." *Green Egg*, September 21, 1975, 31.

———. "Forum Letter." *Green Egg*, June 21, 1976, 31.

Carlson, Allan. "How Did the '50s Ever Beget the '60s?" *The American Enterprise*, May–June 1997.

Carnes, Mark C. *Secret Ritual and Manhood in Victorian America*. New Haven, Conn.: Yale University Press, 1989.

Cathyl-Harrow, Gwyneth, and Judy Harrow. *The Centre of Our Craft: Drawing the Moon*. 4th ed. Calgary: Dayshift-Six Roads, 1998.

Chapin-Bishop. *Right, Sure You're a Fam Trad*. 2001. www.stepchildcoven.org/famtrad.html.

Clifton, Chas S., ed. *The Modern Craft Movement*. Vol. 1, *Witchcraft Today*. St. Paul, Minn.: Llewellyn Publications, 1992.

Clifton, Chas S, ed. *Shamanism and Witchcraft*. 4 vols. St. Paul, Minn.: Llewellyn Publications, 1994.

———, ed. *Living between Two Worlds*. Vol. 4, *Witchcraft Today*. St. Paul, Minn.: Llewellyn, 1996.

——. "Margaret St. Clair: Forgotten Foremother of Pagan Science Fiction." *The Pomegranate: A New Journal of Neopagan Thought* 1, no. 2 (1997): 36–45.

——. "Smokey and the Sacred: Nature Religion, Civil Religion and American Paganism." *Ecotheology: The Journal of Religion, Nature and the Environment* 8, no. 1 (2003): 50–60.

Clifton, Chas S., and Graham Harvey, eds. *The Paganism Reader.* London: Routledge, 2004.

Clitlick, Jefferson. "Letter to the Editor." *Green Egg*, March 21, 1974, 40.

Cohen, Kenneth. "Pagan Theology and Judaism." *Green Egg*, September 21, 1975, 13–16.

Colpe, Carsten. "Syncretism and Secularization: Complementary and Antithetical Trends in New Religious Movements." *History of Religion* 17, no. 2 (1977): 158–76.

Colson, Charles. "The Year of the Neopagan." *Christianity Today*, March 6, 1995, 88.

Connors, Donald F. *Thomas Morton.* New York: Twayne, 1969.

Conway, Flo, and Jim Siegelman. *Snapping: America's Epidemic of Sudden Personality Change.* New York: Dell, 1978.

Cook, Allen T. "A Letter from Colorado." *Ohio New-Church Bulletin*, September 1928.

Corby, Leliah. "How to Form Your Own Coven." *Green Egg*, November 5, 1975, 5.

Covenant of the Goddess Newsletter. "Covenant of the Goddess Membership Requirements and Procedures." October 31, 1982, 10.

Coyle, T. Thorn. *Evolutionary Witchcraft.* New York: Penguin, 2004.

Cuchulain, Kerr. *Michelle Remembers: The Second "Survivor" Story.* Witches' Voice, 2002. www.witchvox.com/whs/kerr_pazder1.html (accessed January 25, 2006).

Cunningham, Scott. *Magical Herbalism.* St. Paul, Minn.: Llewellyn Publications, 1987.

Currier, Mary. "The Myth of the World Soul: Moving Towards an Ecological Psychology." Master of Arts thesis, Regis University, 1997.

Daniélou, Alain. *Shiva and Dionysus.* Translated by K. F. Hurry. London: East-West Publications, 1982.

Davies, Morganna, and Aradia Lynch. *Keepers of the Flame: Interviews with Elders of Traditional Witchcraft in America.* Providence, R.I.: Olympian Press, 2001.

Davis, Erik. "Remains of the Deities: Paganism Is Born Again." *Village Voice Literary Supplement*, November 1993, 19–20.

Devyn. "Mine Host of Ma-Re Mount." *Green Egg*, Beltane 1990, 14.

Dionne, E. J. "How Did the '50s Ever Beget the '60s?" *The American Enterprise*, May–June 1997.

Ebon, Martin, ed. *Witchcraft Today.* New York: New American Library, 1971.

Edghill, Rosemary. *Bell, Book, and Murder: The Bast Novels.* New York: Forge Books, 1998.

Eliade, Mircea. *The Sacred and the Profane.* Translated by Willard R. Trask. New York: Harcourt Brace Jovanovich, 1959.

Eller, Cynthia. *Living in the Lap of the Goddess: The Feminist Spirituality Movement in America.* Boston: Beacon Press, 1993.

———. "The Roots of Feminist Spirituality." In *Daughters of the Goddess*, edited by Wendy Griffin. Lanham, Md.: AltaMira Press, 2000.

Ellwood, Robert S. *Religious and Spiritual Groups in Modern America*. Englewood Cliffs, N.J.: Prentice-Hall, 1973.

———. *Alternative Altars: Unconventional and Eastern Spirituality in America*. Chicago History of American Religion, ed. Martin Marty. Chicago: University of Chicago Press, 1979.

———. *The Sixties Spiritual Awakening*. New Brunswick, N.J.: Rutgers University Press, 1994.

Evans, M. Stanton. "Back to Paganism." *Gazette-Telegraph* (Colorado Springs, CO), September 10, 1976.

Farrar, Stewart, and Janet Farrar. *The Witches' Way*. London: Robert Hale, 1984.

Farrell-Roberts, Jani. *An Introduction to the Craft of the Wise*. http://inquirer.gn.apc.org/craft-intro.html (accessed January 25, 2006).

Faught, Lisa. "Goddesses Rejoice: Pagan Murals Reflect Area's Earthy Era." *San Gabriel Valley Tribune*, May 18, 2003.

Fields, Rick. *How the Swans Came to the Lake*. Boston: Shambhala, 1981.

Fikes, Jay Courtney. *Carlos Castaneda, Academic Opportunism, and the Psychedelic Sixties*. Victoria, British Columbia: Millenia Press, 1993.

Fisher, David. "The Epistle of David the Chronicler." In *The Druid Chronicles (Evolved)*, edited by P. E. I. Bonewits. Berkeley, Calif.: Berkeley Drunemeton Press, 1976.

———. "The Book of Faith." In *The Druid Chronicles (Evolved)*, edited by P. E. I. Bonewits. Berkeley, Calif.: Berkeley Drunemeton Press, 1976.

Fitch, Ed. *Magical Rites from the Crystal Well*. St. Paul, Minn.: Llewellyn, 1984.

———. *The Outer Court Book of Shadows*. St. Paul, Minn.: Llewellyn, 1996.

Fox, Robin Lane. *Pagans and Christians*. New York: Knopf, 1987.

Frew, Donald. "Methodological Flaws in Recent Studies of Historical and Modern Witchcraft." *Ethnologies* 20, no. 1 (1998): 33–66.

Frost, Gavin. "The Dayton Caper: Final Report." *Green Egg*, March 20, 1976, 50–51.

Frost, Gavin, and Yvonne Frost. *The Witch's Bible*. New York: Berkeley, 1972.

———. *Advanced Celtic Witchcraft and Shamanism*. New Bern, N.C.: School of Wicca, n.d.

G'Zell, Otter. "An Editorial History." *Green Egg*, May 1, 1988, 2.

———. "Theagenesis: The Birth of the Goddess." *Green Egg*, May 1, 1988, 4–7, 26.

Gardner, Gerald. *Witchcraft Today*. Secaucus, N.J.: Citadel, 1973.

———. *High Magic's Aid*. New York: Samuel Weiser, 1975.

Garin, Eugenio. *Astrology in the Renaissance*. Trans. Carolyn Jackson and June Allen. London: Penguin, 1990.

Gault, R. K. *1969*. www.cafes.net/ditch/F69.htm (accessed January 25, 2006).

Gawr, Rhuddlwm. *The Quest*. Smyrna, Ga.: Pagan Grove Press, 1979.

Gerstenzang, James. "Religion Lured to Nature." *The Denver Post*, February 9, 1997, 16A.

Gibbons, B. J. *Spirituality and the Occult: From the Renaissance to the Modern Age*. London: Routledge, 2001.

Gillette, Devyn, and Lewis Stead. "The Pentagram and the Hammer." Raven Online. www.webcom.com/~lstead/wicatru.html (accessed January 25, 2006).

Ginzburg, Carlo. *The Night Battles*. Baltimore, Md.: Johns Hopkins University Press, 1987.

Gnostica News. "First Annual Festival Receives International Attention." August 21, 1972, 12–13.

Godl, John. *Remembering Anna Anderson*. 2000. www.serfes.org/royal/remembering AnnaAnderson.htm.

Goodman, Felicitas. *Where the Spirits Ride the Wind: Trance Journeys and Other Ecstatic Experiences*. Bloomington: University of Indiana Press, 1990.

Graves, Robert. *Watch the North Wind Rise*. New York: Avon Books, 1963.

Grey Cat. *Deepening Witchcraft*. Toronto: ECW Press, 2002.

Grounds, Richard A. "Tallahassee, Osceola, and the Hermeneutics of American Place Names." *Journal of the American Academy of Religion* 69 (2001): 309.

Hardman, Charlotte, and Graham Harvey, eds. *Paganism Today*. London: Thorsons, 1995.

Harner, Michael. *The Way of the Shaman: A Guide to Power and Healing*. San Francisco: Harper & Row, 1980.

Harrington, David, and deTraci Regula. *Whispers of the Moon: The Life and Work of Scott Cunningham*. St. Paul, Minn.: Llewellyn Publications, 1996.

Hartsook, Andrew W. *Anastasia: The Truth*. 1999. http://members.ee.net/ahartsook (accessed January 25, 2006).

Hautin-Mayer, Joann. "When Is a Celt Not a Celt?" *Gnosis*, Summer 1998, 59–65.

Hawthorne, Nathaniel. *The Complete Short Stories of Nathaniel Hawthorne*. Garden City, N.Y.: Hanover House, 1959.

Heinlein, Robert A. *Stranger in a Strange Land*. New York: Berkeley, 1961.

Hertenstein, Mike, and Jon Trott. *Selling Satan*. Chicago: Cornerstone Press, 1993.

Heselton, Philip. *Wiccan Roots*. Freshfields, Berkshire: Capall Bann, 2000.

——— . *Gerald Gardner and the Cauldron of Inspiration*. Milverton, Somerset: Capall Bann, 2003.

Hicks, Darryl E., and David A. Lewis. *The Todd Phenomenon*. Harrison, Ark.: New Leaf Press, 1979.

Holzer, Hans. *The Truth about Witchcraft*. 1971. New York: Pocket Books, 1969.

Holzer, Hans. *The New Pagans*. Garden City, N.Y.: Doubleday, 1972.

——— . *The Witchcraft Report*. New York: Ace Books, 1973.

——— . *Confessions of a Witch*. London: W. H. Allen, 1975.

Hopman, Ellen Evert. *The Origins of the Henge of Keltria 1.1*. 2001. www.neopagan .net/OriginsKeltria.html (accessed January 25, 2006).

Huson, Paul. *Mastering Witchcraft: A Practical Guide for Witches, Warlocks, and Covens*. New York: G. P. Putnam's Sons, 1970.

Hutton, Ronald. *The Triumph of the Moon*. Oxford: Oxford University Press, 1999.

——. "A Modest Look at Ritual Nudity." *The Pomegranate: The Journal of Pagan Studies*, August 2001, 4–19.

——. *Witches, Druids and King Arthur*. London: Hambledon & London, 2003.

Ingold, Corby Lance. "Forum Letter." *Green Egg*, March 21, 1976, 39.

James, Simon. *The Atlantic Celts: Ancient People or Modern Invention*. Madison: University of Wisconsin Press, 1999.

Johns, June. *King of the Witches: The World of Alex Sanders*. New York: Coward-McCann, 1969.

Johnson, Paul Christopher. *Secrets, Gossip, and Gods: The Transformation of Brazilian Candomblé*. London: Oxford University Press, 2002.

Jones, Carl. "Rising Goddess: The Nature Religion in the Modern World." *Gnostica*, May–June 1979, 26–41.

Jones, Evan John, with Doreen Valiente. *Witchcraft: A Tradition Renewed*. London: Robert Hale, 1990.

Jones, Evan John, with Chas S. Clifton. *Sacred Mask, Sacred Dance*. St. Paul, Minn.: Llewellyn, 1997.

Kaplan, Jeffrey. "The Reconstruction of the Ásatrú and Odinist Traditions." In *Magical Religion and Modern Witchcraft*, edited by James Lewis, 193–236. Albany, N.Y.: State University of New York Press, 1996.

Keith, W. Holman. "The Priestess." *Green Egg*, February 1, 1974, 28.

——. "Thoughts on Eleusinian Thealogy of Kore, the Divine Maiden." *Korythalia* 1977, 2.

Kelly, Aidan A. "Inventing Witchcraft: The Gardnerian Paper Trail." *Iron Mountain: A Journal of Magical Religion* 1, no. 1 (1984): 19–29.

Kelly, Aidan A. *Crafting the Art of Magic: A History of Modern Witchcraft 1939–1964*. St. Paul, Minn.: Llewellyn, 1991.

——. *Hippie Commie Beatnik Witches: A History of the Craft in California, 1967–1977*. Canoga Park, Calif.: Art Magical Publications, 1993.

——. *Notes on Gardnerian History, 1963–1990*. Los Angeles: Art Magickal Publications, 1994.

——. *The People of the Woods: Some History of the Pagan Way Tradition*. Los Angeles: Art Magickal Publications, 1994. www.oldways.org/paganway.html.

Kenyon, Theda. *Witches Still Live: A Study of the Black Art Today*. New York: I. Washburn, 1929.

Kjos, Berit. "America Is Summoning Pagan Gods." *Colorado Christian News*, September 1993, 11.

Kneitel, Tom. "Gardnerian Aspects." *Green Egg*, June 21, 1974, 18.

Krämer, Heinrich, and Jakob Spenger. *The Malleus Maleficarum*. Trans. Mantague Summers. 1486, 1928. www.malleusmaleficarum.org/part_I/mm01_06b.html (accessed March 6, 2006).

Kriss, Marika. *Witchcraft Past and Present, for the Millions*. Los Angeles: Sherbourne Press, 1970.

Landsburg, Alan. *In Search of Magic and Witchcraft*. New York: Bantam Books, 1977.

LaVey, Anton. *The Compleat Witch*. New York: Dodd, Mead, 1970.
LaVey, Zeena, and Nikolas Schreck. *Anton Lavey: Legend and Reality*. Church of Satan, 1998. www.churchofsatan.org/aslv.html.
Leek, Sybil. *Diary of a Witch*. New York: Prentice-Hall, 1968.
Leland, Charles Godfrey. *Gypsy Sorcery and Fortune Telling*. London: T. Fisher Unwin, 1891.
———. *Aradia, or the Gospel of the Witches*. Translated by Mario Pazzaglini and Dina Pazzaglini. Blaine, Wash.: Phoenix Publishing, 1998.
LeMasters, Carol. "The Goddess Movement Past and Present." *Gnosis*, Summer 1998, 45–48.
Lewis, James. "Numbering Neo-Pagans." In *The Encyclopedia of Modern Witchcraft and Neo-Paganism*, edited by James Lewis and Shelley Rabinovitch. New York: Citadel Press, 2002.
———. "New Religion Adherents: An Overview of Anglophone Census and Survey Data." *Marburg Journal of Religion* 9, no. 1. www.uni-marburg.de/religionswissenschaft/journal/mjr/pdf/2004/lewis2004.pdf (accessed March 6, 2006).
Llewellyn Trade Catalog, Fall 2003. "Grimoire for the Green Witch." St. Paul, Minn.: Llewellyn, 2003.
Luhrmann, T. M. *Persuasions of the Witch's Craft*. Cambridge, Mass.: Harvard University Press, 1989.
Magliocco, Sabina. *Witching Culture: Folklore and Neo-Paganism in America*. Contemporary Ethnography, edited by Kirin Narayan and Paul Stoller. Philadelphia: University of Pennsylvania Press, 2004.
Magliocco, Sabina, and Holly Tannen. "The *Real* Old-Time Religion: Towards an Aesthetics of Neo-Pagan Song." *Ethnologies* 20, no. 1 (1998): 175–201.
Mann, W. Edward. *Orgone, Reich and Eros: William Reich's Theory of Life Energy*. New York: Simon & Schuster, 1973.
Marianacci, Michael. *Sex, Drugs, and Hindu Gods: The Story of the Psychedelic Venus Church*. 1998. http://pw1.netcom.com/~mikalm/psyven.htm (accessed January 25, 2006).
McCoy, Edain. *Witta: An Irish Pagan Tradition*. St. Paul, Minn.: Llewellyn, 1993.
Michelet, Jules. *The Sorceress: A Study in Middle Age Superstition*. Trans. A. R. Allison. 1862. Reprint, Paris: C. Carrington, 1904.
Miller, Richard Alan. "Omega." *Green Egg*, December 21, 1976, 13–19.
———. *The Magical and Ritual Use of Herbs*. New York: Destiny Books, 1983.
Morfitt, Ian. "Naked City." *Fortean Times*, 1999. www.forteantimes.com/articles/119_naked.shtml (accessed January 25, 2006).
Morris, Maerian. "Letter to Caw and the Readership of Green Egg." *Green Egg*, September–October 2000, 36–38.
Morrison, Sarah Lyddon. *The Modern Witch's Spellbook*. New York: Citadel Press, 1971.
Muntean, Fritz. "The Role of St. Margin of Braga in the Moderation of Ecclesiastical Attitudes toward Alternative Religious Beliefs and Practices in 6th Century Gaul and Northern Iberia." MA thesis, University of British Columbia, 1997.

Murray, Margaret. *The Witch-Cult in Western Europe*. Oxford: Oxford University Press, 1921.

———. "Witchcraft." *Encyclopaedia Britannica*, 1929.

Nash, Roderick. *Wilderness and the American Mind*. Rev. ed. New Haven, Conn.: Yale University Press, 1973.

Nathan, Debbie, and Michael Snedeker. *Satan's Silence: Ritual Abuse and the Making of a Modern American Witch Hunt*. New York: Basic Books, 1995.

Newsweek. "Evil, Anyone?" August 16, 1971, 56–57.

Nichols, Mike. *Reflections on Old Guard Paganism*. www.geocities.com/Athens/ Forum/7280/oldgard.html (accessed January 25, 2006).

Niebuhr, Gustav. "Ancient Goddess Isis Makes a Modern Comeback." *The Denver Post*, December 17, 1993, 37A.

NightMare, M. Macha. *The "W" Word, or Why We Call Ourselves Witches*. 1998. www.machanightmare.com/W_word.html (accessed January 25, 2000).

Oboler, Regina. "Nature Religion as a Cultural System? Sources of Environmentalist Action and Rhetoric in a Contemporary Pagan Community." *The Pomegranate: The International Journal of Pagan Studies* 6, no. 1 (2004): 86–106.

Ortega, Tony. "Sworded Behavior." *The New Times*, October 26, 1995, 20–25.

Ouellette, Laurie. "Inventing the Cosmo Girl: Class Identity and Girl-Style American Dreams." *Media, Culture & Society* 21, no. 3 (1999): 359–84.

Oxford Classical Dictionary. Oxford: Clarendon Press, 1970.

Pearson, Joanne. "Wicca, Esotericism, and Living Nature." *The Pomegranate: A New Journal of Neopagan Thought*, November 2000, 4–15.

———, ed. *Belief Beyond Boundaries: Wicca, Celtic Spirituality and the New Age, Religion Today: Tradition, Modernity and Change*. Aldershot, Hampshire: Ashgate, 2002.

Pearson, Joanne, Richard H. Roberts, and Geoffrey Samuel, eds. *Nature Religion Today: Paganism in the Modern World*. Edinburgh: Edinburgh University Press, 1998.

Pei, Mario. *The Families of Words*. New York: St. Martin's Press, 1962.

Pendderwen, Gwydion. *The Faerie Shaman*. Ukiah, Calif.: Nemeton Records, 1983.

Pentagram. "Before Gardner—What?" November 1964.

Petrovski, Leslie. "The Goddess Movement: Woman-Based Spirituality Gains Followers." *The Denver Post*, September 14, 1993, 1–2E.

Piggot, Stuart. *The Druids*. Harmondsworth, Middlesex: Penguin Books, 1974.

Pike, Sarah. *Earthly Bodies, Magical Selves: Contemporary Pagans and the Search for Community*. Berkeley: University of California Press, 2001.

Plowman, Edward E. "The Legend(S) of John Todd." *Christianity Today*, March 1978, 38–40, 42.

Porterfield, Amanda. *The Transformation of American Religion*. Oxford: Oxford University Press, 2001.

Rabinovitch, Shelley, and James Lewis, eds. *The Encyclopedia of Modern Witchcraft and Neo-Paganism*. New York: Kensington, 2002.

Randolph, Vance. *Ozark Superstitions*. New York: Columbia University Press, 1947.

Richardson, Alan, and Marcus Claridge. *The Old Sod*. London: Ignotus Press, 2003.

Roberts, Susan. *Witches U.S.A.* New York: Dell, 1971.

Rose, Elliot. *A Razor for a Goat: A Discussion of Certain Problems in the History of Witchcraft and Diabolism.* Toronto: University of Toronto Press, 1962.

Rousseau, Jean-Jacques. *The Social Contract and the Discourses.* Translated by G. D. H. Cole, *Everyman's Library.* New York: Alfred A. Knopf, 1993.

Salomonsen, Jone. *Enchanted Feminism: The Reclaiming Witches of San Francisco.* London: Routledge, 2002.

Scarboro, Allen, et al., ed. *Living Witchcraft: A Contemporary American Coven.* Westport, Conn.: Praeger, 1994.

Schnoebelen, William. *I Was a Sold-out Goddess-Worshipping Witch!* Fill the Void. www.fillthevoid.org/Wicca/goddess-worshippingwitch.html.

———. *Wicca: Satan's Little White Lie.* Chino, Calif.: Chick Publications, 1990.

Schultz, Donna Cole. "My Quest for Witchcraft in the 1960s." *The Cauldron,* August 2003, 2–6.

Schurmacher, Emile. *Witchcraft in America Today.* New York: Paperback Library, 1970.

Scott, Gini Graham. *Cult and Countercult: A Study of a Spiritual Growth Group and a Witchcraft Order.* Westport, Conn.: Greenwood Press, 1980.

Seymour, C. R. F. *The Forgotten Mage.* Wellingborogh, Northamptonshire: Aquarian Press, 1986.

Sheba, Lady. *The Book of Shadows.* St. Paul, Minn.: Llewellyn, 1971.

Shepard, Paul, and Barry Sanders. *The Sacred Paw: The Bear in Nature, Myth, and Literature.* New York: Viking, 1985.

Shieber, Lewis. "The Caw and Tribalism." *Green Egg,* December 21, 1975, 5–7.

SilverWitch, Sylvana. *Ed Fitch: Revealing the Craft.* 1995. www.widdershins.org/vol1iss2/2.htm (accessed January 25, 2006).

Small, Melvin. Review of *Nixon and the Environment,* by Flippen J. Brooks. www.h-net.org/reviews/showrev.cgi?path=32584973114436 (accessed March 6, 2006).

Smith, Jonathan Z., ed. *The HarperCollins Dictionary of Religion.* New York: Harper-Collins, 1995.

Snyder, Gary. *The Practice of the Wild.* San Francisco: North Point Press, 1990.

St. Clair, Margaret. *Sign of the Labrys.* New York: Bantam Books, 1963.

Starhawk. *The Spiral Dance.* San Francisco: Harper & Row, 1979.

Steiger, Brad. *Sex and Satanism.* New York: Ace Books, 1969.

Steinberg, Geneva. "Wilhelm Reich and Neo-Paganism." *Green Egg,* June 21, 1974, 25–26.

Stevens, Jay. *Storming Heaven: LSD and the American Dream.* New York: Harper & Row, 1987.

Stuart, R. *Entheogenic Sects and Psychedelic Religions.* Multidisciplinary Association for Psychedelic Studies, 2002. www.maps.org/news-letters/v12n1/12117stu.html.

Tannen, Holly. *Between the Worlds.* Gold Leaf Records, 1980.

Tarostar. "Witchcraft and Ecology." *The Cauldron,* November 2003, 16–17.

Teagarden, Diane. "Just My Opinion: Pc Pagans." *Pagan Digest,* Ostara–Beltane (spring) 1994, 8.

Time. "Occult: A Substitute Faith," June 19, 1972, 62–68.

Timmons, Stuart. *The Trouble with Harry Hay: Founder of the Modern Gay Movement.* Boston: Alyson Publications, 1990.

Tiryakian, Edward A. "Toward the Sociology of Esoteric Culture." *American Journal of Sociology* 78, no. 3 (1972): 491–512.

Truzzi, Marcello. "The Occult Revival as Popular Culture: Some Random Observations on the Old and Nouveau Witch." *Sociological Quarterly* 13, no. 1 (1972): 16–36.

Utt, Walter C. "Illuminating the Illuminati." *Liberty,* May–June 1979, 17–19, 26–28.

Vachon, B. "Witches Are Rising." *Look,* August 24, 1971, 40–44.

Valiente, Doreen. *Natural Magic.* Custer, Wash.: Phoenix Publishing, 1986.

Valiente, Doreen. *The Rebirth of Witchcraft.* London: Robert Hale, 1989.

Voigt, Valerie. "Sex Magic." In *The Modern Craft Movement,* edited by Chas S Clifton, 85–108. St. Paul, Minn.: Llewellyn, 1992.

Wallace, C. H. *Witchcraft in the World Today.* New York: Award Books, 1967.

Wanderer, the. "Wiccan High Magick." *Green Egg,* Ostara, March 21, 1974, 5–7.

Warnke, Mike, David W. Balsinger, and Les Jones. *The Satan-Seller.* Plainfield, N.J.: Logos International, 1972.

Webster, Nesta. *World Revolution: The Plot against Civilisation.* London: Constable, 1922.

White, Lynn, Jr. "The Historical Roots of Our Ecological Crisis." *Science* 155 (1967): 1203–7.

Whitehouse, Harvey. *Arguments and Icons: Divergent Modes of Religiosity.* Oxford: Oxford University Press, 2000.

Wilson, Joseph B. *For Those Who Want the Other Side of the Story.* 1734 mailing list, 2003.

WorldNetDaily. "The New Paganism: How Christianity Is Being Replaced by 'Green' Religion, Goddess Worship, Globalism." 2002. www.worldnetdaily.com/news/article.asp?ARTICLE_ID=28468.

Wyman, Anne. "New Life Infuses an Old Religion as Witches, Pagans Join Ranks." *Boston Globe,* October 7, 1982, 2.

York, Michael. *Pagan Theology.* New York: New York University, 2003.

———. "Paganism as Root-Religion." *The Pomegranate: The International Journal of Pagan Studies* 16, no. 1 (2004).

———. "Civil Religion Aspects of Neo-Paganism." *The Pomegranate: The International Journal of Pagan Studies* 6, no. 2 (2004): 253–60.

Zell, Oberon. "Science Fiction, Double Feature." *Green Egg,* March–April 1997, 3.

———. *The Other People.* Index, Wash.: Pathfinder Press, 1998.

Zell, Tim. "The Gods of Nature; the Nature of Gods." *Gnostica,* October 21, 1973, 5–8.

———. "Neo-Paganism: An Old Religion for a New Age." St. Louis: Church of All Worlds, n.d.

Zell, Tim, and P. E. I. Bonewits. "Paganized Songs." *Green Egg,* Oimelc, February 1, 1974, 12.

Index

☾

About the Author

Chas S. Clifton is the editor of *The Pomegranate: The International Journal of Pagan Studies* and serves on the steering committee of the American Academy of Religion's Consultation on Contemporary Pagan Studies. Together with Graham Harvey, he co-edited *The Paganism Reader*. He teaches at Colorado State University, Pueblo.